Keith Lowe is the author of *Inferno*...
and *Savage Continent: Europe in the*...
won the 2013 PEN/Hessell-Tiltma...
published *The Fear and the Freedom*...
been translated into twenty languages.

http://www.keithlowehistory.com/

A *Spectator* Book of the Year 2020
A *Times* and *Sunday Times* Best Book of 2020
A *Mail on Sunday* Book of the Year 2020

'[An] inspired idea . . . Always thoughtful and evocative, sometimes controversial . . . Lowe's sensitive, disturbing book should be compulsory reading for both statue builders and statue topplers. Too many memorials of all kinds seek to promote deceits or half-truths'
Max Hastings, *Sunday Times*

'[A] brilliantly researched and timely book . . . Lowe is not afraid to tread on sensitive ground, but he does so with the integrity that comes from really knowing his material'   *Daily Mail*

'Such a provocative perspective makes Lowe's choice of monuments important. The well-balanced range here enables the retelling of some remarkable war stories, while also providing fascinating insights into the ways different nations have remembered or denied issues around national identity and the glory and horrors of war . . . this is some of the most thought-provoking writing about the Second World War that I have read for a long while'   *Spectator*

'In this timely book, which neatly combines history, art criticism and travelogue, Lowe examines 25 monuments to the Second World War spread across three continents . . . Lowe is a fine guide to these monuments because he feels the moral force – for good or bad – of each site he visits'   *The Times*, **Book of The Week**

'Statues have been in the news this year, finding themselves at the bottom of rivers or boarded up for their own safety. Keith Lowe takes us on a fascinating tour of monuments erected in different countries after the Second World War, looking at what they mean to people and how those meanings change over time'   *Mail on Sunday*, **Books of the Year**

Also by the author

Inferno: The Devastation of Hamburg, 1943
Savage Continent: Europe in the Aftermath of World War II
The Fear and the Freedom

PRISONERS OF HISTORY

WHAT MONUMENTS TO THE SECOND WORLD WAR TELL US ABOUT OUR HISTORY AND OURSELVES

KEITH LOWE

WILLIAM
COLLINS

William Collins
An imprint of HarperCollins*Publishers*
1 London Bridge Street
London SE1 9GF

WilliamCollinsBooks.com

HarperCollins*Publishers*
1st Floor, Watermarque Building, Ringsend Road
Dublin 4, Ireland

First published in Great Britain in 2020 by William Collins
This William Collins paperback published in 2021

1

ISBN 978-0-00-833958-6

Typeset in Minion Pro by
Palimpsest Book Production Ltd, Falkirk, Stirlingshire

Printed and bound in Great Britain by
CPI Group (UK) Ltd, Croydon CR0 4YY

MIX
Paper from
responsible sources
FSC® C007454

For Creo

Contents

Part III – Monsters

Part IV – Apocalypse

Part V – Rebirth

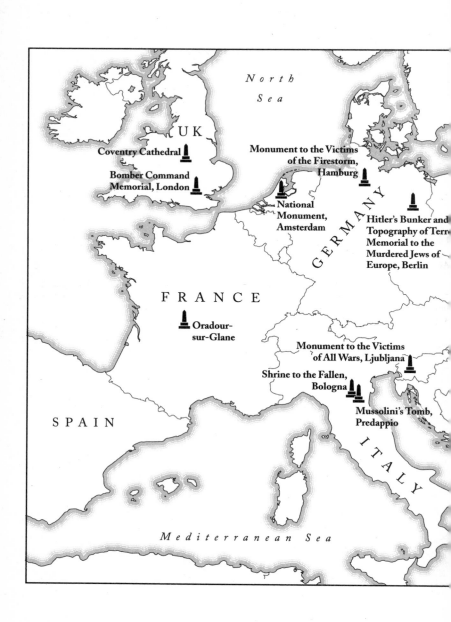

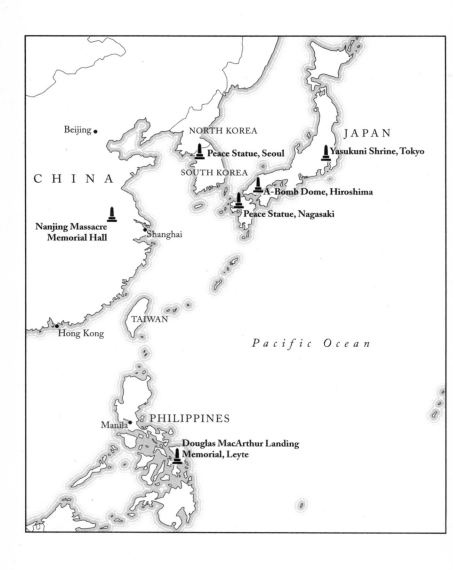

Beijing

NORTH KOREA

JAPAN

Peace Statue, Seoul

Yasukuni Shrine, Tokyo

SOUTH KOREA

CHINA

A-Bomb Dome, Hiroshima

Peace Statue, Nagasaki

Nanjing Massacre
Memorial Hall

Shanghai

TAIWAN

Pacific Ocean

Hong Kong

PHILIPPINES

Manila

Douglas MacArthur Landing
Memorial, Leyte

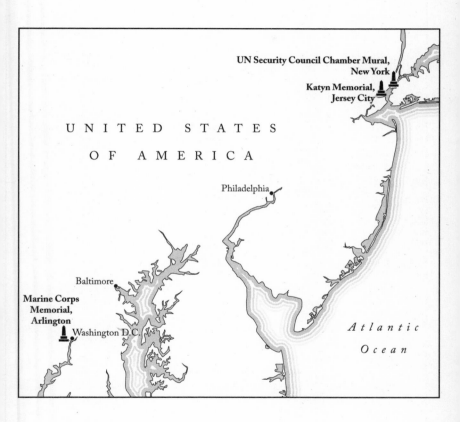

UN Security Council Chamber Mural,
New York

Katyn Memorial,
Jersey City

UNITED   STATES

OF   AMERICA

Philadelphia

Baltimore

Marine Corps
Memorial,
Arlington
Washington D.C.

Atlantic

Ocean

Introduction

In the summer of 2017, American state legislators began removing statues of Confederate heroes from the streets and squares outside public buildings. Nineteenth-century figures like Robert E. Lee and Jefferson Davis, who had fought for the right to keep black slaves, were no longer considered suitable role models for twenty-first-century Americans. And so they came down. All across America, to a chorus of protest and counter-protest, monument after monument was removed.

There was nothing unique about what happened in America: elsewhere, other monuments were also coming down. In 2015, after the removal of a statue of Cecil Rhodes from outside the University of Cape Town, there were calls for the elimination of all symbols of colonialism across South Africa. Soon the 'Rhodes Must Fall' campaign spread to other countries around the world, including the UK, Germany and Canada. In the same year, Islamic fundamentalists began destroying hundreds of ancient statues in Syria and Iraq on the grounds that they were idolatrous. Meanwhile, the national governments of Poland and Ukraine announced the wholesale removal of monuments to Communism. A wave of iconoclasm was sweeping the world.

I watched all this happening with great fascination, but also with a certain incredulity. When I was growing up in the 1970s and 1980s, such occurrences would have been unthinkable. Monuments everywhere were regarded merely as street furniture: they were convenient places to meet and hang out, but few people paid them much attention in themselves. Some were statues of forgotten old men, often with strange headgear and improbable moustaches; others were abstract shapes made of concrete or steel; but either way we did not really understand them. There was certainly no point in calling for their removal, because the majority of people did not care enough about them to make any kind of fuss. But in the past few years, objects that were once all but invisible have suddenly become the centre of attention. Something important seems to have changed.

At the same time as tearing down some of our old monuments, we continue to build new ones. In 2003, the toppling of Saddam Hussein's statue in central Baghdad became one of the defining images of the Iraq War. But within two years of the statue's destruction, a new monument had taken its place: a sculpture of an Iraqi family holding aloft the sun and the moon. For the artists who designed it, the monument represented Iraq's hopes for a new society characterised by peace and freedom – hopes that were almost immediately dashed in the face of renewed corruption, extremism and violence.

Similar changes are taking place all over the world. In America, statues of Robert E. Lee are gradually being replaced by monuments to Rosa Parks or Martin Luther King. In South Africa, the statues of Cecil Rhodes have come down, and monuments to Nelson Mandela have gone up. In eastern Europe, statues of Lenin and Marx make way for depictions of Thomas Masaryk, Józef Piłsudski and other nationalist heroes.

Some of our newest monuments are truly vast in scale,

especially in parts of Asia. At the end of 2018, for example, India unveiled a brand new statue of Sardar Vallabhbhai Patel, who was an important figure in the nation's independence movement during the 1930s and 1940s. Standing at 182 metres (almost 600 feet), it is now the tallest statue in the world. To create such gigantic structures, at such huge cost, implies an incredible level of self-confidence. These are not temporary structures: they have been designed to last hundreds of years. And yet who is to say that they will fare any better than the statues of Lenin or Rhodes or any of the other figures that once seemed so permanent?

It seems to me that several things are going on here at once. Monuments reflect our values, and every society deceives itself that its values are eternal: it is for this reason that we cast those values in stone and set them upon a pedestal. But when the world changes, our monuments – and the values that they represent – remain frozen in time. Today's world is changing at an unprecedented pace, and monuments erected decades or even centuries ago no longer represent the values we hold dear.

The debates currently taking place over our monuments are almost always about identity. In the days when the world was dominated by old white men, it made sense to raise statues in their honour; but in today's world of multiculturalism and greater gender equality, it is not surprising that people are beginning to ask questions. Where are all the statues of women? In a country like South Africa, with its majority black population, why should there be so many statues of white Europeans? In the USA, which has a population as diverse as any on the planet, why is there not more diversity on display in its public spaces?

But beneath these debates lies something even more funda- mental: we can't seem to make up our minds what role our communal history should play in our lives. On the one hand we see history as the solid foundation upon which our world has been built. We imagine it as a benign force, offering us opportunities to learn from the past and progress to our future. History is the very basis of our identity. But on the other hand we view it as a force that stultifies us, holding us hostage to centuries of outdated tradition. It leads us down the same old paths, to make the same mistakes again and again. When left unchallenged, history can ensnare us. It becomes a trap, from which escape seems impossible.

This is the paradox that lies at the heart of our society. Every generation longs to free itself from the tyranny of history; and yet every generation knows instinctively that without it they are nothing, because history and identity are so intertwined.

This book is about our monuments, and what they really tell us about our history and identity. I have picked twenty-five memorials from around the world which say something important about the societies that erected them. Some of these memorials are now massive tourist attractions: millions of people visit them every year. Each of them is controversial. Each tells a story. Some deliberately try to hide more than they reveal, but in doing so show us more about ourselves than they ever intended. What I most want to demonstrate is that none of these monuments is really about the past at all: rather, they are an expression of a history that is still alive today, and which continues to govern our lives whether we like it or not.

The monuments I have chosen are all dedicated to one period in our communal past: the Second World War. There are many reasons for this, but the most important is that, of all our memorials, these are the only ones that seem to have bucked the current trend of iconoclasm. In other words, these monuments continue to say something about who we are in a way that so many of our other monuments no longer do.

Very few war monuments have been torn down in recent years. In fact, quite the opposite has happened: we are building new war memorials at an unprecedented rate. This is not just the case in Europe and America, but also in Asian countries like the Philippines and China. Why should this be? It is not as if our war leaders were any less controversial than some of the figures whose statues have recently been taken down. British and French leaders were just as much champions of colonialism as Cecil Rhodes ever was; American leaders still presided over a racially segregated army; and men from all the Allied forces engaged in acts that would now be considered war crimes. Their attitudes towards women were not always enlightened either. One of our most famous images of the end of the war, *Life* magazine's iconic photograph of a sailor kissing a nurse in New York's Times Square, celebrates what we now know to be a sexual assault. Our collective memory of the Second World War seems to be able to skip over these issues in a way that our memory of other periods can't.

In order to get to the bottom of these questions, I have divided our Second World War monuments into five broad categories. In the first part of the book I will look at some of our most famous monuments to the heroes of the war. I will show how these are the most vulnerable of all our Second World War memorials, and the only ones that show any sign of being toppled or removed. Part II will explore our memorials to the martyrs of the war, and Part III will look at some of the memorial spaces that have been carved out for the war's main villains. The interplay between these three categories is as important as each category itself: the heroes cannot exist without the villains, and neither can the martyrs. In Part IV I will describe memorials to the apocalyptic destruction of the war; and in Part V I will describe some of those to the rebirth that came afterwards. These five categories reflect and reinforce one another. They have created a kind of mythological framework that protects them from the iconoclasm that has ripped through other parts of our collective memory.

I have tried to include a wide variety of monuments, if only to represent the sheer diversity of places that have been used to contain our memories of the past. So I will describe not only figurative statues and abstract sculptures, but also shrines, tombs, ruins, murals, parks and architectural features. Some of the monuments I have chosen were created in the immediate aftermath of the war, while others are much newer – indeed, some are still under construction as I write. Some have an intensely local meaning, while others are of national or even international significance. I have tried to include monuments from many different parts of the world – so, for example, I have included memorials in Israel, China and the Philippines as well as those in the UK, Russia and the USA.

There are great advantages in writing about a period that everyone understands – or, at least, thinks they understand. The Second World War affected every corner of the globe, and most nations around the world commemorate it in one way or another. It is a great cultural equaliser. And yet, as will quickly become apparent in this book, the war is remembered in vastly different ways in different nations. What better way is there to understand the differences between us and our neighbours than to be confronted by our conflicting views on something that we always thought was a shared experience?

Lastly, I have concentrated on Second World War monuments quite simply because of their quality. We sometimes tend to think of monuments as solid, grey, boring, but the sculptures in this book are some of the most dramatic and emotive pieces of public art anywhere in the world. Beneath all the granite and bronze is a mix of everything that makes us who we are – power, glory, bravery, fear, oppression, greatness, hope, love and loss.

We celebrate these and a thousand other qualities in the anticipation that they might free us from the tyranny of the past. And yet, through our desire to immortalise them in stone, they inevitably end up expressing the very forces that continue to keep us prisoners of our history.

Part I

Heroes

We live today in an age of scandal. Our media is so often dominated by stories of corruption among our politicians, our business and religious leaders, our sports stars and screen idols that sometimes it can feel difficult to believe in heroes any more.

It has not always been like this. According to popular memory at least, we once knew exactly who our heroes were. In 1945 we built monuments to the men and women who fought for us in the Second World War, and we continue to build such monuments even today. These monuments speak to us of a simpler time, when people knew right from wrong, and were willing to do their duty for the sake of a greater good.

But how accurate are these memories? Were our heroes really any stronger, braver, or more dutiful than we ourselves are? If we subjected them to the same scrutiny that our politicians and celebrities receive today, would we still be able to see them as heroes?

Our veneration of the Second World War generation says a great deal about how we view our history, and the hold that it still has over us today. In the following pages I will take a look at some of our monuments to heroism around the world, and ask what they say not only about the past, but also about today's values and ideals. I will also explore what happens when those values change over time. Can our heroes ever live up to our expectations? And what happens when our cosy memories of the past clash with a much colder historical reality?

Russia: 'The Motherland Calls', Volgograd

The Second World War was probably the greatest human catastrophe the world has ever seen. Historians have always struggled to find words that can convey even a glimpse of its total scale. We give endless statistics – more than 100 million soldiers mobilised, more than 60 million people killed, more than $1.6 trillion squandered – but such numbers are so large that they are meaningless to most of us.

Monuments, memorials and museums do not rely on statistics: they find other ways to suggest the scale of wartime events. A single well-chosen symbol can often hint at this far better than any words. For example, who can look at the mountain of shoes on display in the Holocaust museum at Auschwitz–Birkenau without imagining the host of corpses from which those shoes were stolen? Sometimes even a tiny object can bring to mind something gigantic. In the Hiroshima Peace Memorial Museum there is a display of clocks and watches that all stopped at the exact moment of the atomic blast. The atom bomb, they seem to say, was so great that it had the power to stop time.

But perhaps the most effective way that memorials convey

the vastness of wartime events is also the simplest: through their own sheer size. Many of the memorials in this book are larger than life. Some are truly gigantic. There is a simple rule of thumb that holds true for most of them: the bigger the event being commemorated, the bigger the monument.

This chapter tells the story of one of the largest of them all: the huge statue that stands on top of Mamayev Kurgan, in the city of Volgograd in Russia. Its size tells us a great deal – not only about the Second World War, but also about the Russian psyche, and the bonds that continue to hold it prisoner.

Mamayev Kurgan is not the site of a single monument, but of a complex of monuments, each more gigantic than the last. The first time I came here, I felt I was entering a realm of titans. At the foot of the hill stands a huge sculpture of a bare-chested man clutching a machine gun in one hand and a grenade in the other. He seems to rise out of the very rock, torso rippling, as tall as a three-storey building. Beyond him, on either side of the steps that lead to the summit, are relief sculptures of giant soldiers springing out of the ruined walls as if in the midst of battle. Farther up the hill is the gigantic figure of a grieving mother, more than twice the size of my house. She is hunched over the body of her dead son, sobbing into a large pool of water, called the 'Lake of Tears'.

The dozens of statues arranged in this park are all giants: not one of them is under six metres (20 feet) tall, and some of them depict heroes three or four times that size. And yet they are dwarfed by the single statue that rises above them all, on the summit of the hill. Here, overlooking the Volga, stands a colossal representation of Mother Russia beckoning to her children to come and fight for her. Her mouth is open in battle cry, her hair and dress fluttering in the wind; and in her right hand she holds a vast sword pointing up into the sky. From her feet to the tip of her sword she stands 85 metres (280 feet) high. She is nearly twice as tall, and forty times as heavy, as the Statue of Liberty in New York City. When she was first unveiled in 1967, she was the largest statue in the world.

This memorial, entitled 'The Motherland Calls!', is one of Russia's most iconic statues. It was the creation of Soviet sculptor Yevgeny Vuchetich, who spent years designing and building it. It contains around 2,500 metric tonnes of metal and 5,500 tonnes of concrete. The sword alone weighs 14 tonnes. So huge was the statue that Vuchetich was obliged to collaborate with a structural engineer, Nikolai Nikitin, to ensure that it did not collapse under its own weight. Holes had to be drilled into the sword to reduce the threat of the wind catching it and causing the whole structure to sway.

Were this monument in Italy or France it would appear absurdly grandiose, but here on the banks of the Volga, in the city that was once called Stalingrad, it feels quietly appropriate. The battle that took place here in 1942 dwarfs anything that happened in the West. It began with the greatest German bombardment of the war, and progressed with attacks and counterattacks by more than a dozen entire armies. Within the city itself, soldiers fought from street to street, and even from room to room, in a landscape of shattered houses. Over the course of five months around two million men lost their lives, their health or their liberty. The combined casualties of this one battle were greater than the casualties that Britain and America together suffered during the whole of the war.

As one stands on the summit of Mamayev Kurgan in the shadow of the gigantic statue of the Motherland, one can feel the weight of all this history. It is oppressive even for a foreigner. But for many Russians this place is sacred. The word 'Kurgan' in Russian means a tumulus or burial mound. The hill is an ancient site dedicated to a fourteenth-century warlord, but in the wake of the greatest battle of the greatest war in history, it carries a new symbolism. This place was one of the major battlegrounds of 1942, and an unknown number of soldiers and civilians are buried here. Even today, when walking on the hill, it is possible to find fragments of metal and bone buried in the soil. The Motherland statue stands, both figuratively and literally, upon a mountain of corpses.

The scale of the war in Russia is one reason why the monuments on Mamayev Kurgan are so huge, but it is not the only reason – in fact, it is not even the main reason. The statues of muscular heroes and weeping mothers might be huge, but it is the giantess on the summit of the hill that dominates them all. It is important to remember that this is a representation not of the war, but of the Motherland. Its message is simple: no matter how great the battle, and no matter how great the enemy, the Motherland is greater still. Her colossal size is supposed to be a comfort to the struggling soldiers and weeping mothers, a reminder that for all their sacrifice, they are at least a part of something powerful and magnificent. This is the true meaning of Mamayev Kurgan.

In the aftermath of the Second World War, the people of the Soviet Union had little to console them. Not only were they traumatised by loss, but they also faced an uncertain future. Russians did not benefit economically from the war as the Americans did: the violence had left their economy in ruins. Nor did Russians win any new freedoms: despite widespread hopes of a political thaw after 1945, Stalinist repression soon started up all over again. Life in Russia after the war was grim.

The only consolation offered to Russian and other Soviet people was that their country had proven itself at last to be a truly great nation. In 1945, the USSR possessed the largest army the world has ever seen. It dominated not only the vast Eurasian land mass, but also the Baltic and the Black Sea. The Second World War had not only restored the country's borders, but extended them, both to the west and to the east, and Soviet influence now stretched deep into the heart of Europe. Before the war, the Soviet Union had been a second-rate power, weakened by internal upheaval. After the war, it was a superpower.

The Motherland statue on Mamayev Kurgan was designed to be proof of all this. It was built in the 1960s, when the USSR was at the height of its strength. It stood as a warning to anyone who dared attack the Soviet Union, but also as a symbol of reassurance to the Soviet people. The giant, it declared, would always protect them.

For the Russian citizens who first stood on the summit of this hill with the Motherland statue at their backs, the vistas looked endless. Everything to the west of them for a thousand miles was Soviet territory. To the east they could travel through nine time zones without once leaving their country. Even the heavens seemed to belong to them: the first man in space was a Russian, and the first woman too. It is impossible to look up at the Motherland statue without also gazing beyond, to the endless skies above her.

Since those days, Russia has never stopped building war memorials. Many of them are on a similar scale to those in Volgograd. In 1974, for example, a statue 42 metres (138 feet) high of a Soviet soldier was erected in Murmansk, in memory of the men who died during the defence of Arctic Russia in July 1941. In the early 1980s, when Ukraine was still a part of the Soviet Union, a second Motherland statue was erected in Kiev. (Like the statue on Mamayev Kurgan, it was designed by Vuchetich. Including its plinth, it stands over 100 metres, or around 320 feet, tall.) And in 1985, in celebration of the fortieth anniversary of the end of the war, a 79-metre-high victory monument (around 260 feet tall) was erected in Riga, the capital of Soviet Latvia.

All these statues and monuments were meant to be symbols of power and confidence. But a generation after the Motherland statue in Volgograd was inaugurated, Soviet power began to waver. In the 1980s, Eastern Bloc countries like Poland and East Germany began to pull away from Soviet influence, culminating in the collapse of Communism in those countries in 1989. Then pieces of the Soviet Union itself began to break off: first Lithuania in March 1990, followed in quick succession by thirteen other states in the Baltic, eastern Europe, the Caucasus and central Asia. The giant was crumbling. The dissolution of the USSR was finally announced on 26 December 1991.

The sense of despair felt by many Russians during this period was palpable. Madeleine Albright, America's Secretary of State at the end of the 1990s, tells the story of meeting a Russian man who complained that 'We used to be a super-power, but now we're Bangladesh with missiles.' For decades, national greatness had been the only consolation for all the loss that men like him had suffered throughout the century. Now this too had been taken away.

In such an atmosphere, Russia's gargantuan war memorials began to look less like symbols of power, and more like Ozymandias in the famous poem by Shelley: relics of past glories, destined to be swallowed, slowly but surely, by the sands of time. But this did not stop the Russian authorities from building them. On the contrary: Russia has never stopped celebrating the glories of the Second World War. In 1995, for example, a brand new 'Museum of the Great Patriotic War' was opened in Moscow. In front of it stands a monument that is even taller than the statue on Mamayev Kurgan: in fact, standing at 141.8 metres (or 465 feet) tall, it is the tallest Second World War memorial anywhere in the world. Other monuments followed. In April 2007, Belgorod, Kursk and Oryol were declared 'Cities of Military Glory' because of the role they had played during the war, and brand new obelisks were erected in each location. The following October, five more cities were given the title, and five more obelisks erected. Within just another five years, more than forty cities across Russia were honoured in the same way, with brand new monuments springing up from Vyborg to Vladivostok.

Why do the Russians continue to commemorate the war in this manner? More than seventy-five years have passed since the final days of the conflict. Is it not time to lay it to rest?

There are a couple of possible explanations for the country's seemingly limitless addiction to massive Second World War monuments. The first is that the trauma caused by the war was so great that Russians simply cannot forget it. They feel compelled to tell the stories of the war again and again, in the same way that individuals who have experienced trauma often have flashbacks. These new memorials, each seemingly bigger than the last, are Russia's way of coming to terms with its past.

I'm sure that this is true, but it is also a little simplistic. For example, it does not explain why the memorials are growing and replicating now more than ever. Is there something about life in Russia today that triggers these concrete flashbacks?

I can't help feeling that there must be a renewed sense of instability, or vulnerability, which is driving Russians to insist ever more stridently upon their wartime heroism. In other words, the monuments that they are erecting today have as much to do with the present as with the past.

Or perhaps this is simply about nation-building. Russia is not the country that it once was. It has lost an empire, and not yet found a new role for itself in the world. For many Russians, the building of war memorials serves as a reminder of the status that their country once had, and perhaps also gives a sense of hope that, one day soon, Russia might rise again. The bigger the monument, the greater the sense of pride – and the greater the nostalgia. The glorification of the war has become a central pillar of Vladimir Putin's programme to forge a new sense of national identity.

This too can be felt at Mamayev Kurgan. During the 1990s, when Russian power was crumbling, the Motherland statue also began to fall apart. Decaying pipes around the 'Lake of Tears' began to leak water into the hill around the statue, making the soil unstable. By the year 2000, deep cracks had begun to appear in the statue's shoulders. A few years later, reports emerged that it was listing 20 centimetres to one side. The cash-strapped Russian government kept promising to pay for reconstruction work, but the money never arrived. Nobody knew whether this official neglect was due to Russia's new-found poverty, or its new-found ambivalence towards its Soviet past.

In recent years, however, the monument has had a new lease of life. When I visited in 2018, the Motherland statue had just been repaired. The other monuments in downtown Volgograd had also been given a facelift, and the whole of the city's Victory Park was closed for refurbishment. In the central square, which is named the 'Square of the Fallen Heroes', school children were practising their marching for a ceremony to honour the Stalingrad dead.

There is pride here, and sorrow, in equal measure. When you climb the hill today, you see people from all over Russia who have come to this place to pay their respects. Families bring children to teach them about the heroism of their great-grandfathers. Young women pose for photos in front of the Motherland statue, and carry red carnations to lay at the feet of the monuments. Military men come in full dress uniform, their medals clanking as they climb the steps.

None of these people can escape the history that has forged them, nor the longing for greatness that has been so integral to their nation's consciousness since 1945. For better or worse, they continue to live in the shadow of the great statue that stands on top of the hill.

The 'Four Sleepers' monument in 2010, before it was taken down

2

Russia and Poland: 'Four Sleepers' Monument, Warsaw

Every nation takes pride in its heroes. The monuments we create to those heroes have a special place in our hearts, because they are representative of all we hold dear: they show us at our very best, with all our most attractive qualities on display. But how we would like to think of ourselves is not always the same as how we really are. And neither is it the same as how we are viewed by others. Our monuments may look glorious to us, but to other people, with other values, they may look distinctly unheroic, even grotesque.

The Russian people are rightly proud of their Second World War heroes, but one does not have to travel far from Russia to find a very different narrative about the role played by that country during the conflict. In neighbouring states like Ukraine and Poland, the Russians are often regarded not as heroes but as colonisers. This narrative too is played out in the story of Europe's monuments. And one monument in particular shows how polarised our different versions of history have become.

* * *

The Monument to Brotherhood in Arms was built in 1945, and erected in Warsaw at the end of that year. It was designed by a Soviet army engineer, Major Alexander Nienko, but was constructed by a group of Polish sculptors. It depicted three larger-than-life soldiers on top of a six-metre plinth (around 20 foot), striding forward, weapons in hand. Standing at the corners of the plinth were four further statues – two Soviet soldiers and two Polish ones – their heads bowed in sombre contemplation. As a result of wartime shortages, the original statues were made of painted plaster; but two years later they were replaced with bronze casts made from melted-down German ammunition. On the plinth itself were inscribed the words: 'Glory to the heroes of the Soviet Army, comrades in arms, who gave their lives for the freedom and independence of the Polish nation'.

This monument was meant to depict a new era of friendship between Poland and the Soviet Union. The two countries had shared an extremely difficult history, stretching right back into Tsarist times. They had actually begun the war on opposite sides: the USSR had initially allied itself with Hitler, and had taken part in the invasion of Poland in 1939. But two years later, when the Nazis had turned against them, the Soviets had sought to build a new relationship with the Poles. They released Polish prisoners and exiles, and allowed them to reform an army. As a consequence, some 200,000 Polish troops fought alongside their former enemies in 1945. The liberation of Warsaw was carried out by Polish soldiers and Soviet soldiers fighting together.

The Monument to Brotherhood in Arms therefore fulfilled several functions at once. It was an acknowledgement of the genuine debt that Poland owed to the Soviets: had it not been for the sacrifices of the Red Army, Poland would not even

have existed in 1945. It promoted hopes for the future: if
Poland and the USSR could collaborate in wartime, then why
not in peacetime too? And, of course, it was a work of political propaganda. The soldiers who stand on the top of the
plinth are Soviets, with the Polish soldiers below them: from
now on, as far as the Soviets were concerned, that would be
the correct hierarchy.

This was the first monument to be built in Warsaw after the
war, but it was soon followed by others. All over the country,
similar memorials began to appear. There were sculptures
celebrating Polish-Soviet friendship, obelisks commemorating
their joint victory over the Nazis, plaques dedicated to their
common war dead, tombs, cemeteries, everlasting flames.
According to a list drawn up in 1994, around 570 monuments
dedicated to fallen Soviet soldiers were built across Poland in
the aftermath of the war. This was all part of an official drive
to build on the wartime collaboration between Poland and the
USSR and forge a new, Communist future together.

Unfortunately, none of these memorials inspired anything like
the love and devotion that similar memorials did in the USSR.
Since they celebrated the exploits and sacrifices of foreign
people, they were not monuments in which Poles themselves
could take much personal pride – at most they were monuments to gratitude and friendship. But when that gratitude
ran dry and that friendship turned sour, the monuments began
to take on an altogether darker meaning.

Most Poles knew very well where they stood in any partnership with the USSR. They saw these symbols of power and
glory and began to suspect that it was not only the Nazis who
had been ground beneath the wheels of Soviet greatness. Soon
they began to take out their frustrations on those symbols.

Soviet monuments were often vandalised, defaced, and covered with nationalist graffiti. They were given derogatory nicknames based on popular memories of the way that Soviet soldiers had behaved during the liberation: names like 'the looters' memorial' or 'the tomb of the unknown rapist'. The Monument to Brotherhood in Arms in Warsaw was no exception. People joked that the statues at each corner were not hanging their heads in mourning, but because they had fallen asleep on duty. Thereafter, the memorial was popularly known as *Czterech Śpiących*, or 'The Four Sleepers'.*

Over the next forty years, the monument continued to stand on its plinth in Warsaw's Praga district. It was occasionally used as a site of remembrance for the war or as a venue for celebrating the more general victory of Communism in Europe. On the thirty-fifth anniversary of the October Revolution, for example, the Warsaw Philharmonic played here, while officials laid flowers at the foot of the monument.

But in 1989, everything changed. During that extraordinary year, Communist governments across eastern Europe began to collapse. The Berlin Wall was breached, dictatorships were toppled, and Soviet monuments everywhere were torn down. For a while the world's newspapers regularly carried photographs of statues falling: Romania's Petru Groza, Albania's Enver Hoxha, Poland's Bolesław Bierut and, all over Europe, Lenin after Lenin after Lenin.

---

* This nickname is more radical than it at first appears. According to popular memory, the Soviet Red Army could have liberated Warsaw as early as 1944, when the local population launched an uprising against the Nazi occupiers. Instead, the Soviets waited until the uprising had been crushed, thereby eliminating any future resistance to their own regime, before finally crossing the Vistula to liberate the shattered city. In other words, they 'slept' while Warsaw burned.

Remarkably, the 'Four Sleepers' monument in Warsaw survived these years unscathed. In 1992 the local authority briefly considered dismantling it; but the idea caused such disagreement – especially when one of the artists who had helped to create it, Stefan Momot, stood up in a meeting to defend it – that the proposal was eventually dropped.

Fifteen years later, however, another attempt was made to remove it, this time on practical grounds. Transport experts were considering the creation of a new tram stop on the exact location of the monument as part of a city-wide transport improvement plan. The tram idea was eventually abandoned, but four years later another transport plan insisted that the 'Four Sleepers' had to be moved to make way for a new underground station. The authorities promised that it would be put back just as soon as the construction of the station was finished. So, in 2011, it was taken down and transported to a conservation workshop in Michałowice.

This, it appeared, was exactly the opportunity that opponents of the memorial had been waiting for. Members of the Law and Justice Party, a right-wing populist movement, were especially vocal. They argued that the monument should never be allowed back to the square, on the grounds that it glorified a foreign power that had subjugated Poland for more than forty years. They called the 'Four Sleepers' a monument to shame, which painted the Polish people as passive bystanders in a Soviet story. It, and all monuments like it, was an insult to Poland, and a falsification of Polish history.

Other figures joined in with the vilification of the monument. Various historians and former dissidents pointed out that the 'Four Sleepers' stood at the centre of a district that had been filled with institutions of state repression. The Warsaw Office of Public Security, a provincial detention centre, the headquarters of the NKVD and a city prison had all stood within 100 metres (328 feet) of the monument. 'In each of these places "the enemies of the state" . . . were interrogated and tortured,' wrote Dr Andrzej Zawistowski of the Polish Institute for National Remembrance. For such people, the monument represented not only the prison of history, but *actual* prisons, where real people had been persecuted.

And yet many others were willing to defend the monument. Socialist politicians argued that the memorial did not glorify Stalinism at all, or commemorate the Soviet leaders who repressed Poland, but merely the ordinary foot-soldiers, who were often conscripted into the Red Army by force. Ageing veterans pointed out that 600,000 of these 'Sachas and Vanyas' had died on Polish soil, and that Polish soldiers were also represented on the monument.

The controversy raged for four years, and involved countless articles in the press, petitions, media debates, demonstrations and acts of vandalism. In 2013, the local authority carried out an opinion poll about whether the monument should stay or go. The results seemed quite emphatic: only 8 per cent wanted the monument to be destroyed, and 12 per cent wanted it moved to a far-off location, but 72 per cent wanted it to be put back in the square. Opponents countered that the sample size had been less than a thousand, and that most people only wanted to keep the monument because it was something they had grown used to. If Poland was to look to the future it needed to free itself from this toxic history.

In the end, it was the nationalist faction that won out. In 2015, the city council announced that it would not return the 'Four Sleepers' monument to Wileński Square after all. Three years later, it was announced that it had been donated to a new Museum of Polish History in the north of the city. According to museum staff, it will finally be on display in 2021 – some ten years after it was removed from its original site.

What is a hero? What is a hero for? Russians see the deconstruction of their war heroes as a personal affront, but heroes are much more than mere representations of actual people; they are also representations of ideas. If you no longer agree with the ideas, then perhaps the heroes must come down.

For Russians, statues like the 'Four Sleepers' represent bravery, liberation, brotherhood – and, of course, greatness. But for Poles and other eastern Europeans, they represent something entirely different: subjugation, humiliation, repression. The truth is that they represent both sets of ideas at the same time, but the emotions surrounding these monuments are so strong that many people are simply not willing to entertain such ambiguity.

The 'Four Sleepers' monument is a single casualty in a war over the memory of 1945 that has swept across Poland in recent years. Dozens of Soviet war monuments were pulled down or destroyed in the exuberant atmosphere of 1989, and dozens more were removed by local councils in the years that followed. In 2017, the national government finally embarked on an official programme to remove those that remained. This went against an agreement made in 1994 between Russia and Poland to respect one another's 'places of memory'. But the Polish government, which by now was dominated by the populist Law and Justice Party, stated that all they were really doing was removing the symbols of foreign power from their towns and cities: they promised not to touch any memorials that marked genuine burial places.

It is not only Poland that has embarked on such a programme. In 2015, for example, the Ukrainian government also passed a law aimed at the complete de-Sovietisation of the country. It included the removal of all Communist symbols and statues of Communist figures, and the renaming of thousands of streets, towns and villages. This was carried out quite quickly. By 2018, the director of the Ukrainian Institute of National Remembrance, Volodymyr Vyatrovych, was able to announce that the de-Communisation of the nation had been achieved.

Similar controversies have hit Soviet war memorials all over eastern and central Europe. The Monument to the Heroes of the Red Army in Vienna is regularly vandalised. The Monument to the Soviet Army in Sofia has repeatedly been daubed with paint – sometimes in jest, but more often in protest over recent actions by the Russian government. The Victory Monument in Riga was bombed in 1997 by a far-right Latvian nationalist group, and since then veterans of the Second World War have repeatedly called for it to be taken down. In Estonia, in 2007, the Bronze Soldier memorial to the 'liberators of Tallinn' was removed from the city centre and relocated in the military cemetery a few kilometres away, sparking two days of protest by Tallinn's ethnic Russian minority.

Many people across eastern Europe regard this iconoclasm as the only way to free their countries from the burden of their Communist past. Given all that they have suffered, this is quite understandable; but, as any psychologist will tell you, history is not so easily escaped. As will become apparent, these people seem to be deconstructing one prison only to build themselves another.

In the meantime, most ordinary Russians struggle to

understand why they should be so hated in eastern Europe. They see the dismantling of monuments to their war heroes as a personal affront. But since they no longer rule in eastern Europe, there is nothing they can do about it.

3

USA: Marine Corps Memorial, Arlington, Virginia

If Russia's monumental heroes reflect that nation's longing for greatness, what of the other post-war superpower? How do Americans tend to view their heroes?

In my working life, I often travel to different parts of the world giving lectures about the Second World War. In one particular lecture I talk about America's mythology of heroism. It is a subject that fascinates me because, to a European like me, it seems so extreme. Americans sometimes seem to regard their war heroes as if they were not human at all, but figures from legend, or even saints. President Reagan spoke of them as a Christian army, impelled by faith and blessed by God. President Clinton called them 'freedom's warriors', who had immortalised themselves by fighting 'the forces of darkness'. TV journalist Tom Brokaw famously proclaimed them 'the greatest generation any society has ever produced'. How can any real-life soldier or veteran possibly live up to such expectations?

I have noticed that reactions to my lecture differ depending on where I deliver it. Whenever I'm in America, my audience tends to listen respectfully in silence: some of them agree with me, and some of them don't. But when I give this lecture anywhere in Europe, the audience tends to snigger. At one point, when I quote at length from a speech given by Bill Clinton to commemorate the fiftieth anniversary of VE Day, they sometimes laugh out loud. American rhetoric, to many Europeans, sounds ridiculous.

It is always nice to get a laugh when you're speaking; but there is something about this particular laughter that worries me. Europeans often make fun of America's insular view of the world, but they themselves are often equally ignorant of America. They don't mean to be disrespectful; they simply can't quite believe that anyone is serious when they speak about their war veterans in this way. But Americans are deadly serious. In the American consciousness, the role that their soldiers played during the Second World War has come to represent everything that is best about their country.

This gulf in understanding between Europeans and Americans is immediately apparent as soon as one looks at their war memorials. America makes monuments to its heroes; Europe much more often makes monuments to its victims. American monuments are triumphant; European ones are melancholy. American monuments are idealistic, while European ones – occasionally, at least – are more likely to be morally ambiguous.

If America does not understand Europe, it is because America never suffered as Europe or Asia did. The vast majority of Americans only ever experienced the war through the images brought home by film units and war photographers, which did not always give the most truthful or complete picture of what was taking place. Some of the most famous American monuments to the war are based on these photographs, and it is no wonder that they portray a rather idealistic view.

If Europe does not understand America, however, it is for very different reasons. Europeans have failed to grasp the fact that American depth of feeling about the war comes not from a sense of history, but from a sense of identity. The war is nothing but a screen upon which they have projected much deeper ideas and emotions that are right at the heart of the American psyche. In other words, when public figures in America wax lyrical about the war, they aren't really talking about the war at all. This, as we shall see, is obvious as soon as one takes a closer look at their war memorials.

One of the best-loved monuments to American heroism during the Second World War is the Marine Corps memorial in Arlington, Virginia. It stands at the very heart of American power, not far from the Pentagon building, with an unrestricted view across the Potomac River to the Lincoln Memorial, the Washington Monument and the US Capitol. It is undeniably one of the most important monuments in the country.

Strictly speaking, this isn't a Second World War memorial at all – it is a memorial to *all* the marines who have fallen since the formation of the corps in 1775. But it was built in the immediate aftermath of the Second World War, and paid for by donations from marines who had served during that war. Furthermore, it is based on one of the most iconic images from 1945 – Joe Rosenthal's photograph of the moment when a group of marines raised a flag on Mount Suribachi during the battle for the island of Iwo Jima.

The memorial depicts six soldiers, their weapons slung over their shoulders, standing on a patch of jagged, unforgiving ground. Like all the statues we have seen so far they are colossal – more than five times taller than an average man.

The figure at the front of the group leans forward, his body almost horizontal, using all his weight to drive a gigantic flagpole into the ground. Those behind him are hunched together, trying also to lend their weight to the task. At the back of the group, one of the marines stretches upwards, his fingers not quite reaching the pole. Beneath them, on the black granite plinth, are Fleet Admiral Chester Nimitz's words summing up the performance of the Marines at Iwo Jima, 'Uncommon valor was a common virtue'.

Like all good memorials, this one tells a story. However, it is a story with many layers, and to understand it properly, one needs to go right back to the beginning of the conflict.

America's war began on 7 December 1941 when the Japanese launched their notorious attack on the US Pacific Fleet at Pearl Harbor. This remains one of the defining events of American history. For ninety minutes, hundreds of Japanese planes bombed American ships, airfields and port facilities, killing more than 2,400 people and wounding almost 1,200 more. Twenty-one ships were sunk, and 188 military aircraft destroyed. The attack came as a complete surprise, because the US Secretary of State did not receive a declaration of war until after it had begun. The sense of shock that this produced in American society is impossible to overstate. Its only recent parallel has been the terrorist attacks of 9/11.

The logic behind this military strike was simple. Japan wanted to take control of the whole Pacific region, and knew that in order to do so they would have to discourage America from stepping in. The Japanese leadership did not think that America had the stomach for a long war in the Pacific, and were willing to gamble that a quick, decisive victory would force them to negotiate a settlement. In other words, Pearl

Harbor was not supposed to start a war with America; it was supposed to prevent one.

Anyone with even a cursory knowledge of US history could have told them that this was a risky strategy. America *never* gives up without a fight. Once they had recovered from their initial surprise, the American military responded with ruthless determination. Over the next three and a half years it clawed its way, step by step, back across the Pacific Ocean. It fought huge naval battles in the Coral Sea and at Midway; it launched submarine strikes against Japanese supply lines; it liberated one island group after another.

The Marines were often at the forefront of the action. The battles they fought to secure Guadalcanal, Tarawa, the Marshall Islands, the Mariana Islands and Palau were some of the most brutal of the whole war. At this time, Japanese soldiers were considered notorious for their viciousness and their refusal to surrender, and inflicted terrible casualties on the less experienced Americans. Before long, the US Marines began repaying them in kind, taking few prisoners, and occasionally massacring them after they had been disarmed. Reports and photographs of atrocities by either side rarely made it back home to America, because US censors wished to spare the public both the anguish and the shame of what was really going on.

Eventually, US forces advanced all the way to the shores of Japan. The first island they reached was Iwo Jima. After four days of savage fighting, a group of marines managed to fight their way to the top of Mount Suribachi, the highest point of the island. To signal that they had reached the summit, they attached a US flag to a length of piping and raised it. Later that day, a second group of marines brought a larger flag up to replace it, and war photographer Joe Rosenthal was there to capture the moment for posterity.

It is this second flag-raising that the Marine Corps Memorial immortalises in bronze. The sculpture is a study in determination. The effort required to plant the flag is plain to see: each one of the six figures appears to be straining every sinew. They are the personification of American grit. The sculpture is also a study in unity: these Americans are all working together in harmony, their hands placed along the same pole, their legs bent in parallel with one another. It is a study in violence – more so, perhaps, than any other American monument to the war. No Japanese soldiers are being killed here, but the force with which the six men are driving the flag into hostile foreign ground is at least suggestive of something darker, which the US censor never allowed the American people to see.

Most of all, however, this is a study in vengeance. The story that begins with Pearl Harbor ends with American troops raising their flag on Japanese soil. In this sense, it is as stark a warning as the statue of the Motherland in Volgograd: this is what happens to anyone who dares attack America.

All these qualities would have been keenly felt by those who stood before the memorial when it was first unveiled in November 1954. Three of the men depicted in the sculpture were present at the inauguration ceremony, as were the mothers of the other three, who had been killed shortly after Joe Rosenthal's iconic photograph was taken. They and the 5,000 other attendees, many of whom had direct experience of the Pacific War, would have had good cause to nurture some of the darker emotions inspired by the monument.

But vengeance and grim determination are not qualities that explain the reverence with which the majority of Americans regard this monument. The thousands of people who come each week to pay their respects, or to watch one of the sunset parades that are performed in front of the monument during the summer months, are not here to celebrate violence. There is clearly something else going on.

To understand this, one must move one's gaze from the figures at the front of the monument to those at the back. These men are not driving a spike into the soil, they are reaching their hands up, as if to heaven. Above them flies the US flag. The figure right at the back is trying to touch the flagpole, his outstretched fingers not quite reaching it. The effect is reminiscent of Michelangelo's famous painting of Adam stretching his hand towards God in the Sistine Chapel in Rome.

Felix de Weldon, the artist who sculpted the memorial, explained the image in a speech at the inauguration in 1954. 'The hands of these men reaching out,' he said, are 'groping for that which may be beyond one's means to attain, needing assistance from the power above, that power which we all need in time of adversity, and without whose guidance our efforts might well be fruitless.' This divine guidance is symbolised by the flag above them, which de Weldon called 'the emblem of our unity, our power, our thoughts and purpose as a nation'.

In other words, the real subject of the sculpture is not the US Marines at all, nor the victory over the Japanese, nor anything else to do with the Second World War. It is the flag which gives the monument its real meaning. This symbol, with its fusion of God and nation, is the real reason why the memorial is so well loved in America.

If there is a gulf of understanding between Europeans and Americans over the memory of the Second World War, then this is one of the issues that lies at the heart of it. Europe and

America learned very different lessons from the war. In the 1930s Europe was exposed to all the dangers of flag-waving. In the violent years that followed it experienced firsthand what happens when fanatical nationalism is allowed to get out of control. As a consequence, flags today are symbols that must be treated with great care. In post-war, post-colonial Europe, anyone who shows excessive passion towards their national flag is generally treated with suspicion. The idea of a monument glorifying the planting of a national flag on foreign soil would be absolutely unthinkable.

In the USA, by contrast, flags are everywhere: outside court-rooms, outside schools and government buildings, in public parks, outside people's homes, on their cars, adorning their clothes. The national anthem, which is nothing less than a hymn to the flag, is sung before every NFL football game; and the pledge of allegiance to the flag is recited by every child from the moment they are old enough to attend school. This has been the case since long before the Second World War; but the war cemented the holy bond between Americans and their flag.

What Europeans fail to understand is that, to most Americans, the flag means much more than mere nationhood. It is a symbol of virtues they believe to be universal: hope, freedom, justice and democracy. Between 1941 and 1945, Americans watched the progress of their flag across Europe and the Pacific, saw liberation spreading in its wake, and knew that they were doing something remarkable. After the war they were magnanimous to those they had defeated, nursing their economies back to health, and quickly handing them back their independence. This is the final meaning of the Iwo Jima memorial: when an American soldier plants a flag on foreign soil it is not an act of domination, but of liberation.

Americans understand this instinctively. That is why, since 1945, America has paraded its flag so proudly in Korea, Vietnam, Grenada, Somalia and Afghanistan. It is why, during the liberation of Baghdad in 2003, a modern marine climbed the statue of Saddam Hussein in Firdos Square and wrapped a US flag around his face. Americans believe passionately in the values they promote, which are no different from the values for which they fought the Second World War.

Unfortunately, other parts of the world see things rather differently. As we shall see next, however glorious an American flag seems when flown in the USA, it begins to look very different when planted on foreign soil.

4

USA and the Philippines: Douglas MacArthur Landing Memorial, Leyte

Just as the Soviets had monuments erected in their honour in other countries after the war, so too did the Americans. There are several in western Europe, most famously in Normandy near the beaches where the Allies landed on D-Day. There are also several in the Pacific, in places like Guadalcanal and Papua New Guinea, which saw some of the most vicious fighting of the war.

Unlike the Soviets, however, the Americans did not impose their own visions of glory upon the nations that they liberated. They did not seize positions on hill tops and in town squares, so that their monuments would dominate the urban land-scape. On the whole, they confined their memorials to the cemeteries where US servicemen lay buried. As a conse-quence, American monuments have never aroused the same animosity that monuments to the Soviets have: what nation could possibly object to their liberators paying quiet tribute to their dead?

Every now and then, however, a different kind of monument to American heroism is raised on foreign soil, and things suddenly become much more controversial.

One such monument can be found in the municipality of Palo, on the coast of Leyte in the Philippines. It consists of seven statues, standing in a pool of water near the shore. They are larger-than-life representations of the American officers and aides who led the liberation of the country from the Japanese in 1944. Among them is the Filipino president of the time, Sergio Osmeña – but he is not the main figure. Standing front and centre, taller than all the others, is the Supreme Commander of the Allied Forces for the South West Pacific Area, General Douglas MacArthur. He stands upright, chest out, shoulders back, as he strides purposefully towards the shore. His eyes are hidden behind dark glasses, but it is clear that his gaze is fixed on the land he is liberating.

The Douglas MacArthur Landing Memorial is based on a photograph that was taken on this very coastline in 1944 when its liberators first waded ashore. Like most monuments devoted to American soldiers, it represents a variety of heroic virtues: perseverance, bravery, goodness, redemption, victory. Unlike most other monuments, however, it locates those virtues not in a generic hero or American everyman, but in a real-life historical figure. And not just any figure: Douglas MacArthur was one of the most controversial generals of the war.

Had the Americans themselves erected this memorial, it would have raised a few eyebrows. But the fact that it was commissioned and paid for by the Filipino government is even more interesting. No other monument says more than this one about the fallibility of American heroes, or how they are viewed by the nations they liberated.

* * *

'I have returned': Gaetano Faillace's famous photograph of
MacArthur striding ashore at Leyte in 1944

Douglas MacArthur was a towering figure in the history of
both the Philippines and the US Army. His father was military
governor of the islands during their first days as a US colony,
and MacArthur himself served there several times, first as a
junior officer and later as commander. In the mid-1930s he
was appointed field marshal of the Philippine Army – the first
and only American ever to have held this rank. But what
would make him truly famous, and indeed infamous, was the
role that he played here and in other parts of Asia during and
after the Second World War.

MacArthur's war began on the morning of 8 December
1941, when the Japanese attacked the Philippines just a few
hours after they had struck Pearl Harbor. MacArthur, who
had only recently been put in charge of all US Army forces
in the Far East, was taken completely by surprise. Most of his
planes were destroyed on the ground before they even had a

chance to take off. Soon his coastal defences on Luzon were also overwhelmed, and his troops were forced to fall back in disarray.

They retreated to the Bataan peninsula, a mountainous stretch of jungle just across the bay from Manila, where they hoped to hold out until help arrived from the US Navy. But that help never came. For three and a half months MacArthur's men fought a series of desperate skirmishes against the Japanese with barely enough food and supplies to sustain them. Eventually they could hold out no longer. At the beginning of April 1942, around 80,000 starving men gave themselves up to the Japanese. Over the next two weeks at least 5,000 would die on an infamous 'death march' to internment camps in the north of the island. Thousands more were to die in squalid conditions as they waited out the rest of the war in captivity.

MacArthur himself escaped this fate at the last minute. Under the cover of night, he and a few key staff boarded a handful of patrol torpedo boats on the island of Corregidor and fled south to Mindanao. From here they caught one of the last flights out of the Philippines to safety in Australia.

Almost as soon as he arrived on Australian soil, MacArthur announced his determination to redeem himself. 'I shall return,' he told reporters on the station platform while he was changing trains at Terowie in South Australia. Over the next two and a half years he devoted himself to fulfilling this promise. Building up a force of eighteen American divisions, he fought desperate battles in Papua New Guinea and the Admiralty Islands. Gradually he clawed his way north towards the Philippines.

His return was just as dramatic as his escape. On 20 October 1944, backed up by the power of the US Seventh

Fleet, MacArthur began landing 200,000 men on the island of Leyte. While the battle was still raging, MacArthur himself boarded one of the landing boats and headed towards the shore. When it hit ground a few yards from the shoreline, he and his staff stepped down into the water and waded through the surf. The sound of small arms fire could be heard all around them, but MacArthur continued to walk fearlessly up onto the beach.

In the following days, a photograph of him striding through the waves would make front pages all over the world, accompanied by gushing articles which sang his praises to the skies. 'The successful Philippines invasion is more than a great military victory, it is a personal triumph for MacArthur,' announced one Australian newspaper. 'With a crusader's zeal and singleness of purpose rarely encountered, he concentrated everything into redeeming his pledge to the Filipino nation and to the haggard, battleworn Americans overrun on Bataan and Corregidor.'

MacArthur himself seemed to sense the huge historical importance of the moment. After he had waded ashore, he made his way to a radio and broadcast an extraordinary speech full of religious imagery. 'To the people of the Philippines,' he announced, 'I have returned . . . The hour of your redemption is here . . . Rally to me! . . . The guidance of divine God points the way. Follow in His name to the Holy Grail of righteous victory!'

This is the story told by the memorial that stands on the beach today. It depicts an American hero: compassionate but tough, determined not to give up on a desperate cause, unafraid to get his hands dirty, or his shoes wet, in the pursuit of liberating his people. Symbolically speaking, MacArthur *is* America. He is shown here bestowing upon the Philippines the most precious gift that America had to offer – the gift of freedom. But he is more than America, too: he is a father returning to save his children, a shepherd returning to save his flock. Looking at the memorial today, there is more than a touch of the Messiah about the way that he and his disciples stand in their pool of water: they appear to be walking on top of the water rather than wading through it. Behind them is nothing but sea and sky: it is as if they have descended not from a landing craft but from heaven itself.

Most memorials endow a kind of mythical power to the events of the past – that's the whole point of them. But imbuing a real historical figure with such qualities is a dangerous game. No man can possibly live up to such ideals, let alone a man as flamboyantly flawed as Douglas MacArthur.

There are other ways of telling the story which are not nearly so flattering to MacArthur. Many historians believe that his leadership, particularly at the beginning of the war, was greatly overrated. Why were his men not prepared for an attack? Why was their retreat to Bataan such a shambles? And why did he take such credit for the return to the Philippines, when it was only the victories of commanders in other branches of the military – particularly the US Navy – that made it possible?

Far from being the selfless, moral paragon of contemporary news stories, MacArthur is often accused of carelessness towards his men. At the beginning of the war, while his troops were starving on Bataan, he set up his command post on the well-stocked and well-fortified island of Corregidor. Records show that he only visited his beleaguered men on the mainland once. Embittered by his absence, they began calling him 'Dugout Doug', and composed disparaging songs about him, sung to the tune of 'The Battle Hymn of the Republic':

Dugout Doug, come out from hiding
Dugout Doug, come out from hiding
Give to Franklin the glad tidings
That his troops go starving on!

The care he took of civilian lives was not always exemplary either. During the landings at Palo he ruthlessly shelled the coastline, regardless of the civilians who lived there: it was only thanks to an American spy called Charles Parsons that local residents evacuated the area before the bombardment began. Later on in the campaign, MacArthur's forces bombarded Manila so comprehensively that by the end there was little left to liberate: around 100,000 Filipinos are thought to have been killed, and the historic heart of the city was reduced to rubble. When viewed from this perspective, MacArthur's record is not nearly as admirable as it at first appears.

If MacArthur was an exceptional military leader, he was also a highly narcissistic one. It was not mere chance that made the photograph of MacArthur wading ashore so famous: he himself gave it a helping hand. The picture was taken by his personal photographer, Gaetano Faillace, and promoted by his personal team of public relations officers. This team was notorious for stretching the truth in order to make the general look good. They often pretended that MacArthur was at the front with his men when he was actually hundreds of miles away in the comfort of Australia. They gave him credit for other people's successes, much to the chagrin of the US Navy, the Marine Corps, and even his own subordinates. According to George Kenny, MacArthur's air force chief, 'unless a news release painted the General with a halo and seated him on the highest pedestal in the universe, it should be killed.'

After his death, questions also began to arise about

MacArthur's moral character. In a groundbreaking article in the *Pacific Historical Review*, historian Carol Petillo revealed that the general had accepted a mysterious payment from the pre-war president of the Philippines, Manuel Quezon, of half a million dollars. The payment was made in the desperate days of early 1942, when Filipino leaders like Quezon were scrambling to escape falling into the hands of the Japanese. MacArthur had already told Washington that he was not willing to rescue Quezon; but after he received the money, Quezon was indeed evacuated. Most historians would stop short of suggesting that the money was a bribe to get MacArthur to change his mind; but all agree that there is something distasteful about an American leader accepting such a huge sum of money during the darkest days of the war, when his own men, just a few miles away on the Bataan peninsula, were starving.

Once one knows all this about Douglas MacArthur, is it possible to look at the memorial in the same way? The monument was supposed to celebrate the virtues of bravery, perseverance and morality, but what if it inadvertently celebrated a different set of qualities – vanity, arrogance and corruption? And what if these qualities also ended up being identified, via MacArthur, with America?

It is unlikely that the artist who created the monument asked himself any of these questions. Filipino sculptor Anastacio Caedo was commissioned to build the memorial in the mid-1970s, when memories of the war were still strong in the Philippines and MacArthur was still universally held in high regard. MacArthur was always the central figure in the monument. By his own admission, Caedo did not know the identity of all the men he was sculpting – he was simply trying to make a three-dimensional image of Faillace's famous photograph.

Caedo wanted to make the sculptures out of bronze, but there was not enough time or funds to get them ready for the inauguration. He therefore cast them in reinforced concrete and painted them with metallic olive-drab paint. (Today's bronze statues are a later replacement.) The unveiling was to take place in October 1977, but first there were political hurdles to negotiate. The president's wife, Imelda Marcos, ordered major changes to the memorial at the last moment. Caedo's sculpture included a giant landing craft as a backdrop to the seven statues, exactly as the wartime photographs showed; but the First Lady ordered the backdrop torn down, saying that the monument 'should honour men, not barges'. Caedo, who had spent eight months building this element of the memorial, reportedly burst into tears when it was dismantled.

It was not only Imelda Marcos who took a direct interest in the memorial. Her husband, President Ferdinand Marcos, was also heavily involved both in the planning of the monument and in the celebration of it when it was unveiled. In a speech at the inauguration, he made it clear what the memorial was supposed to symbolise: 'Let this Landing Memorial . . . be a tribute to the American fighting men who crossed the vast Pacific in fulfilment of a promise to return,' he said. Furthermore, 'Let it be a renewal of the Filipino people's bond of friendship with the people of the United States of America.'

Other public figures of the time expressed similar sentiments. The Filipino foreign minister, Carlos Romulo, emphasised how important the memory of MacArthur was for Filipino–American relations. 'We owe him a debt of gratitude that we cannot forget,' he said in an interview in 1981. 'His name is revered and idolised in the Philippines.'

There was a certain amount of national self-interest in

making such statements. During the 1970s, the Philippines was in thrall to American investment, American financial and military aid, and American credit. The country was moreover home to dozens of American military bases, from which US troops dominated the western Pacific and the South China Sea. In such an atmosphere, it certainly made sense to pay tribute to 'American fighting men' like MacArthur. Corrupt Filipino officials also had darker reasons to sing America's praises. Many of them, starting with President Marcos himself, were making a fortune out of bribes from American businesses, or from skimming development aid as it entered the country. The occasional grand gesture towards the USA was probably considered a sound investment.

However, alongside such cynical motivations, there was also a great deal of sincerity. Corrupt or not, Marcos and his administration did not impose the memorial upon his nation: it was always backed by popular sentiment. And probably personal sentiment too: it is impossible to escape the suspicion that government leaders had their own private reasons for wanting to see MacArthur honoured in this way. President Marcos had served under the general during the war, and claimed to have been personally decorated by him (although such claims later turned out to be more than a little exaggerated). Marcos was every bit as narcissistic as MacArthur, and repeatedly tried to wrap himself in the general's reflected glory. His wife, Imelda, also had a personal interest in the memorial: she had grown up in Leyte, very close to where the landings took place, and had witnessed the liberation first hand. Carlos Romulo, meanwhile, was even closer to MacArthur; so close, in fact, that he himself appears in the monument (he is the helmeted figure standing at the back of the group).

In commissioning this memorial, interfering in its design, and celebrating it so wholeheartedly, those at the centre of government were not only honouring an important moment in Filipino history; nor were they merely acknowledging an important military, political and economic alliance. They were also dramatising one of the most important moments in their own lives.

* * *

Times change. When I first visited the Philippines in 1990, a fresh wind had already begun to blow. Marcos had gone, ousted by a popular uprising in 1986; his government had been revealed as one of the most fantastically corrupt and violent regimes of the post-war era; and a new, democratic government under Cory Aquino had begun investigating his crimes. The whole country was struggling to come to terms with its immediate past.

At the same time, resentment of American power was running high, particularly regarding the presence of American military bases on the islands. US soldiers were no longer regarded as heroes, but as a humiliating imposition upon a sovereign nation. The Filipino press often carried stories about the exploitation of women around the huge air force and naval bases at Angeles City and Subic Bay. The national conversation was all about taking back control from a giant, neo-colonial power.

Anti-Americanism also found its way into academic circles. Several historians, among them the renowned Renato Constantino, had begun to challenge the popular view of the liberation at the end of the Second World War. They claimed that the Philippines had not needed rescuing by outsiders, and that the Filipino resistance had been on the verge of defeating the Japanese on their own. MacArthur was no longer the unequivocal hero he had once been: in some quarters he was regarded as a symbol of continued American imperialism, stepping ashore in Leyte not to liberate the Philippines, but to reclaim it.

Over the following years, successive governments decided to try to commemorate a much more Filipino-focused view of history. New monuments were built, most notably a Filipino Heroes Memorial (inaugurated in 1992) and a monument to the victims of the liberation of Manila (in 1995). In more recent years memorials have even been built to the Hukbalahap – a wartime guerrilla movement that fought against not only the Japanese but also the return of the Americans.

If the Philippines were to follow the same pattern as other countries, the next step would be clear: there would be calls on politicians to shake off their colonial history and tear down the memorial to MacArthur. In one or two other Asian countries something similar has already happened. In South Korea, for example, where MacArthur was long revered as the commander who turned the tide of the Korean War, his statue in Incheon has been the focus of repeated demonstrations against American influence in the country. In 2005, riots broke out around the statue, with protesters calling for it to be torn down.

So far, however, the Filipino people have stopped short of such moves, at least as far as the MacArthur Landing Memorial is concerned. The authorities still treat this monument with great care and respect. When one of the seven statues (that of Carlos Romulo) was toppled by a typhoon in 2013, it was immediately repaired by the government and restored to its position. War veterans and their families continue to visit the memorial every year on 20 October, accompanied by dignitaries from Manila, Washington, Canberra and Tokyo. Down on the beach there are regular re-enactments of the battle, and the nearby city of Tacloban holds an annual Liberation Day parade.

Despite all his faults, and the long-running arguments between historians, MacArthur is still a hero in the Philippines – if only for the single moment when he stepped upon the shore of Leyte. Today the statues in Palo representing him and his aides are a little tarnished by weather and corrosion. They have been soiled by the birds that occasionally land on them. But they stand nevertheless, their eyes focused on the Philippine shore, their faces still a picture of grim determination.

5

UK: Bomber Command Memorial, London

The USSR and the USA were not the only major victors of the Second World War: Britain also belonged to this elite club of heroes. Of the so-called 'Big Three', Britain was the only one to have been engaged in the war right from the very start. It therefore holds a special place in Allied history.

Britain's capital, London, was for many years the epicentre of the Allied war effort. As a consequence, it has become home to dozens of different war memorials devoted to all manner of people and nationalities. There are monuments to the civilians who died in the Blitz, to the city's firefighters, its railway workers and its air raid wardens. There are large installations dedicated to the Canadian soldiers who fought for Britain, to the Australians, to the New Zealanders and to the soldiers from India and the rest of the British Empire. Every branch of the military seems to have its own monument here, from fighter pilots and tank crews to Gurkhas and Chindits. There are statues of generals, admirals and air marshals. There is even a memorial to the animals that served during the war.

However, one monument in London stands out among all

the others. The RAF Bomber Command Memorial in Green Park is one of London's newest: it was only inaugurated in 2012, long after almost all the others were built. It is also by far the largest Second World War memorial in the city: over 8 metres (26 feet) high and 80 metres (262 feet) long, it is probably twice as big as its nearest rival. But what really makes the memorial unique is its design. Unlike London's other war monuments, which all stand out in the open, this one is semi-enclosed. It conceals its message inside an elaborate structure of Doric columns and classical balustrades: it looks more like a Greek temple than a war memorial. Inside, taking the place of Mars or Apollo, are the statues of seven airmen, standing in a group as though they have just returned from a mission. It is quite clear from their size, their stance, and the way that each of them gazes confidently into the distance that these men are supposed to be heroes. As you enter the temple-like structure, you are forced to look up at them as if they were objects of worship. Above their heads, the roof is open, so that nothing stands between them and heaven. If ever there were a temple to British heroism, this surely is it.

The Bomber Command Memorial is one of the most important monuments in London, but it is also one of the most problematic. Despite the heroic pose of the statues within, it is not at all clear *why* these men should be considered heroes. Unlike so many other statues devoted to the war, they are not raising a flag, or wielding a sword, or stepping onto a beach to liberate a nation. In fact, they are not in any kind of dynamic pose at all: they are just standing there. On the wall, carved deep into the stone, is an inscription telling us that 55,573 similar men were killed during the war. But this does not explain their heroic stance either: dying in large numbers like this implies some kind of victimhood, not heroism. On the opposite wall is a quote from Winston Churchill, claiming that 'the bombers alone provide the means of victory'. But how? And why? What exactly did these men do to win our adulation?

To understand what this memorial is commemorating, you need to know something about the bomber war, and the leading role that Britain took in this type of combat during the Second World War. But to understand why it looks as it does, why it is so much bigger than every other British war memorial, and what it is really trying to say, you need to understand the political atmosphere in the UK at the beginning of the twenty-first century, and the forces that led to the building of the monument in the first place.

Britain's bomber war is one of the most controversial episodes in the country's recent history. It began with the best of intentions. The British government made a solemn promise to spare civilians wherever possible, and only sent its bombers to strike specific military installations. But bombing specific targets in those days meant getting in close and bombing in broad daylight. In such circumstances the slow bomber planes were easy targets for flak guns and fighter planes: casualties among British aircrews were catastrophic.

So the Royal Air Force changed tactics. It began bombing at night instead, and from higher altitudes. This kept British planes and crews safer, but it also made their bombing far less accurate. According to a government report in 1942, only one in three British bombs landed within *five miles* of its target.

Far from being Churchill's 'means of victory', therefore, bombing was turning out to be a costly failure. The RAF seemed to be faced with two alternatives, both of them equally hopeless. They could attack in daylight and be shot down, or they could attack by night and miss their targets.

It was at this point that a new commander-in-chief took charge at Bomber Command – a brusque, uncompromising leader named Arthur Harris. It was Harris who championed the idea of a different kind of bombing: to forget about picking out individual military targets, and simply bomb entire cities instead. There was a certain brutal logic to this. If bombing were to work then it would have to be acknowledged as the blunt instrument that it was. By bombing large areas, the RAF could destroy not only the factories and installations that were supplying Germany with arms, but also the homes of the workers who staffed those factories. Killing the workers them- selves was part of the plan: in a total war, factory workers were considered a target just as legitimate as the soldiers they supplied.

But Harris went further. By devastating entire cities, he believed that he could break not only the German economy, but also the will of the German people to continue fighting at all. According to this reasoning, shops, restaurants, schools and hospitals were legitimate targets. The purpose was to drive Germany to despair. Thus, ordinary civilians were no longer collateral damage – they had themselves become targets.

Harris knew that he was crossing a moral line, but believed that the ends justified the means: if he could bring an early end to the war, he reasoned, then his brutal policy might end up saving more lives than it took. He was quite open about this, and wanted to enlist the support of the British people. The only reason he did not explain his strategy publicly was that the government prevented him from doing so. Churchill and his cabinet wholeheartedly endorsed the strategy; but they wanted to keep up the pretence that Bomber Command's targets were always strictly military.

Unfortunately German morale never collapsed as Harris hoped it would. The war dragged on, and city after city in Germany was devastated. According to military historian Richard Overy, some 600,000 civilians were killed beneath Allied bombs, not only in Germany, but also in those countries that the Allies were liberating. It was a horrific death toll, outnumbering the British victims of German bombs by almost ten to one. At the time, however, the British public did not seem to care too much. Every successful bombing was reported in the newspapers with triumphant glee. Bomber crews went on publicity tours of British factories, and the stories they told the workers were invariably greeted with cheers. The loss of German civilian life was deemed a price worth paying.

Towards the end of the war, however, the atmosphere suddenly changed. The turning point was the bombing of Dresden in February 1945. During a press conference after the raid, a senior officer let slip that it had been conducted partly to destroy 'what is left of German morale'. In the following days, stories began to appear claiming that the British were conducting 'terror bombing'. Questions were asked in the House of Commons. After the American press got hold of the story, the Royal Air Force was put under considerable international pressure to explain its actions.

It was not long before the British establishment turned its back on the men of Bomber Command. Churchill drafted a memo to his chiefs of staff berating them for indulging in 'acts of terror and wanton destruction' (although he toned down his rhetoric in the final version of the memo). The hypocrisy of this memo is really quite something. Churchill had always known what strategy Harris was following, but had never before expressed much concern about it. After the Allied victory in May 1945, Churchill praised every branch of the armed forces in his victory speech – but made almost no mention of Britain's bombers. In his bestselling memoirs, published after the war, Churchill omitted the bombing of Dresden. It was as if he hoped that the episode could be erased from public memory simply by not talking about it.

Naturally, the men who flew the bombers were quite disoriented by this sudden change of heart. As the official historian of the bomber war, Noble Frankland, put it, 'Most people were very pleased with Bomber Command during the war and until it was virtually won; then they turned around and said it wasn't a very nice way to wage war.'

The indignation this caused over the following years cannot be overestimated. I have known and interviewed dozens of British bomber crew, and most of them have spoken bitterly about the way they were shunned by the establishment after 1945. Many were upset that they were never granted their own specific medal, but instead had to make do with a more generic campaign medal that was granted to everyone in the air force. They saw this as yet another way in which their contribution to the war was being discreetly brushed under the carpet. Worse still was the way that they were treated by the general public. During the war, a bomber crewman who walked into a pub in uniform would rarely have to buy his own drinks; but after 1945 he would have to think twice before admitting to what he'd done during the war. In the 1960s especially, when a new generation was questioning the actions of its parents, students sometimes mocked the claims of bomber veterans that they were 'only following orders'. Right-wing historians like David Irving also drew deliberate, if dubious, parallels between Nazi atrocities and the actions of the RAF. The men of Bomber Command, once heroes, were suddenly being treated as villains.

Eventually this backlash against veterans of the air war fizzled out, and a more nuanced view began to take hold. In the late 1970s, historians like Martin Middlebrook and Max Hastings led the way in rehabilitating the men of Bomber Command in the minds of the public. Since then there have been dozens and dozens of popular histories by authors like Robin Neillands, Mel Rolfe and Kevin Wilson. In the years when I used to work in military publishing I collaborated with many of these authors, and indeed commissioned some of their books myself.

In the 1990s and 2000s a succession of British TV dramas and documentaries about the bomber war brought this nuanced view of history into the mainstream. Viewers of the BBC drama *Bomber Harris*, or the Channel 4 documentary *Reaping the Whirlwind*, were invited to put themselves in the shoes of the airmen before making moral judgements. Gradually the British public was learning to come to terms with an uncomfortable history.

Sensing that the public was ready to support them, the Bomber Command Association began in 2009 to campaign for a memorial. They were granted their wish three years later, in the summer of 2012, when the Bomber Command Memorial was finally inaugurated.

Had this been all there was to the story, the Bomber Command Memorial would not have been nearly as interesting, or as problematic, as it is today. It might have ended up resembling some of the memorials to the bomber war in other parts of Britain and Germany. For example, it could have been a monument to reconciliation, like Coventry Cathedral's 'Cross of

Nails' (see Chapter 24). It might have been an anti-war sculpture, like the Dammtordamm monument in central Hamburg. At the very least, it might have made a nod to the dark moral choices that Britain was forced to make because of the war. But then a new wave of popular sentiment swept over the issue, making any such nuance almost impossible.

The problems began when the newspapers started to become involved. The Bomber Command Memorial was to be built with private funding, so three daily newspapers – the *Telegraph*, the *Mail* and the *Express* – ran campaigns to raise money. Since these are all newspapers of the political right, the memorial was largely supported by right-wing donors, particularly Lord Ashcroft, the former deputy chairman of the Conservative Party, who contributed £1 million. The political left, by contrast, were scarcely invited to have a say – and nor, to their shame, did they particularly seem to want one. Thus, what should have been a project that brought people together from across the political spectrum ended up being a highly partisan *cause célèbre*.

In order to drum up support for the memorial, the three newspapers, especially the *Daily Mail*, began to publish highly emotive stories about how the men of Bomber Command had been snubbed. Articles began to appear calling them 'Forgotten Heroes', or 'the black sheep of the British popular memory of the Second World War' – despite the fact that they were neither forgotten, nor any longer regarded as 'black sheep'. Online rumours began to spread suggesting that the local council was blocking the construction of a memorial because its planners were ashamed of Britain's bomber crews, or that Germany was putting pressure on the British government to veto the project – stories that had little foundation in truth.

When historians insisted that there should be at least some

mention of the controversial aspects of bombing, they were derided as milksops with no sense of national pride. Columnists claimed that the men of Bomber Command were under attack once again, this time by the forces of political correctness. (In the end, the builders of the memorial did agree to add an inscription mentioning 'those of all nations who lost their lives in the bombing of 1939–1945'. But it was in an awkward position, high up near the roof, and obscured from view by the statue. It was quite obviously an afterthought.)

I watched this happening with a certain amusement, but also with growing incredulity, because I knew from years of research that the vast majority of what was being said was complete nonsense. I was particularly struck by the way that the veterans of Bomber Command were portrayed. The British press always labelled them 'heroes', but in fact were depicting them as victims. None of the men I had interviewed over the years felt nearly as sorry for themselves as the newspapers seemed to feel for them. On the whole they had been sensible men, who had long since come to terms with the way they had fought the war and were generally satisfied with the way that British society had belatedly come to accept them. So where was all this indignation coming from?

The truth is that the Bomber Command Memorial, like all the monuments in this book, says at least as much about the society that erected it as it does about the people it supposedly commemorates. There is nothing modern or contemporary about it, like so many of the other recent memorials that stand nearby: this is a monument to nostalgia. Its classical columns and balustrades evoke a bygone era when Britain was still a great colonial power. The architect, Liam O'Connor, made much of the fact that the style of the memorial echoed the façades of the houses opposite – houses that were built at the height of Britain's imperial splendour. Its size and prominence are the result of a deliberate attempt to create something physically impressive, just as Britain once used to do in the days of Admiral Nelson and Queen Victoria.

The statues, too, are an exercise in nostalgia. Their stance and attitude evoke the stoic heroes of British war films of the 1950s – films like *Reach for the Sky* and *The Dam Busters*. These are heroes who don't have to be seen doing anything dramatic: the drama is all beneath their strong, silent surface. We do not make heroes like this any more.

British people still speak of the Second World War as their 'finest hour', but deep down they also understand that it was the end of something. The Second World War cost Britain its empire, its prestige, and its pre-eminent place in the world economy. After 1945, it was no longer the workshop of the world; and it was never again able to dictate world events as it had done during the previous two centuries. Britain was left virtually bankrupt by the war, and was forced for years to rely on financial aid from the USA. No wonder the British feel indignant, snubbed, cheated by history. No wonder they can't quite make up their minds whether they are heroes or victims.

This has been one of the major themes of post-war life in Britain, and one that the nation still has not come to terms with. During the war itself, officials were already joking that the USA, the USSR and Great Britain were not really the Big Three, but the Big Two and a Half. In the 1960s, the former American Secretary of State Dean Acheson famously said that 'Great Britain has lost an empire and not yet found a role'. The nation regained some of its pride in the 1980s and 1990s, during the age of Thatcherism and 'Cool Britannia', but at the start of the twenty-first century it once again feels itself in the shadow of others: the USA, China, the European Union.

This is the true meaning of the Bomber Command Memorial, with its heroes staring out between Doric columns like prisoners in a cage. They are a group of heroes who appear to have nothing heroic to do. They have finished their mission, but have been cheated of their glory, and now they merely stand there, gazing across London's Green Park, waiting stoically to see what new disappointments might be looming on the horizon.

6

Italy: Shrine to the Fallen, Bologna

The themes on display at London's Bomber Command Memorial are part of a much greater pattern that is evident not only in the UK but all over the world. In the twenty-first century, every nation likes to believe itself a nation of heroes; but deep down, most nations are beginning to think of themselves as victims.

This process has been decades in the making. In the immediate aftermath of the Second World War, heroism was still in great demand. But in the years since then, many nations have come to realise that heroism comes with responsibilities. For example, the USA, the one undisputed winner of the war, has found itself obliged to act as the world's policeman ever since. Britain too felt obliged to keep the world's peace after 1945, despite the fact that it could no longer afford to do so.

There are other dangers, too. Heroes always run the risk of being exposed as the flawed human beings they really are; and, once exposed, they can quickly fall from grace – much as the old Soviet heroes have recently fallen from grace in eastern Europe. In an effort to stave off this trend, some nations have resorted to defending their Second World War heroes with a manic vigour. One need only look at the way that the USA mythologises its 'greatest generation', or that Britain continuously mythologises the figure of Winston Churchill, to see how much work it takes to maintain hero status.

Other nations, however, have given up portraying themselves as heroes altogether. Instead they have increasingly begun to choose another motif for their memorials, equally powerful, and equally pure – that of martyrdom. This is a much easier identity to maintain. It allows a nation to keep the moral high ground without having to shoulder any of the work or responsibility for maintaining peace; and it is an easy way to deflect criticism. In the next part of the book I will discuss the growth of victimhood as a national motif, which comes with its own drawbacks and dangers.

First, however, I want to explore one final monument to heroism, which shows a very different side of what it is to be a hero.

The Shrine to the Fallen in Bologna, Italy, is a much more intimate memorial than any I have described so far. Based on the simplest of ideas, it consists of some 2,000 portraits and names of local resistance fighters attached to the wall of the municipal building in Piazza del Nettuno, right in the centre of the city. This was the site where captured partisans were publicly executed during the war. Since 1945 it has become a commemorative site not only for those who died here, but also for those who died fighting the Nazis and Italian Fascists all over the region.

Unlike any of the other monuments in this book, this one was not erected by the state, or by a museum, or by any other kind of remembrance organisation. It was not planned in advance, but born in a spontaneous burst of emotion. It was put together by local people to commemorate the lives and deaths of those they had known and loved. It highlights something about the war that does not come across in most larger, state-sponsored memorials: the Second World War was not only a titanic conflict between giant armies on the battlefield, it was also an intensely local war fought in the hills and the forests, and on the streets of towns far behind the front lines. The war had a different flavour in Italy from that of Poland or France; and it had a different flavour in Bologna from that of Naples or Milan. The Shrine to the Fallen was not constructed to express national virtues or ambitions; it was simply an expression of local pride, and local loss. It is reminiscent of something that we all do privately in our living rooms at home – display the portraits of those we most love. This is who we are, it says. These people are family.

The war in Italy was much more complicated than it was in other parts of Europe. Italy had begun the war as an ally of Germany, but ended up being occupied by German forces when it tried to change sides in 1943. After the Allies invaded the south, the Germans set up a puppet government under Benito Mussolini in the north, and the country was effectively split in two. In the midst of this upheaval, a resistance movement grew up. All kinds of groups joined the partisans, but the driving force behind it was the Italian Communist Party, which sought not only to liberate the nation from the Germans, but also to overthrow the Fascists who had ruled Italy since the 1920s, and to institute widespread social change in the process.

As a major centre of the Resistance, Bologna suffered more than most places in Italy. In the last year of the war, the region was awash with intrigue and violence. In nearby Marzabotto, an entire village was massacred by the Waffen-SS in reprisal for local resistance activity – at least 770 men, women and children were shot in cold blood, or burned to death in their houses. Within Bologna city centre there were more than forty different public shootings, involving around 140 men and women. Piazza del Nettuno was a favourite spot for both the Nazis and the Italian Fascists to carry out these executions. Between July 1944 and the end of the war at least eighteen people were shot here. Their bodies were left on display as a warning to the local population; and to drive the point home, a sarcastic notice was placed on the wall proclaiming it a 'place of refreshment for partisans'.

However, if such violence was supposed to deter people from joining the Resistance, it did not work. By the end of the war the Bolognese people had had enough. On 19 April they rose up in insurrection, and within two days had taken control of the city. According to official figures, by this time more than 14,000 local people were actively fighting for the partisans, of which more than 2,200 were women. Bologna was in the vanguard of a nationwide movement: a few days later, on 25 April, insurrection spread to all parts of northern Italy.

As the Germans and their Fascist puppets fled the city, the people of Bologna were at last able to mourn their losses publicly. The families of those who had been executed returned to Piazza del Nettuno and set up a shrine to their loved ones. Someone pushed an old green table against the wall, upon which people could place little mementos, flowers and framed photographs of those who had died. An Italian flag was hung on the wall, and more photographs were pinned to it.

In the coming days, this shrine grew and grew. Within a couple of months there were hundreds of photographs spreading for 20 metres along the wall. It quickly became not only a place of mourning for those who had been killed on this spot, but also a place of respect for all those who had died in the name of freedom. There were photographs and tributes to all kinds of people: teenage boys executed for resistance activities, women in their sixties who had died heroically in combat, men in their prime who had died in training accidents or had been tortured to death by the authorities. The full range of the partisan experience was represented here.

It was not long before the new city authorities decided that the shrine should become a permanent feature affixed to the medieval wall of the Palazzo d'Accursio. In 1955 the paper photographs were taken down and replaced with weatherproof tiles, each one displaying the name or portrait of a single man or woman. Today there are more than two thousand tiles on that wall, along with sixteen larger tiles reproducing photos of the time. It is an enduring reminder of the suffering and bravery of the people of Bologna.

As the saying goes, everything is political. The Shrine to the Fallen may have begun as a simple symbol of mourning; but there was always more to it than that. It was inevitable that it would include some political overtones; after all, it had been built to commemorate those who had died for their beliefs. Political themes were therefore present in the shrine from the beginning, and would continue to characterise it over the following decades.

The liberation of Bologna in April 1945 was a chaotic and violent event. According to Edward Reep, an American war artist who witnessed the liberation of the city, one of the first acts to take place in Piazza del Nettuno in April 1945 was not

one of mourning at all, but one of vengeance. Before the
shrine was first set up, a Fascist collaborator was shot here:
his fresh blood was still visible on the wall. In other words,
the political violence that had characterised the war years was
not quite over; it was just that the boot was now on the other
foot. In the long aftermath of the war, similar violence would
continue to rear its head from time to time all over Italy.

The original shrine in 1945

According to Reep, political symbols were incorporated
into the shrine even while it was first taking shape:

Within minutes, an Italian flag was hung on the wall, above
and to the left of the blood stain . . . The House of Savoy
emblem had been ripped away from the white central panel
of the flag; pinned in its place was a stiff black ribbon of
mourning. This became a dual gesture: it signified the end of

the monarchy and Fascism, and it became a memorial to those who had given their lives in the long struggle for liberation.

It was upon this flag that mourners first pinned their photographs.*

In the following years, the Shrine became one of many monuments in Bologna dedicated to the partisans. In 1946, a bronze statue of Mussolini on horseback was melted down to create two new statues of Italian Resistance fighters: they can be seen today at Porta Lame, north-west of the city centre. In 1959, an Ossuary to the Fallen Partisans was built in Certosa Cemetery by architect Piero Bottoni, and in the 1970s two more monuments were built: one in Villa Spada, and another at Sabbiuno, just south of the city. In addition, several streets and piazzas were renamed after the war. For example, the piazza named after King Umberto I became 'Piazza of the Martyrs of 1943–1945'.

All this was part of a deliberate attempt not only to demonstrate the city's moral and social rebirth after the war, but also to redefine its very identity. Monarchist and Fascist symbols were torn down, and symbols of the Resistance were put up in their place. If Bologna was to be a city of heroes, they were not to be the old, elitist heroes. From now on it would be workers and students who were celebrated – ordinary people, with faces like those on display in Piazza del Nettuno.

Under the gaze of all those dead heroes, the people of Bologna were more or less obliged to follow the future laid out for them by the memory of their wartime struggles. In

---

* In 1946, Reep painted a prize-winning picture of this shrine, which launched his career as an artist. Today it is part of the permanent collection of Washington, DC's National Museum of American Art.

the first post-war municipal elections, held in March 1946, they elected a member of the Resistance as their mayor. Giuseppe Dozza would lead the city council for the next twenty years; and his party, the Italian Communist Party, would remain the major force in Bolognese politics for most of the rest of the century.

In the 1970s and 1980s the city once again came under attack. During the *anni di piombo* – the 'years of lead' – the whole of Italy became embroiled in political violence. Many other cities suffered terrorist attacks at the hands of the Communist 'Red Brigades'; but Bologna came under assault from neo-Fascists. In 1980, a bomb was set off at the main railway station, killing eighty-five people and injuring some two hundred more. Two smaller-scale attacks also happened in 1974 and 1984, killing a dozen or so people each time. The reason was clear: Bologna had been targeted because it was a left-wing city.

To commemorate these attacks, a new plaque was put up in Piazza del Nettuno close to the Shrine, listing the names of the dead. Unwittingly, however, the new plaque marked a subtle shift in the city's memorial landscape. The original Shrine to the Fallen had never given the impression of a people that felt sorry for themselves, despite the terrible atrocities they had suffered during the war. The wording above it states clearly, in large metal letters, that the wartime partisans were heroes who had died in a just cause: 'for liberty and justice, for honour and the independence of the fatherland'. The wording on the new plaque, however, carried no such message. Here, the dead were simply 'victims of Fascist terrorism'. They had not died in a cause. There was no semblance of heroism. When the two memorials are taken together, the lines between heroism and victimhood no longer seem so clear-cut. The senseless violence of the 1980s is reflected back in time to the equally senseless violence of the war years, and even the partisans begin to look less like heroes and more like martyrs.

In recent years, there have been even greater shifts in the city's identity. The old certainties of Bolognese political life have long since broken down: Communism died here, just as it did all over Europe, with the end of the Cold War. Since the turn of the century there has been little continuity between the city's wartime past and its present: largely speaking, the Communists have given way to the more moderate Social Democrats. The tides of globalisation are also visible, not only in the university, which has always welcomed students from all over Italy and the world, but also in the general population. More than 10 per cent of the people living in Bologna today come from other countries, and that percentage is growing all the time.

In such a world, the 2,000 portraits on Piazza del Nettuno no longer have the power that they once did. They are obviously from a bygone era. Their faces look stiff, formal – nothing like the smiling selfies that today's generations routinely post on social media. Why should these old portraits be relevant any more? Why should today's city be held prisoner to *their* history, and *their* ideas?

And yet they still dominate the wall of this medieval piazza. Local politicians making their way to and from the town hall must walk past them every day. Students who gather on the steps of the public library sit in their shadow. Like the photographs of long-dead aunts and uncles in countless homes across Bologna, they gaze down on the inhabitants of this left-wing city, silently reminding them of who they are, and where they have come from.

Coda: The End of Heroism

Heroes are like rainbows: they can only really be appreciated from a distance. As soon as we get too close, the very qualities that make them shine tend to disappear.

None of the monuments I have described so far reflect the nuances of historical reality. The greatness of the Russian Motherland was always built on shaky foundations. America's devotion to its flag, while glorious to Americans themselves, always looked a little dubious to everyone else. Britain needed its famous stiff upper lip not only to win the war but also to weather the disappointments that would follow. And resistance movements – not only in Bologna, but all over Europe and Asia – usually did far more dying than they ever did resisting. But none of this really matters, because these monuments were never meant to express historical reality. They are representations of our mythological idea of what it means to be a hero, that's all. They are as much expressions of identity as they are of history.

In some ways our monuments to our Second World War heroes seem quite timeless. The values they express – strength, stoicism, brotherhood, virtue – are no different from the values that all societies have held dear since ancient times. But in other ways they seem hopelessly dated: indeed, some of them, like the Bomber Command Memorial in London, already looked old-fashioned from the moment they were first unveiled. It is no coincidence that all the monuments I have mentioned in this section are conventional statues, or photographs, or statues based on photographs. This is the way that heroes are generally commemorated throughout the world. Compared to some of the monuments I will describe later, they are rather unadventurous.

Heroes represent our ideals. They must be brave but gentle, steadfast but flexible, strong but tolerant; they must always be virtuous, always be flawless, always be ready to spring into action; and as our communal champions they must represent all of us, all the time. No individual can possibly live up to such expectations. Neither can any group.

And yet some nations have been bequeathed these responsibilities by history. As the undisputed victor of the Second World War, America has been called upon to act the hero ever since. To a lesser degree, the UK and France have also felt obliged to take a leading role in international affairs, particularly when it comes to their former colonies. Even Russia sometimes feels obliged to live up to its status as a great power. The efforts of these nations are not always appreciated, and unsurprisingly so: no modern-day international policeman can ever live up to the Second World War ideal.

Times change. Values, even timeless values, go in and out of fashion: who today celebrates qualities like stubbornness, inflexibility, or the willingness to endure silently? Inevitably some of the heroes we used to revere seem faintly tragic, or even slightly ridiculous, to modern sensibilities. Communities also change. Our heroes are supposed to represent who we think we are, or at least who we would like to imagine ourselves to be, but when we begin to adopt new political outlooks, or when our communities absorb people of different classes, religions or ethnicities, it becomes hard to identify with the old heroes any longer.

All this highlights a strange paradox: our heroes, who in our minds seem so strong and indestructible, are actually the most vulnerable figures in the historical pantheon. It does not take much to knock them from their pedestals.

There are other, more robust motifs. As I have already hinted, many groups are now much more likely to portray themselves as martyrs than as heroes. In most cases, the groups in question have little choice in the matter: we are all prisoners of our history, and these are the roles that the tragic events of the past have bequeathed them. Nevertheless, as will become clear, martyrdom turns out to be a much stronger identity than heroism ever was. Heroes come and go. But a martyr is for ever.

Part II

Martyrs

In 1945, every nation believed itself a nation of heroes. However, there is no escaping the fact that in most places the Second World War was not glorious – it was brutal. Whole populations had been bombed, starved, enslaved and humiliated. Millions had died in the most unheroic of settings – not on the battlefield, but in their homes, in gas chambers, or cowering in bomb shelters. Hundreds of thousands of women had been raped. Hundreds of thousands of children had been orphaned. These people were not heroes: they were victims.

Memorials to the victims of the war are some of the most important remembrance sites we have. Most of them have been created for very good reasons. Suffering must be acknowledged. A well-designed memorial can provide a place for people to mourn what they have lost, and remember those who have died. It can bring a divided nation together in its common grief. And it can allow a humiliated population at least some space to forgive themselves: not everyone can be a hero, particularly when they have been rendered powerless by massive forces beyond their control.

However, there is a darker side to such memorials that is rarely confronted. On the one hand they offer us the chance to acknowledge our painful past and rise above it; on the other hand they invite us to wallow in that past until our souls are enchained by it. They can allow us to take ownership of our suffering and thereby control it; or they can allow us to give in to our suffering, abandon all responsibility, and look around for someone else to blame. Remembering the past like this can lead us to dangerous places. Rather than inspiring unity, it can promote division. Rather than bringing us peace, it can rouse us to anger.

There has been a shift in our memorial culture in recent decades. Where once we used to erect monuments to our Second World War heroes, nowadays we much more readily erect monuments to victims and martyrs. There are straightforward political reasons for this. Martyrs, like heroes, inspire loyalty. But while a nation of heroes is obliged to take responsibility for its place in the world, a nation of martyrs is free to be as selfish as it wishes. Martyrs cannot be criticised. Their faults must always be forgiven. Their past suffering is like a perpetual 'Get out of jail free' card, absolving them of all sins.

Unfortunately, this apparent freedom is something of an illusion. As will become apparent in the following chapters, there are costs as well as benefits to such ways of thinking. Nations that view themselves as martyrs are in thrall to their history just like everyone else.

7

Netherlands: National Monument, Amsterdam

The people of the Netherlands suffered greatly during the Second World War. In 1940, their country was invaded by a massive, unstoppable force which inflicted massive damage, particularly in cities like Rotterdam, which was flattened by bombing. For the next five years they suffered the full consequences of Nazi occupation: the stripping of their sovereignty, the rounding up of Jews and other 'undesirables', the exploitation of the Dutch people and the brutal repression of dissent. When resistance activity increased towards the end of the war, the Nazis retaliated by cutting off all shipments of food and fuel to the west of the country. A famine quickly descended: around 18,000 people are thought to have died in what soon became known as the 'Hunger Winter', and hundreds of thousands more were left severely malnourished. By the time the country was finally liberated in May 1945, the Netherlands was on its knees.

In the aftermath of this terrible conflict, the new Dutch government commissioned the building of a monument to ensure that the people never forgot the humiliation and suffering they had been forced to endure. From the very beginning the National Monument was intended to be the most important in the country. It was to be built in the historic heart of Amsterdam, in Dam Square. Its central motif was to be Dutch martyrdom.

The first component of the memorial was built as early as 1946. It was a curved wall, in which were a series of niches, each containing an urn. Each urn was filled with soil taken from a site where Dutch people had been tortured and executed. Originally there were eleven urns in all – one from each province – making this a truly national monument. A few years later a twelfth urn was added containing soil from the Dutch East Indies (present-day Indonesia), in recognition of the suffering that Dutch citizens had also experienced at the hands of the Japanese.

A few years later, a stone pillar was built in front of this curved wall. It was 22 metres (72 feet) tall, and adorned with sculptures created by John Rädecker, one of the Netherlands' most prominent artists. Rädecker's design says a great deal about how the Dutch saw themselves in the aftermath of the war. The main image, which sits on the front of the pillar, consists of four men in chains, one of whom has his arms outstretched like a crucified Christ figure. On either side of this sculpture stand two statues representing the resistance: a bearded figure on the left, who embodies the resistance of the intellectuals, and a muscular figure on the right who represents the workers' resistance. By their feet sit three howling dogs, symbolising fidelity. Above the central image stands a woman holding a child, symbolising the new life that was possible after the end of the war. Above her head is a wreath, symbolising victory. Finally, on the back of the column is a series of doves ascending to heaven, symbolising peace.

The National Monument in 1958, two years after it was first built

The memorial therefore offers several messages at once. The Dutch resisted oppression. They were unified in their suffering. They were faithful to an ideal. And in the end their suffering paid off: they were rewarded with victory, peace, and the opportunity for rebirth.

All in all, it is a very well thought out monument. Its central images are mostly religious in nature. The doves are reminiscent of the Christian symbol for the Holy Spirit; the woman and child are like classical images of the Madonna; and, most importantly, the Christ-like figure represents the martyrdom of the people – tortured, enchained and sacrificed, in the faith that the end of the war would bring them resurrection. It is impossible for a Christian to stand before this monument without feeling the same kind of religious awe that he or she might feel in a church. It is a transcendent vision of the Netherlands during the war: it is the nation as Messiah.

There is just one problem. Not everyone in the Netherlands was Christian, even in 1945. And not everyone who was persecuted by the Nazis died on Dutch soil. By portraying the nation in this way, the monument excludes a variety of groups who do not fit into Rädecker's definition of what it was to be Dutch. The most important of these groups was the one sector of the population that suffered most: the Jews.

If you are looking for a figure to represent martyrdom during the Second World War, there is no better place to start than with Europe's Jews. In the Netherlands they made up only 1.5 per cent of the population; and yet, by the end of the war, they accounted for half of all Dutch casualties. Jews were singled out like no other group in the country. They were hunted down mercilessly, hounded onto trains and sent east to concentration camps. Here, they were either murdered on arrival or slowly worked to death. Around 110,000 were deported in this way. Only about 5,000 ever returned.

Today it seems obvious that any monument to remember the dead should not only include such people, but give them pride of place. So why does the Dutch National Monument ignore them? Were they deliberately excluded? Was it merely an unfortunate oversight? Or was something else going on?

To get an idea of how this might have been allowed to happen, it is worth considering the stories of some of those 5,000 Holocaust survivors who returned to the Netherlands in 1945. At the end of the twentieth century, Dutch historian Dienke Hondius interviewed dozens of these people about their experience of returning home, and found that their stories were broadly similar. Almost all of them felt ignored in 1945. Almost all felt a pressure not to talk about what they had suffered. Worst of all, many found themselves the target of a perverse and misplaced kind of envy. 'You were lucky,' one Jewish survivor was told by an acquaintance in 1945. 'We suffered such hunger!' Another was denied an advance from his employer on the grounds that in Auschwitz, 'You had a roof over your head and food the whole time!'

A charitable excuse for such insensitivity is that it was largely born of ignorance. Unlike in eastern Europe, where the Holocaust took place right under the noses of the people, in the Netherlands there was only ever a vague understanding of what had happened to Jews after they had been deported. Many Dutch people did not acknowledge Jewish suffering because they were scarcely aware of it. It is quite possible that this ignorance extends to the National Monument, whose creators simply did not think to include Jewish suffering as a separate category to be represented.

There are, of course, darker possibilities. Anti-Semitism was prevalent in the Netherlands even before the war, but years of Nazi propaganda were bound to have had some effect on the nation and its people. If no one bothered to think about what had happened to Jews during the war, it was partly because they were not interested. It is conceivable that one of the reasons why Jews were left off the National Monument was because they were not considered worthy. At an unconscious level at least, perhaps they were not really considered Dutch at all.

However, contemporary documents point to another, more political explanation for why the experience of Jews was overlooked. In 1945 there was a great push to bring a divided nation back together. A myth grew up that the Dutch people had suffered as one – a single people, united in their martyrdom. This is the central message of the National

Monument, with its Christian images and its samples of earth taken from atrocity sites in each of the Dutch provinces. Such a myth suited almost everyone, from former collaborators who wanted a chance to be brought back into the fold, to an exhausted public that was eager to put the war behind them.

Unfortunately, however, the Jews did not fit into this comfortable myth – indeed, any acknowledgement of what had happened to them automatically made a mockery of it. Deep down, everyone knew that Jews had been singled out during the war, and that they had suffered in quite a different way from everyone else. Not only that, but they felt ashamed at their failure to come to the Jews' aid. Rather than acknowledge these uncomfortable truths, it was much easier simply to ignore the issue altogether. And so, at a national level at least, Dutch Jews suddenly became invisible.

Whatever the reasons for their exclusion from the National Monument, there was little that Jews in the Netherlands could do about it. Even in Amsterdam, which had once been a thriving Jewish centre, there were now so few Jews left that they were in no position to make much of a fuss. On the whole, they simply kept their heads down and tried to rebuild their lives in silence. After all they had been through, most Jews were unwilling to draw attention to themselves. They were resigned to being invisible.

It was years before the fate of the Jews was properly acknowledged in the Netherlands, but eventually things did change. It began with the publication of Anne Frank's diary in 1947. This Jewish teenager had been forced into hiding, along with her family, for more than two years. They lived in the back rooms of the building where Anne's father had his business, accessed through a secret doorway hidden behind a bookcase.

The family was finally discovered in August 1944, and deported to concentration camps in Germany and occupied Poland. Anne Frank died in Belsen at the beginning of 1945, but her diary survived, and would go on to be an international bestseller.

If Amsterdam's living Jews were silenced and sidelined after the war, this book at least gave them some kind of voice. In the late 1950s, Anne's father, Otto Frank, the only member of his family to survive, purchased the house where they had hidden during the war and converted it into a museum. It opened in 1960 and has gradually grown in importance ever since. Today it attracts more than a million visitors each year, and is one of the most visited museums in the country.

Other commemorations of the Jewish experience of the war eventually followed. In 1962, a new monument to Jewish victims was opened up at the Hollandsche Schouwburg, a former theatre in Amsterdam that had been used as a deportation centre during the war. A memorial wall was erected, listing the surnames of the 104,000 Dutch Jews who had been killed. The inscription on the wall makes it clear that these were not people who had 'died for the Fatherland', but who had been taken away to be murdered. They were not heroes, but victims.

In 1977, a monument to the Jews who had died at Auschwitz was built at the Ooster cemetery. Later, in 1993, this was moved to the Wertheimpark in the Jewish Quarter, and greatly enlarged. It consists of a series of broken mirrors, laid over an urn containing ashes taken from Auschwitz concentration camp. Consciously or otherwise, it makes up for the lack of any similar urn built into the memorial wall of the National Monument in Dam Square.

The commemoration of Jewish suffering in Amsterdam continues in our own century. Since the mid-2000s,

'Stolpersteine' have become a feature of dozens of Amsterdam streets, as they have in many other cities across Europe. These are small brass cobbles, placed in the ground outside the former homes of Jews who were deported during the Holocaust. They are engraved with the names of the Jews who once lived here, the date of their arrest, and their ultimate fate. Today there are more than four hundred of these across Amsterdam.

Finally, as recently as 2016, a National Holocaust Museum opened in Amsterdam, also in the former Jewish Quarter. The suffering that once went ignored here is now commemorated more than any other.

No memorial exists in isolation. In the aftermath of the war, the Dutch government built a single monument that they believed would express the unifying qualities of Dutch suffering during the Second World War. They failed. But in the years since then, Amsterdam has made up for its exclusions and oversights. Today the city has a rich memorial culture that includes many of the victims ignored in the immediate aftermath of the war. For example, Amsterdam was the first city in the world to build a public monument to the gypsies persecuted by the Nazis during the war. Unveiled in 1978, it stands in the Museumplein. Amsterdam was also the first city to build a 'Homomonument' in 1987: a memorial to those persecuted by the Nazis because of their sexuality.

When you stand before the National Monument in Dam Square today, it is worth remembering that this important memorial, with its dramatic Christian imagery, is just the headline: the rest of Amsterdam contains a network of subtexts. The city, like many other cities in Europe, is indeed a city of martyrs; but those martyrs come in a variety of shapes and sizes.

Wu Weishan's sculpture of a mother and dead child at the entrance
of the Nanjing Massacre Memorial Hall

8

China: Nanjing Massacre
Memorial Hall

When did the Second World War begin? The answer to this question depends very much on whom you ask. For Americans, the war began in December 1941, with the bombing of Pearl Harbor. For Europeans it began earlier, in September 1939, with Hitler's invasion of Poland. But for the Chinese the beginning came earlier still, in July 1937, when Japanese and Chinese troops first exchanged fire at the Marco Polo Bridge, just outside Peking (modern Beijing). Unlike earlier incidents, which had usually ended in an embarrassing Chinese capitulation, this one prompted Chiang Kai-shek, the Chinese nationalist leader, to launch a full-scale attack against Japanese troops elsewhere in the country. So began more than eight years of conflict that would cost millions of lives and leave much of eastern China in ruins.

Today, Chinese memories of the war are dominated by what happened in these opening few months. This was the period in which several of the greatest battles took place, and in which Chinese troops inflicted the greatest damage on Japan: there are many tales of heroism for the Chinese to feel pride in. Chiang committed all his best resources at the beginning

of the war, in the hope that he might at least give the Japanese
a bloody nose, and perhaps even draw the support of the
international community on his side. However, at this stage
of the war his troops were no match for Japan's strength and
technical superiority, and it was not long before this heroic
Chinese story gave way to tragedy.

One episode in particular stands out. In November 1937,
just a few months after the conflict had begun, Chinese
forces were driven back to their capital city, Nanking
(modern Nanjing). At the beginning of December, the
Japanese began to surround the city. After fierce fighting
around the city walls, Chiang decided to abandon his position. Tens of thousands of Chinese troops were forced to
escape across the Yangtze River. Those who could not flee
fought on, or surrendered, only to be slaughtered in a series
of mass executions along the river bank. Others tried to hide
among the general population by putting on civilian clothing,
but they were ruthlessly hunted down by Japanese troops,
who conducted inspections of all the men they came across.
Anyone deemed to have a 'military posture' was pulled out
of the crowd, as were men with calloused hands or shoe
sores; and anyone with strap marks on their shoulders was
assumed to have recently been carrying a military backpack
or a rifle. Naturally there were plenty of ordinary civilians
who fell foul of such inspections, and who were taken off
to their deaths.

Neither did the massacres end with those suspected of being
military men. In the aftermath of the battle, Japanese troops
lost all discipline and fell to sacking the city. Women of all
ages were raped and then murdered, as were children and
even infants. There are numerous eyewitness accounts of pregnant women being bayoneted and slit open, and photographic

evidence to back up those accounts. Some Japanese soldiers even took their own photographs – not as evidence, but as souvenirs.

Unsurprisingly, the city quickly descended into chaos. In desperation, civilians began streaming into the city's international zone in the hope that they might find some protection among Nanking's European residents. A small group of twenty or so schoolteachers and missionaries did what they could to help. They negotiated with the Japanese to allow them to set up a 'Safety Zone' for refugees. When Japanese troops came looking for women, they stood between the soldiers and their prey. There is no question that the Japanese were more cautious around the Europeans – they did not want to provoke any kind of incident with the West at this stage. Nevertheless, atrocities continued even in the international Safety Zone for several weeks after the defeat of the city. The testimonies of neutral Europeans, who were able to take photographs and even cine film of the massacres, provide some of the most compelling evidence of the atrocities that took place.

It is not known precisely how many people were murdered during those tragic weeks in December 1937 and January 1938, but it is certainly in the tens if not hundreds of thousands. According to the war crimes tribunal held after the war, around 200,000 were massacred, and at least 20,000 women raped. The official Chinese figure today is 300,000 dead. Some Japanese scholars dispute the higher figures, but nobody – or at least, nobody with any academic credibility – denies that the massacre took place. What has come to be known as the 'Rape of Nanking' was one of the most shameful episodes in the history of the war in China.

* * *

The Chinese institution that leads the way in commemorating these events is called the 'Memorial Hall of the Victims in Nanjing Massacre by Japanese Invaders'. It is truly huge. The site consists of a museum, two mass graves, an academic institute, a series of memorial squares and a peace park. There are dozens of memorial statues and sculptures here, some of them quite epic in scale: the tallest is some 30 metres (98 feet) high, and the longest is 30 metres long. In all, the memorial site occupies more than 28,000 square metres of land, close to the heart of the city. It attracts a remarkable eight million visitors every year.

The first sight that greets you, even before you have entered the complex, is the statue of a mother in torn clothing, carrying the limp body of her dead child. Her head is thrown back in anguish, her mouth a silent wail. The statue, which was sculpted by Chinese artist Wu Weishan, is at least 10 metres (32 feet) tall, and dominates the entrance to the site on Nanjing's busy Shuiximen Street. There is something visceral about the anguish expressed in the sculpture. The despairing slump of the woman's shoulders, the vulnerability of her long, exposed neck, and the lifelessness of her child, which she no longer has the energy to hold up – all this is a statement about what awaits you inside the memorial site.

Once you have followed the crowds past this statue, you come to a series of other statues by the same artist, depicting refugees fleeing the city in 1937. Their faces are contorted in terror. Some of the sculptures show figures dragging or carrying wounded or dying loved ones. Some show corpses of women or children.

There are gruesome statues all around the site. In one place, a giant arm bends out of the ground, its hand clutching life-lessly at the stones that surround it. Nearby a huge severed head lies beside a wall pocked with bullet holes. A stone cross 16 metres (52 feet) high looms over one of the memorial squares, like a tombstone, marked with the dates of the massacre. A statue of a lonely mother stands in a field of stones, searching for the bodies of her dead family. Elsewhere there is a bronze pavement, marked with the cast footprints of 222 witnesses to the massacre.

Everything about the place screams victimhood. To drive the point home, the official number of victims appears several times in metre-high letters. Inside the museum this number – 300,000 – is cast in bronze and lit from above in an otherwise darkened room. In the memorial square it is written in eleven different languages on a granite wall. It is carved in stone on one of the memorial's giant staircases; and it is written in black paint across the side of one of the many sculptures. It is repeated like a mantra throughout the memorial site, as if daring anyone to challenge its authority.

As with all such numbers, there is an element of deception going on here. The figure of 300,000 is high enough to be horrifying, round enough to be memorable, and low enough to be plausible – but in reality, nobody knows how many people were slaughtered in Nanjing at the end of 1937. For the Chinese, the number 300,000 is a symbol in which they can invest emotional energy, while allowing them some respite from contemplating the distressing reality of the individual details of murder and mutilation. For the Japanese, particularly for right-wing deniers of the massacre, the number conveniently gives them something to argue with. How exactly was this number reached? Does it include military as well as civilian casualties? Does it include people from the surrounding region, or only those from Nanjing's city centre? How can so many people possibly have been killed

This iconic number is reproduced repeatedly across the memorial site

when the official population of Nanjing at the time was only around 190,000 – or were refugees also included in the head count? All these questions are valid, but they also provide a useful distraction from the horror of what Japanese soldiers actually did.

At the centre of the memorial site is a museum which contains over a thousand relics and photographs of the massacre. The most important part of the museum contains graphic photographic evidence of the atrocity. There is a picture of a nineteen-year-old pregnant woman who had been raped and stabbed thirty times in the face, belly and thighs – miraculously she lived to tell the tale, but she lost her baby. There are relics and remains found at the sites of mass graves around the city. There is even a mass grave right here, inside the museum: a dark pit containing twenty-three skeletons that was discovered during the construction of the building's extension in 2007.

In a separate building beyond the museum is a second mass grave site containing the remains of 208 corpses. After seeing their skeletons, visitors are invited to a meditation hall, where they can contemplate the full horror of the things they have just seen and meditate on the names of some of the hundreds of victims that are recorded here.

The overall experience of visiting this place is quite over-whelming, even for foreigners with no personal connection to Nanjing. For those who call the city home, and for those whose parents or grandparents were caught up in these events, it must be close to unbearable. The museum designers obvi-ously understood this, and have done their best to ease visitors out of the disturbing sights they have just witnessed. After coming through the darkness of the mass grave sites and the meditation hall, visitors emerge into a bright and beautiful 'Peace Garden' surrounded by mature trees which sway in the breeze, masking the sound of the traffic outside. A long pool lined with yellow flowers reflects the colours of the sky; and at the far end of the garden a statue of the goddess of peace rises above the city.

Nevertheless, it is difficult to leave this place without an acute sense of trauma. It is not the statue of peace that one remembers when one returns home, but the statue of the bereaved mother at the entrance to the museum, whose silent scream seems like a metaphor for the anguish of an entire city.

The first time I visited the Nanjing Memorial Hall was in April 2019. I had been invited to Nanjing by its curator, Zhang Jianjun, who wanted me to present some of my work to his colleagues. While I was there he offered to show me around with the help of one of his tour guides.

Whenever I meet a Chinese scholar of twentieth-century

history, the question I ask them is this: why did it take China forty years to get around to commemorating the events of the Second World War? It was not until the 1980s that any public memory projects really took off. The Nanjing Memorial Hall is a perfect example: it was not opened until 1985. What took them so long?

Over the years, some of the answers I have received to this question have been quite prosaic. A few historians have told me baldly that China had quite enough to deal with during those four decades, including a civil war, the Korean War, the Great Leap Forward and the Cultural Revolution: there was simply no time or energy to revisit the events of the Second World War with any degree of thought. Others have brushed my question aside with the observation that China is not so different from many western countries: few of the world's great Holocaust museums and memorials existed before the 1980s either. It takes time for any nation to come to terms with past traumas.

Some of the scholars I met in Nanjing took a more political view of my question: they told me that while the Chinese Communist Party was so focused on class war, memories of a nationalist war against Japan were not considered politically useful or interesting. Chairman Mao is reputed to have thanked the Japanese for invading China because ultimately it helped him to seize control of the country. It was not until after Mao's death that it became possible to revisit the traumas of 1937; and it was only in the 1980s that Communist leaders realised the potential of Chinese wartime suffering as a motif that might be used to bring greater unity to the nation.

When I asked Zhang Jianjun why he believed there had been such a delay in commemorating the events of 1937, the answer he gave me was not entirely unexpected, but was nevertheless disturbing. Before 1982, he explained, there was no appetite for reopening old wounds. But in that year, according to Zhang, the Japanese Ministry of Education committed a seemingly wilful act of provocation: they altered their school history textbooks in order to downplay Japanese responsibility for the war. 'People here would like to forget these unhappy past events,' he told me. 'Personally, I think that if the Japanese government had never revised their text-books denying the massacre, we probably would never have had a memorial museum, because it would not have been necessary.'

Zhang's remarks, although true in spirit, gloss over a more nuanced history. There was indeed a huge international controversy about Japanese school textbooks in 1982, but it was based on a misunderstanding: the revisions Zhang referred to never exactly took place. He was absolutely right that Japanese textbooks tended to play down the invasion, but in the 1980s this was not a new phenomenon. The more egre-gious revisions and omissions had largely taken place decades earlier: the typical Japanese textbook of the 1950s and 1960s barely mentioned the massacre in Nanjing, and only ever in the blandest of terms. To put it simply, in 1982 no real revisions took place because there was nothing much to revise.

What the Chinese authorities were reacting to in 1982 was not the mainstream Japanese point of view, which was in fact beginning to change in favour of the Chinese, but rather the *backlash* against that point of view. As Zhang pointed out to me, right-wing nationalists in Japan became much more vocal in the 1980s, and a few of them were also very violent. They sent death threats to those who spoke about Japanese guilt, and occasionally even acted upon such threats. But the reason for their violence was that they had so demonstrably lost the argument about Japan's wartime history. By the end of that decade, the overwhelming majority of Japanese academic thinking had rejected right-wing rhetoric and accepted Japan's collective guilt for the war: and indeed, since then, almost all Japan's history textbooks have been revised to *include* the Nanjing Massacre.

The Nanjing Memorial Hall therefore seems to have been created out of several impulses at once. First, it fulfilled an academic need for greater understanding – and public documentation – of an important moment in Chinese history. Second, it provided a much-needed public acknowledgement of a trauma that had scarred a whole community. Lastly, however, it also played a political role in a new rivalry between Japan and China that began to emerge in the 1980s, and which was being expressed through the symbolism of the Second World War. For better or worse, the Nanjing Memorial Hall has become an aspect of that rivalry, as Japan and China compete over memories of their collective past.

In the past three decades there has been an explosion of historical consciousness in China, particularly in the public memory of the Second World War. The Nanjing Massacre has been at the heart of this revolution: it has become a national symbol of Chinese martyrdom. Thousands of books have been written about the atrocity over the last thirty years, and thousands of films, TV dramas and documentaries have been made. Today, Chinese TV companies make some two hundred programmes a year dramatising the 1937–45 war, the vast majority of which use the Nanjing Massacre as their central motif. The reason why the Nanjing Memorial Hall is so huge – and the reason why it sees such a phenomenal number of visitors each year – is that it is not merely a local institution, but a national one. Nanjing stands for all the atrocities that took place during the war, no matter where in China they occurred. Since 2014 the anniversary of the Nanjing Massacre has been a national holiday.

In Japan, by contrast, the pace of change has been much slower and more erratic. Some members of the general public, particularly those on the political right, have been reluctant to acknowledge the darker facts of their history. They do not generally deny that war crimes occurred, but they have begun to question whether the scale of those crimes was as great as the Chinese claim they were. They have also become extremely suspicious of Chinese motives for continually bringing up the past. As some Japanese politicians point out, there have been many Japanese apologies over the years – from individuals, from institutions and from the government itself – and yet the Chinese never seem to be satisfied. In recent years, right-wing revisionism has begun to gain ground again, especially on social media. The Nanjing Memorial Hall has been accused, quite unfairly, of being an institution whose only function is to point an admonishing finger directly at Japan.

Herein lies one of the great problems of our times. The only way that the Chinese sense of martyrdom can ever be assuaged is through apology, followed by apology, followed by apology – and each apology must be absolutely unequivocal. Germany has managed to do this with its neighbours in Europe; why can't Japan follow suit? But at the moment this is not something that even mainstream Japan, let alone Japan's right wing, is prepared to do.

In the absence of any such unconditional surrender from Japan, feelings in China are only likely to grow stronger. This is simply human nature: victims cannot overcome their past when those who wronged them insist on calling their most traumatic memories into question. All they can do is to reaffirm their own stories more loudly and more vehemently. The louder the Chinese shout, the more defensive the Japanese become. Along the way, objective history is increasingly smothered by a seemingly endless cycle of accusation and denial.

Given the poisonous history between these two countries, it would be easy to become gloomy about their future relations; but in fact there is also cause for hope, especially at a local level. The Nanjing Memorial Hall carries out a huge amount of reconciliation work with partners in Japan; and thousands of Japanese people come here each year to pay their respects. Relations between the curators of this institution and their counterparts in Japan are generally very good.

There is evidence of this spirit of cooperation elsewhere too. During my visit to Nanjing, I happened to meet a local historian – a quiet, thoughtful man named Liu Xiaoping, whose knowledge of his home city was truly encyclopaedic. Liu offered to show me another memorial to the massacre, off the beaten track, next to a main road by the river. This was the site where 9,800 Chinese soldiers were executed during the massacre. In 1985 a memorial stone was placed here to mark the site, along with an abstract tripod sculpture, topped with a carved stone wreath of flowers.

Today the monument is well-tended, with neatly cropped hedges that screen it slightly from the busy road; but thirty years ago, soon after it was erected, it fell into disrepair. Local people paid little attention to it, and used the site to dump rubbish.

According to Liu, the reason why it is so well looked after today is that a group of Japanese tourists came here to pay their respects and express their remorse. They were so shocked to discover the state it was in that they alerted the local government, which stepped in to tidy the place up. It was Japanese concern that rescued this place, and the Chinese local officials worked together with them to make sure that the memory of the massacre was respected here.

Neither the Chinese nor the Japanese will ever escape the history of what happened in Nanjing at the end of 1937. But it is small gestures like these that provide the best hope for making that history seem just a little more bearable.

The original Peace Statue sits outside the Japanese embassy in Seoul, but dozens of duplicates, like this one, stand in parks and cities all over the country

South Korea:
Peace Statue, Seoul

If the relationship between China and Japan is occasionally strained, then that between South Korea and Japan sometimes appears even worse. Korea was a Japanese colony between 1910 and 1945, and was ruthlessly exploited by the colonisers, especially during the Second World War. Today, however, South Korean politicians often use the past as a weapon to attack contemporary Japan. In recent years, claim and counter-claim between the two countries have degenerated into another seemingly endless cycle of finger-pointing.

At the centre of this storm of mutual indignation stand two monuments. In Japan, much nationalist sentiment about the war years is focused on the Yasukuni Shrine – a place that arouses nothing but outrage in South Korea. (I shall discuss the various controversies around this institution later, in Chapter 14.) For Koreans, meanwhile, painful memories of the past are expressed in the form of a bronze statue in down-town Seoul – a statue that many Japanese people, especially on the political right, have come to hate.

At first sight it is difficult to see what could possibly be offensive about the Peace Statue. It is a bronze sculpture of a young woman – little more than a girl, really – sitting on a chair with her hands clenched. She is wearing a traditional Korean dress. On her shoulder is a little bird, representing peace and freedom. She stares straight ahead of her, with an impassive but determined expression on her face. Beside her is a second, empty chair: an invitation to sit beside her, perhaps, or else a symbol of another, missing, person.

On the face of it, there should be nothing controversial about this statue at all. The girl does not appear particularly angry or upset; she is not scowling, or gesturing in any way that could be considered offensive. Even the title of the monument seems quite benign: what could possibly be wrong with a 'Peace Statue'?

It is only when one knows who this girl represents that one begins to understand why she provokes such emotion. She is in fact a depiction of a 'comfort woman' – the Japanese euphemism for a prostitute who serviced Japanese soldiers during the war. Between 1937 and 1945, tens of thousands of Korean women were tricked into becoming 'comfort women'. They were often promised good jobs in factories far from home, before being abducted and held in brothels as sex slaves. Rather than cracking down on such trafficking, the Japanese authorities turned a blind eye. Indeed, according to some accounts at least, the Japanese military not only colluded in this vast system of sexual slavery, but may even have set it up deliberately.

What makes this statue so controversial is that it sits on the pavement directly opposite the Japanese embassy in Seoul. The girl's face may not show any signs of anger or hurt, but she is staring directly at the diplomatic mission, and her clenched fists speak volumes. Koreans call it a 'Peace Statue', but it is quite clearly much, much more than that.

* * *

There has always been a very strong undercurrent of anti-Japanese sentiment in Korea. Before the twentieth century, the country had frequently been in conflict with its neighbour, often having to rely on China or Russia to provide a counterbalance to Japanese power. After 1905, however, when Japan had defeated the last of its regional rivals, Korea fell entirely within the Japanese sphere of influence. The country was formally annexed into the Japanese empire in 1910; and thus began thirty-five years of colonial exploitation.

The zenith of this exploitation came during the Second World War, when Japanese rule began to intrude on all aspects of Korean life. Between 1939 and 1945, some 200,000 Korean men were drafted into the Japanese Imperial Army, and at least a further 1.5 million were conscripted to work in Japanese factories. Women were also forced into all kinds of work for the Japanese. According to a proclamation in 1941, all Korean women between the ages of 14 and 25 were obliged to give up thirty days of work for the government each year – a system that seemed only to encourage the abuse of young girls. By the end of the war women of all ages were being forcibly drafted by the Japanese for much longer periods. A proportion of these women never made it to the factories, but were kidnapped and imprisoned in Japanese military brothels.

Unfortunately, the end of the Second World War did not bring an end to Korea's troubles. Unlike the people of neighbouring China, or of other colonial countries like Indonesia and Vietnam, Koreans never had the satisfaction of taking part in their own liberation. The Japanese ruled right up to the last moments of the war, at which point they were replaced by other outsiders: the Russians in the north and the Americans in the south. Koreans themselves seemed to have little control over their own destiny.

In the years that followed, two opposing systems were imposed upon Korea, each of them equally brutal, and each sponsored by a different superpower. In the north, the Soviets installed the Communist dictator Kim Il-sung, whose dynasty has ruled there ever since. In the south, the Americans sponsored a series of brutal military dictatorships that lasted until the 1980s. Conflict between the two systems erupted violently in 1950 with the onset of the Korean War, which went on to claim the lives of at least 1.2 million people. Despite the bloodshed nothing was resolved, and to this day Korea is split in two.

None of these later tragedies can be laid at Japan's door; however, as is frequently pointed out, they would never have happened were it not for the way that Japan had first subjugated Korea, and then involved the country in the Second World War.

Soon there were other reasons for Koreans to be resentful. In the 1950s, 1960s and 1970s, while Korea was still reeling from its recent upheavals, its neighbour saw unprecedented economic growth. Soon Japan was once again the undisputed powerhouse of the region, not only provoking a great deal of envy, but reviving unpleasant memories from the past.

Alongside economic power came political power. In 1965, Japan offered the South Korean government around $800 million in grants and loans as compensation for its brutal rule before and during the Second World War. In return it asked for a normalisation of relations, and the end of any future claims on Japan. South Korea's military dictatorship had no mandate from the people to sign such a treaty, but under pressure from the USA it did so anyway. In the coming weeks a series of anti-Japanese demonstrations burst onto the streets of Seoul.

For many South Koreans, their country's renewed subservience to Japan and the USA was symbolised by a huge new sex industry catering mostly to Japanese tourists and American servicemen. It seemed that Korean women – and by extension Korea itself – had not yet managed to shake off foreign exploitation.

Given such a history, it seems obvious today that the image of the 'comfort woman' was set to become something of a national symbol in South Korea. This image of a woman who had been dominated, raped and enslaved by outsiders – but who had nevertheless managed somehow to maintain her dignity – is a perfect metaphor for Korean suffering in the twentieth century. All these things are expressed by the Peace Statue in Seoul.

But I am getting ahead of myself: at the beginning of the 1980s nothing was quite so obvious. In fact, until the end of that decade very few people in South Korea had ever heard of 'comfort women'. Few of the women themselves had ever dared to tell their stories, for fear of the humiliation it would bring upon their families. Neither did the South Korean authorities ever encourage them to come forward. The whole issue was hidden away under a pall of shame.

The silence was not broken until 1988, after the country had started down the path towards democratic reform. That year, a Korean Church group organised an academic conference on sex tourism, where a scholar named Yun Chung-ok presented her research about how Korean women had been treated during the Second World War. Her paper caused something of a sensation. In the ensuing media storm, the Korean and Japanese governments were suddenly inundated with requests for more information.

In Japan, unfortunately, the initial reaction was to deny everything. In 1990, the Japanese government claimed that the comfort woman system had never been the work of the government or the military, only of private entrepreneurs.

Then a former comfort woman named Kim Hak-sun stepped forward to tell her story, and the issue suddenly became much more real. Kim was first raped in 1941 at the age of seventeen, after being abducted by a Japanese soldier. She had been travelling in Beijing with her foster father, trying to find work, when the two of them were arrested and separated from one another. For the next four months she was imprisoned in a military brothel, before she escaped with a Korean travelling salesman, whom she later married.

In the following months and years, hundreds of other women from all over Asia came forward to tell similar stories. Some of them, like the Filipina Lola Rosa, were imprisoned in brothels as a punishment for resistance activities. Others, like the white Dutch expatriate Jan Ruff O'Herne, were kept almost as military trophies for groups of Japanese officers. But the vast majority were ordinary peasants, factory workers or schoolgirls who were either abducted by soldiers or enticed away from their families by unscrupulous middlemen. Their stories are uniformly horrific. The Korean Council for Women Drafted for Military Sexual Slavery, an NGO based in Seoul, has gathered dozens of testimonies involving not only repeated rape but also other extremes of physical violence. Similar organisations in China, Indonesia and the Philippines have also gathered such stories. Later these issues were brought up by the United Nations Commission on Human Rights, and an investigation was carried out by the Geneva International Commission of Jurists.

The findings of all these groups, as well as those of Japanese academics, were unequivocal: the Japanese military might not have formally conscripted Korean women as sex slaves, but they had certainly planned, built and operated a network of brothels where Korean women had been imprisoned. Furthermore, it was clear that key figures at the very top of the army had been aware that many of these women were being recruited against their will.

As these facts gradually became known in South Korea at the beginning of the 1990s, they caused widespread outrage. In Seoul, local activists decided to take their outrage onto the streets. When the Japanese prime minister, Kiichi Miyazawa, visited the country in January 1992, a demonstration was organised outside the Japanese embassy, where protesters held up banners demanding an unequivocal, legal apology.

Before long, such demonstrations became a weekly occurrence, with crowds gathering outside the embassy every Wednesday at noon. These demonstrations were held each week for more than twenty-five years – in fact, at the time of writing they are still being held. Whenever possible, a group of old ladies, the former 'comfort women' themselves, takes pride of place, sitting at the front of the demonstration. These women have been hailed as living symbols of Korea's national victimhood. Collectively, they are known as the people's 'grandmothers'.

It was in this context that the Peace Statue was erected. In 2011, the organisers of the Wednesday demonstrations wanted to commemorate the upcoming anniversary of their protest: 14 December that year would mark their 1,000th demonstration in front of the Japanese embassy. They commissioned a pair of artists, a married couple named Kim Seo-kyung and Kim Eun-sung, to create a memorial to be placed on the site where the demonstrators gathered. At first it was thought that they might design a simple memorial stone with some kind of inscription on it, but when the Japanese government began to protest at such an object being placed outside its embassy, the artists reacted by proposing something more prominent: a statue.

Had the statue been erected in a different location – outside a church, perhaps, or a government building, or at the site of a former military brothel – it might have had a gentler meaning. As an expression of victimhood, it might have given Koreans a place to mourn, to reflect on their troubled past, and to heal old wounds. It might even have helped in the process that its sculptors say they wish to promote – the search for some kind of peace. But from the very beginning the statue was intended for *this* site only. As a consequence it can never be considered simply as an expression of victimhood or a symbol of peace. It is also the embodiment of a highly emotional protest directed against Japan.

The problem with a bronze statue, or for that matter a stone plaque, is that it implies a kind of permanence. Unlike a protest, even a weekly protest that continues for years, a memorial does not go home on Wednesday evening, or gradually disperse over time. It stays on the pavement outside the embassy twenty-four hours a day. It states a single, seemingly eternal truth, regardless of any political concessions that might be made by either side: South Korea will always be the victim, and Japan will always be the perpetrator.

The Japanese argue that this is unfair. They say that they have repeatedly made financial reparations, and have repeatedly apologised for the wrongs that were done to Korea before and during the war. This is undeniably true. In the mid-1990s the Japanese government helped to establish the Asian

Women's Fund, an organisation devoted to publicising the 'comfort woman' issue and compensating the victims with 'atonement money'. Around the same time the Japanese prime minister, Tomiichi Murayama, expressed his apologies several times, not only during state visits to South Korea but also in individual letters to the victims themselves. Subsequent Japanese prime ministers have done likewise. Even Shinzo Abe, who is known for his right-wing nationalist views, went out of his way in December 2015 to express his 'most sincere apologies and remorse to all the women who underwent immeasurable and painful experiences and suffered incurable physical and psychological wounds as comfort women'.

As Korean protesters point out, however, this is not quite the whole story. They argue that some of the Japanese apologies have been half-hearted at best, and are often drowned out by loud and offensive denials by Japanese nationalists in the media. Yes, money was paid to former victims of the 'comfort woman' system via the Asian Women's Fund, but it should have been paid directly by the Japanese government itself. Taking this indirect path was just another example of the Japanese government trying to wriggle out of its legal responsibilities. A new fund, set up more directly by the Japanese government in 2015, has also been rejected.

The crux of the matter is that, while the Japanese seem willing to accept moral responsibility for the past, they have never yet accepted direct, legal responsibility. This is what South Korean activists crave more than anything else. They want an official admission that the Japanese government deliberately planned to enslave Korean women, set up a system to do so, and knew from start to finish exactly what they were doing.

Unfortunately, without conclusive documentary evidence

to prove precisely that, this is not something that the Japanese are prepared to do.

In the meantime, the Peace Statue will continue to sit in the street in downtown Seoul, staring at the Japanese embassy in silent accusation. Since 2011 it has become a permanent feature of the city.

Today other cities have also taken up the cry. According to the artists, there are now dozens of other identical statues in parks and cities all over South Korea. In 2018, one of these statues was erected outside the Japanese consulate in Busan, in direct imitation of the protest in Seoul. Not only that, but they have also started to appear in other countries as well, including the USA, Canada, Australia and Germany.

This is martyrdom as a weapon. South Korea's victims know that they have the moral high ground, and that continued protest – perhaps even perpetual protest – is the best way to make sure that their stories are heard.

The women who were repeatedly raped between 1937 and 1945 will never be able to escape their history. The best they can hope for is that, through monuments like the Peace Statue, Japan will never be able to escape it either.

10

USA and Poland: Katyn Memorial, Jersey City

In Jersey City, overlooking the Hudson River, stands one of the most dramatic Second World War memorials in the world. Ten metres (32 feet) high, standing on a granite plinth, is a bronze statue of a bound-and-gagged soldier being stabbed through the back with a bayonet. He appears to be in the throes of death. His body is arched in pain, and his face is tilted up towards heaven. The point of the bayonet emerges through the left side of his chest, exactly where his heart is.

The memorial commemorates an atrocity committed in 1940 by the Soviet secret police: the massacre of thousands of Polish officers in the Russian forest of Katyn. Ever since it was first installed in 1991, it has divided local opinion. Some residents complain that it is ugly and vulgar, and that its depiction of violent death is simply too graphic. But others have always defended it as darkly beautiful. The feelings of discomfort it provokes, they say, are exactly the emotions that a good war memorial should inspire.

In May 2018, however, the statue suddenly became the centre of a quarrel that went far beyond local sensibilities. It began when the mayor of Jersey City, Steven Fulop, announced plans to move the monument to a different place nearby. The area was being redeveloped, and the spot was earmarked as the location of a new, riverside public park. The statue had to be moved to make way for this new development.

A group of Polish Americans immediately protested against the move, and launched a lawsuit against the city council: it was their memorial, and they did not feel properly consulted. They were backed up by other local residents, who opposed the redevelopment plan more generally.

Within days, the issue had escalated into a full-blown international incident. The Polish ambassador to the USA complained on social media about the monument's relocation. Politicians in Poland accused Jersey City of disrespecting Polish heroes, and condemned their plans as 'really scandalous'. Mayor Fulop hit back by accusing one of these politicians of being a 'known anti-Semite' and 'holocaust denier', prompting the politician in question to take legal action. Soon, tempers were flaring all round. The developer tasked with renovating the area denounced the monument as 'gruesome'; the artist who designed it called the developer a 'schmuck'.

For neutral observers, this unseemly spectacle raises all kinds of questions. Why were local people so quick to take offence, when all that seemed to be happening was that the memorial was being moved from one prominent place to another, just a few hundred metres away? Why all the fuss now, more than seventy years after the Second World War was over? And most importantly, what was this statue doing in New Jersey in the first place? The events it commemorates involved no US citizens, and took place 4,500 miles away from US soil. So why was it even there?

So many different themes demand attention here, both local

and international, that it is difficult to know where to start. But the element that binds them together into such an insoluble tangle is history. There could be no better demonstration of how impossible it is to escape our history, especially when that history involves an element of victimhood.

It is worth taking a moment to consider what exactly the memorial commemorates, because, like many memorials, this one is not quite as straightforward as it seems.

At the very beginning of the Second World War, while Poland was defending itself from the German invasion, it was attacked again, this time by the Soviets, from the rear. In other words, it was 'stabbed in the back'.

Within a few weeks, the country was split down the middle: the Nazis ruled in the west, the Soviets in the east. The Soviet occupiers were just as cruel as the Nazis. Between September 1939 and March 1940, their secret police arrested hundreds of thousands of people. This included anyone who might pose a future threat to their rule: Polish landowners, businessmen, priests, lawyers, teachers and other members of the intelligentsia. The majority were deported to Siberia and Kazakhstan, and abandoned there to fend for themselves. Tens of thousands starved to death. These events are commemorated on the back of the plinth by a bronze relief depicting a woman and three children, barefoot and dressed in rags. Above them are the words '1939 Siberia', and below a description of the series of betrayals carried out by the Soviet Union which led to their banishment.

While these people were being deported, other groups suffered a much more gruesome fate. Polish soldiers and policemen were often simply executed. The most notorious killing grounds were in the Russian forest of Katyn, where several thousand Polish army officers were murdered and piled into mass graves. These terrible events are quite literally at the heart of the monument: buried within its granite base is soil taken from the forest where the atrocities were committed.

During the rest of the war, Poland was to suffer a series of other 'stabs in the back'. For example, at the Big Three conference at Yalta, at the beginning of 1945, Stalin demanded a large area of eastern Poland to be incorporated into the Soviet Union. In return, Poland would be compensated with new land taken from defeated Germany. The deal was struck in the absence of any consultation with the Poles themselves, and its consequences were huge. After the war, around 1.2 million Poles were forcibly expelled from the eastern regions of Poland and sent west. Over a million more who had been abroad in 1945 suddenly found themselves without a homeland to return to. They included hundreds of thousands of Polish soldiers and airmen who had spent the war fighting for the Allies, and slave labourers liberated from German factories and work camps. These people felt betrayed not only by the Soviets who had taken their lands, but by the British and Americans who had stood by and let it happen.

The final insult came with the Soviet subjugation of Poland in 1945. Despite promises that the Polish people would be free to choose their own form of government, the Soviets imposed a puppet administration. For the next forty-four years, Poland would be a vassal state, serving the interests of the Soviet Union. Free elections would not take place again until the fall of Communism in 1989.

The memorial in Jersey City commemorates all these events. While it is ostensibly dedicated to the Katyn massacres, the word 'Katyn' has itself become a symbol of every betrayal that the Poles were forced to suffer during the second half of the twentieth century. The soldier who is being bayoneted upon his plinth represents much more than the thousands of Polish officers killed at Katyn in 1940. He represents Poland itself, in all its tragic martyrdom.

It is tempting to leave the analysis here: the monument is a national symbol, representing national suffering. But to the people who built it, it is much more than that. It is intimately bound up not only with Polish history, but also with the local history of Jersey City, and the personal history of those who came here in the aftermath of the war.

In 1945, there were more political refugees from Poland than from any other European country. Of the 200,000 or so who ended up in the USA, around 10,000 settled in New Jersey, where there was already a thriving community of Polish immigrants. They found jobs, built new lives for themselves, learned to speak English and embraced American life. But they never forgot their heritage. Many joined Polish-American cultural and political groups, such as the Polish American Congress and the Polish Roman Catholic Union of America. For immigrants whose lives had been so fractured by the Second World War, such organisations offered them the chance to forge a new identity for themselves. They helped them learn to be both Polish *and* American.

In the early 1980s a group of Polish veterans gathered to discuss ways of commemorating the various tragedies they had lived through, particularly the massacre at Katyn. The group included men like Walter Sosulski and Ryszard Winowski, who had fought with the western Allies in Italy; and Stanisław Paszul, who had not only fought with the Polish resistance against the Nazis but had also spent many years in

Soviet gulags in Siberia. They got together with other Polish Americans and tried to come up with ideas for a memorial in the heart of their community.

In 1986 they formed a non-profit corporation devoted to raising money. They hired sculptor Andrzej Pitynski to design something dramatic, and worthy of the strength of emotion they felt. After lobbying the city council for permission to display their memorial in public, they were eventually granted a spot in Exchange Place, a riverside location with a view across the Hudson towards Manhattan. The Katyn Memorial was finally inaugurated in June 1991.

Jersey City was a very different place in those days. It was still a largely working-class city, whose residents worked in the many local factories, freight terminals and warehouses that lined the Hudson. This was reflected in the group that had championed the memorial, which included not only journalists and teachers but also carpenters and foundry workers.

In the following years, however, new businesses began to move here in search of cheaper real estate than they could find across the river in Manhattan. New residents quickly followed: yuppies, hipsters and white-collar workers in the financial industries. These people could not understand why there should be such a graphic representation of violent death at the centre of their community. Gentrification began to sweep the city, driving up prices and driving out many of the older, blue-collar residents. The redevelopment of Exchange Place, where the Katyn Memorial is situated, was just the latest instance of this gentrification. An important element of the protest against moving the memorial was nothing to do with Polish identity or memories of the Second World War, but about local identity and memories of a community that was fast disappearing.

There are markers of this very local identity on the memorial itself. In 2001, when two airliners were flown into the Twin Towers in Manhattan, visitors to the Katyn Memorial had an unrestricted view of the unfolding disaster across the river. Three years later, a plaque was added to the base of the memorial commemorating 9/11. It shows a relief sculpture, in bronze, of the New York City skyline, with smoke billowing from the twin towers of the stricken World Trade Center. 'Never forget!' reads the inscription beneath it. 'Pray for all the innocent victims and heroes who died in the terrorist attack on America, September 11, 2001.'

What does this plaque have to do with Katyn, or Poland, or the Second World War? The answer is, absolutely nothing. But it has everything to do with local memories of yet another 'stab in the back'.

International history, national history, local history, personal history – each of these layers of history is represented in this one memorial. And each layer is suffused with trauma and deep feelings of suffering and betrayal. The Katyn monument is one of the most emotionally charged memorials in the world. Is it any wonder, then, that Steven Fulop's surprise announcement that the monument would be moved away from Exchange Place – purely for the sake of commercial redevelopment – was greeted with such defensive outrage?

In the days after the announcement was made, debates about it took place in the local and national newspapers, on social media, in the city council, on Polish radio, and between Polish and American diplomats. At the centre of this storm of emotion stood the local Polish-American community, many of whom felt betrayed all over again. What had seemed like a minor detail to councillors – the movement of a memorial from one prominent location to another – affected Polish Americans in ways they could not possibly fathom. These survivors of the war knew what it was to be uprooted and moved against their will. The decision to move their memorial without consulting them was just another reminder of a deeply traumatic history.

Across the Atlantic, in Poland, there was a much better understanding of the emotions involved, but even here they did not quite get the full picture. Poland embraced the Katyn Memorial as a symbol of Polish identity, when in fact it was something slightly different – it was a symbol of *Polish–American* identity. It commemorates a specific kind of loss, and a specific kind of martyrdom, unique to those Poles who were forced into exile after 1945.

It is no coincidence that the Katyn Memorial in Jersey City is much more graphic, and much more dramatic, than any of the numerous Katyn memorials that exist in Poland itself. The people who built it had lost not only friends and family, but also their homeland and their sense of belonging. Some of them never saw Poland again after 1945. Their very Polishness was therefore defined by this memorial in a way that other people, even other Poles, could never truly understand.

Finally, there was a local dimension to the controversy that could only be fully appreciated by Jersey City residents. The city's old-timers already felt betrayed by their council, whose gentrification drive appeared to be putting the needs of newcomers and big businesses above their own. To such people, the Katyn Memorial was the symbol of a local identity that, ironically, was itself being stabbed in the back.

Even some council members were swept up in these emotions. One city councillor, Rich Boggiano, was particularly vocal about leaving the memorial where it was. 'I'm sick and tired of all these new people coming here,' he told the local newspaper, 'wanting to change everything about Jersey City.'

Once people get riled up, it is difficult to calm them down again. The city council tried to rectify their mistake and started to consult local Polish-American community leaders, but it was too late. They promised to move the monument just one block south, to the foot of York Street, but indignant protesters refused to negotiate. Anyone who argued in favour of the move was shouted down. When the president of the Katyn Memorial Committee said at a press conference that he was willing to accept the council's offer, he was booed. When the Polish ambassador tried to pour oil on troubled waters, and offered his support, Councillor Boggiano called him a 'piece of shit'. The Polish president himself gave the relocation his blessing, but was immediately denounced by local protesters as a traitor to their cause: in May 2018, when he made a personal visit to the memorial, he was greeted there by demonstrators with cries of 'Shame!'

The forces that fuelled this maelstrom of protest were memory and martyrdom – which in the minds of the protesters combined to form a single entity called 'history'. At council planning meetings they accused the city of trying to 'erase history'. At their public demonstrations they unfurled huge banners which read 'Respect Our History'. This history was more important to them than progress, or harmony, or compromise, or anything else; and any threat to it was regarded as a threat to their very identity.

Eventually, after several heated meetings, two petitions and the scheduling of a public referendum, the city council backed down. The subject of the monument had simply become too toxic, and threatened to disrupt too much other business. In

December 2018, seven months after the controversy had begun, the council voted unanimously to leave the statue where it was, 'in perpetuity'.

There are different ways of viewing this story, depending on your political point of view. You might see it as a victory for the common citizen, standing up fearlessly against the combined forces of power and money. Or you might see it as a defeat for the forces of progress, held to ransom by a hysterical mob. Either way, it demonstrates one fundamental truth: in the day-to-day running of our communities, we are all prisoners of our history. When we forget that truth, or try to ignore it, it inevitably comes back to bite us.

For the protesters who won this battle, their memorial now has yet another meaning, and one that speaks not of suffering but of empowerment. For once, the martyr has come out on top. The psychological consequences of their victory are potentially profound. Today, the people of Jersey City are able to identify themselves not only with the blindfolded soldier but also, on a symbolic level at least, with the invisible hands that hold the rifle and its bayonet.

In the words of one resident, posted on a local internet forum: 'I love that memorial. Welcome to Jersey City. Don't fuck with us.'

A NÉMET MEGSZÁLLÁS ÁLDOZATAINAK EMLÉKMŰVE

11

Hungary: Monument for the Victims of German Occupation, Budapest

One of the problems with the Peace Statue in Seoul is the way that it focuses all the blame for what happened to Korea's 'comfort women' upon Japan. Of course, the Japanese military will always bear ultimate responsibility; but there were many others who contributed to this tragedy. According to their own accounts, Korean women were often abducted not by Japanese soldiers but by Korean collaborators or middlemen. After the war, the shame these women suffered was perpetuated by their own society. And the financial reparations that they might have received from the Japanese government in 1965 were actually pocketed by the Korean government to pay for public infrastructure projects. None of these things are expressed in the Peace Statue. It's always much easier for a nation to blame outsiders than to look at itself.

That is one of the problems with figurative monuments and memorials: they often simplify history too much. In the pursuit of a single, dramatic story about our past, they can obscure other, more nuanced stories. Furthermore, this obfuscation is sometimes more than an accident. Cynical politicians occasionally erect monuments that seem deliberately designed to whitewash the past, and the motif of the martyr is often their main tool. Martyrs have moral power. Martyrs are untouchable. In the twenty-first century, almost every nation wants to portray itself as a martyr.

Europe's most controversial memorial in this regard is probably Budapest's Monument for the Victims of the German Occupation. It was erected in 2014 by Hungary's Fidesz government to commemorate the moment when, seventy years earlier, the German army seized control of the country. During the German occupation, hundreds of thousands of Hungarians were killed. Either they were deported to concentration camps, or they died on the battlefield while fighting under German leadership. This monument is supposed to stand in memory of all those who died.

The design consists of two main figures arranged before a classical colonnade. In the foreground is the archangel Gabriel, a symbol of Hungary, standing with his arms outstretched. One of his wings has been broken off, leaving only the fluttering end of his body cloth to suggest where it once was. His face shows an expression of serene suffering, and his eyes are shut. In his hand is a golden orb topped with a double cross – another symbol of Hungary – which he is holding up rather carelessly, seemingly oblivious of the fact that it is about to be snatched from his grasp.

Above him, swooping down from the top of the colonnade, is the second figure in the allegory: an eagle representing Germany. In contrast to the serene and innocent angel below him, everything about this eagle is aggressive. Its outstretched talons are sharp; its feathers are nothing like the soft feathers of Gabriel's wings – they are more like blades. Around its ankle is a metal ring with the date on it: 1944.

The message of the sculpture is not difficult to work out. Serene, peaceful Hungary is being attacked by a ruthless and aggressive Germany. Hungary is being portrayed as an innocent victim – a wounded angel. Germany, and only Germany, is guilty of violence.

There have been so many objections to this monument, from so many different people, that once again it is difficult to know where to begin. Architects, planners and political geographers criticised its location, which they said was unsuitable for a national monument. It stands on a narrow strip of land at the southern edge of Budapest's Szabadság Tér (Liberty Square), with a narrow road running directly in front of it, making it difficult to see and impossible to approach. Artists criticised its aesthetics, which they said were an uneasy mix of Viennese baroque and social-realist kitsch. Prize-winning sculptor György Jovánovics called it a 'messy nightmare'.

But the main objections concerned its flawed symbolism. Nobody denied that March 1944 was indeed a tragic moment for Hungary, but they certainly questioned the way that the monument was portraying the event. Was Hungary such an innocent angel at the time? And was Germany the only aggressor? Did not other events that happened around this time tell a very different, and much more uncomfortable story?

Even before the monument was built, a group of prominent Hungarian historians wrote an open letter to their government complaining that its symbolism was 'based on a falsification of history'. They were joined by a variety of politicians, international organisations and local Jewish groups who also issued open letters in the press saying similar things. There were protests on the international stage too. Diplomats in the USA and Israel expressed outrage at the proposed monument, and a group of American senators wrote a collective letter to the

Hungarian government urging them to consult representatives of the Jewish community before going ahead with their design. In the European Parliament the monument quickly became the subject of furious debate.

As all these groups pointed out, the history of the occupation was much more controversial than the monument suggested. They wanted to remind the Hungarian government that, far from being a victim of Germany, Hungary had actually spent most of the war as its ally. The German occupation had only taken place in 1944 because Hitler had wanted to prevent the possibility of the Hungarians making a separate peace with the Allies, and in the event it had not been a particularly violent affair. In fact the Germans arrived unopposed, and took over with no bloodshed at all. Resistance to German rule was virtually non-existent.

The real victims of the German occupation were not to become apparent until later. Contrary to the impression given by this memorial, the vast majority of victims were not Hungarians in general, but quite specifically Hungarian Jews. One of the first German administrators to arrive in Budapest on 19 March, the very day of the occupation, was Adolf Eichmann, the main architect of the Holocaust. Within four months he and his team had organised the deportation of 438,000 Jews to Auschwitz. According to Holocaust historian Saul Friedländer, 90 per cent of these Jews – some 394,000 people in total – were exterminated upon arrival. Later on, some 20,000 Roma people were also taken off to be murdered, along with a small number of 'degenerates' and political prisoners.

Contrary to the impression given by the monument, the Germans were not the sole perpetrators of these crimes. It is true that the Holocaust did not begin in Hungary until after the German occupation, but it would never have taken place so quickly had Hungarians not willingly collaborated. In truth, the groundwork for the Holocaust had already been laid years before. The first anti-Semitic laws were introduced in Hungary as early as 1920, when Miklós Horthy's government imposed strict legal limits on the number of Jewish students allowed in universities. From 1938 onwards a series of other anti-Semitic laws followed. Hungarian Jews were defined, labelled and registered. They were officially excluded from jobs in government, and their opportunities in the media and in the legal and medical professions were tightly restricted. They were denied the right to vote. From 1941 they were forbidden from marrying non-Jews or having sexual relations with them. Even after the occupation it was not the Germans who rounded Jews up, beat them, packed them onto trains and then shared out their property: all these things were done by Hungarian policemen and local government officials.

Soon, Hungarian fascists also joined in more directly with the killing. In October 1944, after Horthy was finally forced from office, the Germans installed a Hungarian fascist as prime minister. Ferenc Szálasy was the leader of the Arrow Cross Party, a popular far-right group that advocated an even more violent form of anti-Semitism. Within a month of taking power, Szálasi's followers were rounding up Jews and shooting them on the banks of the River Danube. The worst atrocities occurred just a few hundred metres away from the site of today's Monument to the Victims of the German Occupation, where between 10,000 and 15,000 were murdered and thrown into the river. (There is, incidentally, another memorial here, the Shoes on the Danube Bank – sixty pairs of empty shoes lined up by the water's edge to represent some of the people who were killed.)

In the light of all this, how could the monument's creators possibly justify the portrayal of Hungary as an innocent victim – a wounded angel, whose only sin was not to have seen the occupation coming? How could they justify grouping the victims of the Holocaust together with other so-called victims of the German occupation, including politicians who until 1944 had willingly collaborated with the Nazis?

Other objections to the monument had less to do with history than they did with contemporary politics. No sooner had its construction been announced than people began to ask why it was necessary at all. There had been no great popular campaign to erect a memorial to the victims of the occupation. Why was the government so keen to erect one now? And why the hurry?

The monument was first approved in a government decree on 31 December 2013, but officials originally wanted it to be commissioned, constructed and inaugurated in time for the seventieth anniversary of the occupation on 19 March – a mere eleven weeks later. Critics claimed that the real reason for this impossible deadline was not the anniversary at all, but the upcoming general election at the beginning of April. The ruling party at the time – Viktor Orbán's Fidesz Party – already had an unassailable majority in the parliament, which everyone expected to continue after the election. Nevertheless, Fidesz had long been under pressure from the radical right-wing Jobbik party, which already commanded nearly 17 per cent of the popular vote. The creation of a monument to Hungarian martyrdom was exactly the sort of populist gesture that might lure some of these voters over to Fidesz.

There were also serious questions about how the monument

had been commissioned. Over the previous few years, Orbán's government had been repeatedly accused of authoritarianism by other politicians and campaigners, and the monument seemed to be a perfect case in point. It had never been discussed or debated in parliament. It had not been presented to Hungarian experts, and there was certainly no consultation with the public. Neither was the contract for building the memorial put out to tender: a construction company had simply been appointed. Nor was there any kind of competition to find a suitable artist: the minister in charge had simply handed the project to Péter Párkányi Raab, a sculptor who had been a favourite of the Fidesz Party for years. Párkányi Raab came up with a design within a few days, and it was rapidly approved by a committee consisting of just five people. In other words, the whole project was the result of a top-down decision, rushed through by government decree, and imposed on the Budapest cityscape without any public scrutiny.

In such a context, it is hardly surprising that people began to protest. At first the objections came in the form of private letters to the government and open letters published in the press. The strength of public feeling over the issue seems to have taken the Fidesz government completely by surprise, and for a while in March 2014 they called a temporary halt to construction of the monument. But it was not long before they changed their minds. Two days after their victory in the election that April, they decided to press ahead regardless.

Frustrated by the government's refusal to engage with anyone's concerns, a group of artists and civic activists decided to take matters into their own hands. Since they seemed unable to influence what the official monument looked like, they decided to do the next best thing and build one of their own. Unlike the official memorial, theirs would not be made from stone and metal, but would consist of photographs, handwritten stories and personal relics from 1944, all of which were to be donated by members of the general public. They set up a Facebook group, and invited people to bring along 'symbols of their souls'. They specifically asked people not only to bring emblems of their personal victimhood, but also symbols of repentance, of forgiveness for the past.

Before long, the group had gathered hundreds of such items, which they arranged in front of the construction site. There were prayer books, shoes, pairs of spectacles and battered old suitcases. There were yellow stars made of cloth, of the sort that Jews were forced to wear during the war. Hundreds of people brought small stones, as they might to a Jewish grave, some of them inscribed with the names and details of individuals deported to Auschwitz. Others brought flowers, plants and candles.

The organisers called their counter-monument a 'Living Memorial', because of the way that it changed and evolved from day to day. At the centre of their display sat two white chairs, facing one another. These were supposed to symbolise the invitation to sit down and discuss the past, and the way that it was being portrayed in the present – exactly the sort of conversations that had been missing during the commissioning of the official monument. True to this symbolism, the group began to organise formal public discussions at the site. Artists and critics gave talks about different monuments around the world, and compared them to the monument being built in Budapest. Poetry slams took place in the open air beside the memorial. Holocaust survivors and their relatives were invited to share their memories;

20 July 2014: the day the monument was first erected. The 'counter-monument' lies before it, on the ground and attached to the railings, along with a banner reading 'Falsification of history is the moral equivalent of well-poisoning'

and commemorations were held for the victims of the Roma genocide.

By the time the government contractors were completing the official monument, the unofficial counter-monument was already well established. It consisted of hundreds of items, spread along more than 30 metres of roadside. Hundreds, possibly even thousands of local people had already come to visit it.

The final elements of Fidesz's grandiose sculpture were winched into place during the night of 20 July 2014, but by that point the government already seemed to be losing interest in the project. Their monument has never been formally inaugurated, and no official government events have ever taken place at the site. It has been on the receiving end of so much criticism, not only in Hungary but around the world, that it was difficult to keep standing up to defend it. Calls to have the monument pulled down continue to this day. In 2018, the leader of the Socialist Party pledged to take the monument down if he was elected; and one or two candidates from other parties followed suit.

The 'Living Memorial' by contrast seems to have gone from strength to strength. It continues to grow and evolve even today; and various groups and activists still hold regular events here. The range of topics debated on the chairs beside the memorial has expanded: this is now a forum not only to debate Hungarian history, but also to explore a range of contemporary social, political and artistic issues. But the heart of it remains the slightly chaotic collection of personal relics and photographs that line the pavement opposite the arch-angel Gabriel, which has become something of a local tourist attraction.

The history of the Second World War is still a deeply painful and controversial subject in Hungary. The period of the German occupation in 1944–5 was a particularly dark episode: it was a time when a deeply flawed government was obliged to make a series of impossible political and moral choices while being increasingly powerless. There is not a great deal for Hungarians to feel proud of here.

As my friend Áron Máthé at Hungary's Committee of National Remembrance once pointed out to me, 'It is not possible to build a nation on a sense of guilt.' When the Fidesz government commissioned the Monument to the Victims of the German Occupation, it was attempting to paper over the complications of Hungary's troubled history and find common ground. There might have been some cynical intent in all this, but I have no doubt that there were many good intentions behind it too.

However, if a nation can't be built on a sense of guilt, neither can it be built on the falsification of its history. It is not good enough merely to proclaim yourself a martyr: the facts also need to stack up. Neither is it good enough to appropriate someone else's victimhood and proclaim it as your own: that is not something that the real victims will ever be prepared to stand for. The Monument to the Victims of the German Occupation was originally conceived as a symbol of national martyrdom – but today, in part because of the 'Living Memorial' that stands opposite, it has become little more than a symbol of national hypocrisy.

The events of 2014 in Budapest demonstrate two fundamental truths about monuments. The first is that it doesn't matter if you construct a monument with a specific message in mind: it is impossible to predict how it will be used and interpreted by the public once it is up.

The second is that if you build a monument in an attempt to rewrite history, it won't work. One way or another, history always catches up with you in the end.

The gatehouse of Auschwitz–Birkenau, from inside the camp

12

Poland: Auschwitz

Of all the many victims of the Second World War, there was probably no single group that suffered more than the Jews. Between 1939 and 1945 around two-thirds of Europe's Jews were exterminated. Almost six million people were killed all over the continent, but particularly in the eastern European 'Bloodlands' of Poland, Lithuania, Belarus and Ukraine.

Today there are hundreds of memorials marking their places of execution, but none is more famous than the museum and memorial at Oświęcim in Poland. Before 1939 very few people outside Poland had ever heard of this small town; but during the German occupation it was renamed Auschwitz, and it became home to one of the largest concentration camps in history. As a consequence, the word 'Auschwitz' has since become a byword for horror and suffering. Today, it is perhaps the world's best-known symbol of victimhood.

Auschwitz was not a single concentration camp, but a complex of camps. At its peak it was spread over forty separate sites, mostly centred around factories and farms, where prisoners of many different nationalities and religions were forced to work in abject conditions as slave labour. From 1942, however, Auschwitz also began to be used for a second purpose: it became a centre for the mass murder of Europe's Jews.

When most people think of Auschwitz today, they are thinking about the two main camps: Auschwitz I and Auschwitz II (otherwise known as Birkenau). The original camp at Auschwitz I was established in 1940 on the site of an old army barracks. In the beginning it was used as a jail for Polish political prisoners, but as time went on it also began to serve as a concentration camp for Russian prisoners of war, Jews, gypsies and a dozen other ethnic groups and nationalities. There was a summary court here, administration blocks, workshops and warehouses where the prisoners were expected to work.

The camp first became a centre for mass killing towards the end of 1941. Until that summer, the Nazis had generally carried out mass executions by shooting – not so much in concentration camps as in forests, fields, quarries and other remote places across eastern Europe. However, shooting large numbers of people was time-consuming, inefficient, and stressful for the executioners. So the Nazis began to look for other ways of killing.

In Auschwitz, SS prison guards discovered that groups of prisoners could be killed much more efficiently by grouping them together in a single room and gassing them with Zyklon B, the powerful insecticide that was used to fumigate the prisoners' clothing. The first experiments were carried out on Russian and Polish prisoners, in the basement cells of Block 11, the prison block. However, since the place was difficult to ventilate, and a long way from the camp crematorium, another block was converted to be used specifically for this purpose. Auschwitz now had its first gas chamber.

As the war progressed, the camp expanded rapidly. To relieve the congestion, a second camp was built on the site of a nearby village called Brzezinka – or Birkenau, as the Germans called it. This was originally conceived as a camp for holding Soviet prisoners of war, but when the Nazis began transporting huge numbers of Jews here in 1942 they realised that it could also double up as a place to exterminate their racial enemies. So they converted two remote farmhouses into gas chambers, and constructed a series of purpose-built crematoria, with gas chambers attached. Any Jews who could not be exploited as slave labourers were simply brought here and murdered.

Over time, the Nazis honed the execution process into a model of efficiency. Transports of Jews were unloaded from trains that came directly to the camp, and were sorted into groups on the platform. Those deemed fit for work were funnelled off to live in the camp's vastly overcrowded barracks: they would spend the following months being exploited as slaves until they were too weak to continue. Those considered economically worthless – children, pregnant mothers, the elderly, the weak – were relieved of their possessions, stripped, shaved, gassed and cremated. It was like a production line in a factory. Between 1942 and 1944 over a million people were killed here. At its peak, in the summer of 1944, Auschwitz–Birkenau was capable of processing thousands of bodies each day.

Auschwitz remained in operation until the end of 1944, when the advance of the Soviet Red Army meant that the camp had to be evacuated. When the Nazis finally left in January 1945, they tried to destroy the evidence of what they had done. The inmates were force-marched to other concentration camps closer to Germany. Documents were removed or destroyed, warehouses were torched, gas chambers and crematoria were dismantled or blown up. In their hurry to retreat, however, the camp guards left plenty of physical evidence behind, particularly in the original camp of Auschwitz I, which remained largely intact. They also failed to kill all the witnesses to their crimes. Unlike some of the other killing centres for Jews, Auschwitz was never exclusively a death camp, but also served as a work camp for slave labour. As a consequence, thousands of labourers who survived the war were able to bear witness to the terrible sights they had seen there.

In the decades since then, countless people have come forward with evidence of the atrocities that were carried out at this notorious place. In 1947, the post-war Polish authorities decided to preserve what was left of the site for future generations. Auschwitz I was made into a museum, curated by people who had themselves been imprisoned there during the war. Nearby Auschwitz II, which by this time had been largely dismantled, was preserved as a memorial site.

Today, the two sites combined have come to represent the Holocaust as a whole. They became a UNESCO World Heritage Site in 1979, and are now considered among the most important symbols of martyrdom anywhere in the world.

Visitors who come to Oświęcim today can see for themselves the evidence of what happened here. Along the way they can experience a tiny slice of that horror. They can pass beneath the notorious wrought-iron gates at Auschwitz I, upon which the famous lie was written – *Arbeit macht frei* ('work makes you free'). In the museum they can see a mountain of shoes stolen from those who were about to be killed. There are rooms full of personal possessions taken from the victims –

battered suitcases, spectacles, children's toys and clothes, shaving brushes, kitchen utensils. There are more sinister displays too – a vault full of human hair, a vast heap of prosthetic limbs, a pile of empty Zyklon B canisters. Visitors can enter the punishment block, where prisoners were beaten and tortured, and where the first experiments with mass murder took place. They can stand beside the wall where prisoners were shot. And, most disturbingly of all, they can enter a reconstruction of one of the gas chambers and stand in the very place where thousands of people were killed.

At nearby Auschwitz II–Birkenau, you can continue your tour by visiting the epicentre of the Nazi system of organised murder. You can walk along the infamous railway track that brought more than a million Jews to their doom. You can stand on the very ramp where the selections took place. You can gaze through the barbed wire at the rows and rows of chimneys, sticking straight out of the ground like admonishing fingers, which are the only remains of the hundreds of barrack huts that used to house tens of thousands of human beings. The scale of the place is truly immense. It is the size of a small city – more than 80 hectares of ground devoted to negation and death.

It is impossible to enter the site without feeling the weight of history bearing down upon you. The moral crime that was committed concerns not only Jews, or Slavs, or Gypsies, or any of the other groups who were murdered here: it makes victims of us all. It is an affront to humanity itself: indeed, it is because of places like this that a new legal term was created after the war, 'crimes against humanity'.

These things are expressed so well at Auschwitz that the site has attracted visitors in ever greater numbers. But such success has itself brought problems. In recent years Auschwitz has begun to drown under the sheer number of visitors it receives. Before 2007, the site received less than a million visitors each year; today that number has more than doubled. Every day, particularly in summer, bus after bus of visitors arrives, and thousands of people are funnelled through the gates to the museum. There is now not nearly so much time to stand and absorb the horror of the place. Tour guides rush their groups through at a steady pace because they have to make room for the groups pressing them from behind. Ironically, such phenomenal success threatens to undermine everything that the museum is supposed to represent.

It is safe to say that not everyone approaches the site in the spirit of sombre contemplation that it deserves. Hundreds of school groups come here as part of their education, predominantly from Poland – but also from Israel, Germany, the UK and other countries – and not all of them treat the place with the appropriate solemnity. Teenagers will be teenagers, after all: they are more concerned with living life than with lingering so long in the presence of death.

There are few places to buy food here, so visitors sometimes bring picnics to enjoy in the car park, or in the shade of one of the birch trees that surround the site. It's not an unreasonable thing to do. The journey from Krakow to Oświęcim takes at least an hour and a half each way, and people need to eat. Nevertheless, I can't help wondering if there is something disrespectful about enjoying a good meal in a place where so many people starved to death. Last time I was here I watched a group of men relaxing in the sun near the entrance to Auschwitz I, drinking cans of beer.

Such occurrences seem to me to be a part of something greater that has happened here. Auschwitz today finds itself on people's holiday itineraries alongside palaces, art galleries, water parks and beer festivals. As many people come here each year as visit the Uffizi in Florence. Even the memorial site itself boasts that it is now by far the most popular museum in Poland. If Auschwitz is a prisoner to its history, it is also a prisoner to tourism.

There are other concerns about the popularity of Auschwitz. In past years, the memorial site was still mostly the domain of scholars, and Holocaust historians, and people trying to find out about where their own family members had died. In such circumstances, it was much easier to embrace a wide range of stories from those who had suffered here. No two stories were ever quite the same: the range of experience was vast.

Today there is much less time for visitors to take in the intricacies of life in the camp. The differences between the various categories of prisoners get lost. It is harder to appreciate how different life could be if one was in the camp orchestra, or the camp choir, or the hospital, or the medical experimentation units, or the *Sonderkommando* – Jews forced to work around the gas chambers and the crematoria clearing away the dead bodies. Visitors who rush through can only ever get the basic facts of what happened, and inevitably a standardised version of the story emerges: arrival, selection, death. Isn't the reduction of so much human experience to such a narrow narrative in itself dehumanising?

There are many other ways in which the story could be told, ways which only emerge if you are able to linger here a little longer. Jews were never merely victims during the Holocaust: many were also heroes. There were many places in eastern Europe where Jews stood up for themselves and fought back, and Auschwitz was no different. Jews resisted the Nazis in Auschwitz in various ways, ranging from simple acts of human kindness to violent confrontation with the camp guards; in 1944 the *Sonderkommando* staged a major rebellion. In the 1950s, these were the kinds of stories that many Jews themselves preferred to tell. They did not want to be portrayed merely as the passive victims of an inhuman system: such a thought was far too painful.

Among the heroes there were also those who were not quite so pure and innocent as today's accepted version of the story suggests. Some Jewish leaders collaborated in the deportation of Jews to Auschwitz. Some bought time for themselves and their families by feeding others to the monster first. At Auschwitz there were plenty of inmates who collaborated with camp guards and informed on their fellow Jews for the sake of a crust of bread. These people must be mentioned not to blame them in any way, but rather to emphasise their human fallibility. Regardless of what the Nazis always said, there was never anything particularly special about the Jews. There was and is no archetype here. Jews are just as human as everyone else.

When one drills right down into the individual experiences of the Holocaust, one can find the most surprising stories, rendered all the more poignant by their contrast with the standardised version that we have all come to know. For example, in his memoir of the Holocaust, historian Otto Dov Kulka remembers afternoons at Auschwitz when he would gaze up at the blue sky and feel overwhelmed by its beauty. Despite all that happened to him here, these are happy memories; but he was always forced to ask himself whether it was morally permissible to have happy memories of this place.

Such individual moments are lost when we are forced to

rush through the displays of the Auschwitz museum. For the sake of efficiency, today's museum administrators are obliged to push greater and greater numbers of people through their system. Surely this too evokes disturbing echoes of the past.

Auschwitz has become such a globally recognised symbol that it is now stamped upon our collective memory in a way that no other memorial site can rival. In a world of victims, this is the undisputed capital city. This too brings problems, because, unfortunately, alongside status comes envy.

There have always been plenty of people who can see the moral power of a place like Auschwitz, and who want to acquire some of that power for themselves. The first group who tried to claim ownership of Auschwitz after the war were the Polish Communists. When the first commemorative plaques were put up at Birkenau, there was no mention of Jews: the plaques referred instead to the '4 million people' who had 'suffered and died here at the hands of Nazi murderers'. Tour guides at the museum also used to speak only of 'victims' and 'people', with no mention of their ethnic or religious origins. In a Communist narrative of the war, the specific fate of the Jews was irrelevant. Instead, the concentration camp was portrayed as a place where ordinary Poles, along with their brothers and sisters from other countries, had been exploited until every drop of economic worth had been squeezed from their bodies. Auschwitz was the ultimate symbol of capitalist exploitation.

In the 1970s, Polish Catholics also tried to appropriate the site as their own. It was certainly true that tens of thousands of Catholics died here. One of them, a Franciscan friar named Father Maximilian Kolbe, was even canonised as a saint because of the way he had volunteered to take the place of a stranger who had been sentenced to death. In 1972 Cardinal Karol Wojtyla, the future Pope John Paul II, held a major Catholic service here in honour of Father Kolbe. Wojtyla returned seven years later, after being elected Pope, to give another, even bigger service. A cross was erected on the ramp where Jews had once been selected for life or death, and the Pope proclaimed Auschwitz to be 'the Golgotha of our time'. In 1984, a group of Carmelite nuns went further still, and established a convent right beside the perimeter fence at Auschwitz I. Many Jews were profoundly uncomfortable about the fact that they were being forced to compete with Catholics over whose stories should be given greater prominence, and which religious symbols – if any – should be allowed to go on display. Here, in the place where Jews had been exterminated, the very Jewishness of their experience was being taken from them. It was not until the mid-1990s that the Catholic Church finally backed off. Most of the crosses erected around the site were taken down, and the convent was moved elsewhere.

Today Auschwitz is universally recognised as a place predominantly of Jewish suffering, just as it should be. Once again, the balance of historical truth has won out in the end.

But that does not mean that the controversies are at an end. In recent years people have begun to question Auschwitz's pre-eminent status among the world's monuments to the Second World War. Why should this place be more important than the Nanjing Memorial Hall? Why should the suffering of the Jews be considered substantially worse than the suffering of Korea's comfort women?

The argument goes well beyond the Second World War. What about the million or so Armenians massacred by Turkish soldiers earlier in the century? What about the six million or so Ukrainians starved to death by Stalin in the 1930s? What about all those who died in the killing fields of Cambodia in the 1970s, or in the Rwandan and Yugoslavian genocides of the 1990s? When there are so many other victims in the world, why should we continue to regard the Holocaust as special?

These questions come up again and again in our international institutions, and there is no satisfactory answer to them. It is fruitless to weigh the traumas of one victim against those of another: suffering cannot be measured out like grains of rice. The memorials I have described over the past six chapters represent only a tiny proportion of the world's monuments to victimhood. Great or small, each and every one deserves recognition.

And yet, for better or worse, there remains something unique about Auschwitz. During my research for this book I visited mass graves, killing sites and victims' memorials all over the world, but Auschwitz feels different from all of them.

First there is its sheer scale: it's difficult to think of another site where so many people were killed in such a concentrated area. Auschwitz–Birkenau is huge, close to 900,000 square metres in total. And yet every square metre represents at least one victim.

Then there is the unique character of the atrocity that unfolded here. It was not born of military frenzy, like the Rape of Nanjing; nor merely out of political expediency, like the shooting of Polish officers in the forest of Katyn. The main method of killing here was not particularly bloodthirsty compared to what happened in other places – in fact, quite the opposite: the distinguishing feature of Auschwitz was not its passion, but its coldness. It is the impersonal, machine-like indifference of this kind of murder that makes it so unbearable to contemplate.

This is perhaps one of the reasons why the Jewish victims of the Holocaust have become such a symbol for our age. They were not only prey to men with guns; they were also fodder for a vast political and industrial system that had reduced them to mere units to be processed and eliminated. In this sense, they were the victims not only of war, but of modernity. If you can bear to follow this thread to its logical conclusion, it leads to all kinds of other victims in other times and places, from the slave trade in the eighteenth century to the sex trade in the twenty-first century. The victims of the Holocaust are representative of a much greater phenomenon that has never entirely gone away.

In 2005, the United Nations recognised the universal nature of this symbolism by instituting an International Holocaust Remembrance Day. This is now observed every year on 27 January – the anniversary of the liberation of Auschwitz. According to UN thinking, the victims of the Holocaust are not only Jewish victims – they are archetypal victims. They represent humanity as a whole, in all its precariousness.

I would love to believe that this is also in part why Auschwitz itself is such a global symbol. It would be heartening to think that more than two million people come here each year simply to pay their respects to a universal victim, and pledge to make sure that the suffering those victims endured never happens again. But I know that this is not quite true. Because the atmosphere that pervades the site is not only one of sadness and mourning, but also one of dread. This is another thing that makes Auschwitz unique. It is impossible to walk around the site without feeling the presence of some gigantic evil, at once both repellent and beguiling.

Many people come here because they want to experience this presence, and remind themselves of what it feels like to be alive. This is one of the reasons why so many Jews come each spring to walk from Auschwitz I to Birkenau in a demonstration called the March of the Living. There can be nothing more life-affirming than to visit such a place of death and stand right at its heart, vibrantly and defiantly alive.

But I suspect that there are also darker motivations for wanting to experience the presence of such evil. Who among us is not impressed by the power of death, particularly death on such a gigantic scale? Is there not a part of us that secretly longs to appropriate just a sliver of that power for ourselves?

Every year people are caught stealing buttons or fragments of cloth from the museum site at Auschwitz, which they intend to take home as souvenirs. In 2010 a Swedish neo-fascist went so far as to steal the famous wrought-iron sign above the Auschwitz gates, intending to sell it to a collector of ghoulish memorabilia. His crime made headlines all over the world, but I can't help wondering if the meaning behind it was all that different from what every visitor does when he or she comes here. We all take photos. I myself have hundreds of photos of Auschwitz in my collection. What could I possibly want with such souvenirs?

If Auschwitz makes victims of us all, then it also makes monsters of us all. By coming here, we necessarily implicate ourselves in both sides of this sickening story. In other words, Auschwitz is not only a memorial to the victims of the Holocaust, but also a memorial to its perpetrators. And that, as I shall explore next, is a much more disturbing thought altogether.

Part III

Monsters

What makes a monster? By all accounts, the devil can be quite charming when he needs to be. Men like Hitler and Stalin did not win power only through force: they were also charismatic, eloquent, and able to mesmerise millions through the power of their rhetoric. They certainly did not see themselves as evildoers, but as men of action. According to their own warped logic they were simply trying to take back control from the sinister global forces – capitalists, imperialists, Jews – that they believed had made victims of their people. The reality of what they were doing, however, was the demonising of these groups and the fuelling of genocidal hatred.

Rather disturbingly, many of the qualities of a monster are the same ones we look for in our heroes and martyrs: strength, cunning, determination and an unwavering devotion to their cause. But in a true hero or martyr, these qualities stand beside other virtues, such as compassion, mercy, and a willingness to stand up for the rule of law and the universal norms of morality. A monster has contempt for such things. During the 1930s and 1940s, powerful fanatics pursued their aims with an utter disregard for the rights, the dignity and the lives of millions. They killed without thought or conscience. They treated human beings like objects to be used and then discarded; indeed, they often treated them not as humans at all, but as vermin to be exterminated. In such men, obsessive devotion to a cause is not a quality to be admired. It has become a sickness, one which cloaks all their actions in the same dark atmosphere that is so palpable in the grounds of Auschwitz–Birkenau.

* * *

Nobody deliberately sets out to make a monument to a
monster. Some of the monuments in this part of the book
were created when their subjects were still considered heroes,
and only began to look dubious in later years, after the crimes
of their subjects became more widely understood. Some of
them became monuments almost by mistake, simply because
of the attitudes of those who come to visit them. Some are
barely monuments at all: they include shrines, tombs and
other sites of memory that have become associated with the
darker aspects of the war. By including them in this book I
hope to widen our understanding of what constitutes a monument in the first place.

Is it ever right to visit such locations? Should they be
shunned, or even erased – just as the men they call to mind
tried to erase their own enemies? Can we ever escape these
symbols, or are we bound forever to remain prisoners of their
memory?

Of all the monuments described in this book, these are the
most problematic. They throw up moral dilemmas that are
impossible to solve. But by confronting these dilemmas I hope
we can at least learn valuable lessons about what happens
when the qualities we so admire in our heroes and martyrs
are taken to extremes.

13

Slovenia: Monument to the Victims of All Wars, Ljubljana

In the centre of Slovenia's capital city, Ljubljana, stands one of the most interesting and problematic memorials I have ever come across. Unlike all the other monuments discussed so far, this one does not try to lock up the nation's past in a figurative image. There are no statues, no portrayals of people frozen in action. In fact, the memorial is entirely abstract. But this does not make it any less controversial.

The Monument to the Victims of All Wars consists of two giant slabs of stone, set in an open-sided courtyard. The slabs stand close together but do not touch; they are parallel, and yet slightly askew from one another. One monolith is almost square, some 12 metres (39 feet) high and 12 metres wide; the other is narrower, rectangular, and made of much thicker blocks. However, their differences are greatly outweighed by their similarities: they are built from exactly the same stone; beneath the ground they share the same foundations; and though they are of different shapes, they are exactly the same height, weight and volume. They are like a pair of perpetually warring siblings, always independent, always in opposition, and yet inextricably linked to each other.

Unlike some other memorials, this one is not designed to grab the attention. The last time I visited it, in November 2018, I stood and watched it for a couple of hours, and in all that time not one person stopped to look up at it. Nobody waited for their friends on the wedge-shaped step that forms its southern edge. Nobody lingered in the shade of the great stone slabs to eat a sandwich. The memorial dominates one side of Congress Square, right in the heart of the city; but it seems to be impregnated with a quality that repels attention.

This is no accident. Politically speaking, invisibility is one of the monument's greatest strengths. When one considers what might have stood here instead, and the dark history that still grips at the heart of Slovenian nationhood, it is easy to understand why this particular design was chosen.

I was fortunate enough to be present at the birth of this monument. In May 2015 I was invited to the Slovenian parliament to witness the unveiling of the design. I sat in a large chamber along with a selection of journalists and politicians, and watched the president, Borut Pahor, make a speech. A scale model of the monument sat in the centre of the room. Afterwards we were all invited to take a closer look, have a glass of wine and shake hands with the designers.

In my naiveté, I thought that the reception would be a fairly jolly affair; but in fact it was not jolly at all. There was something quite uncomfortable about it that I, as an outsider, did not entirely understand. When I spoke to some of the MPs at the reception, none of them seemed very pleased with the design of the monument. It was too bland, they said. It was not *satisfying* as a memorial. It didn't say anything about heroes or villains, or the victims of the war. None of them could fully explain what they didn't like about it, or what they might have preferred instead. Nevertheless, most of them seemed to feel the same.

It was at this point that a Slovenian historian who was also present took me to one side. Mitja Ferenc, a professor from the University of Ljubljana, was the man who had invited me to the event in the first place. After talking to me for a while, he said something along the lines of, 'Let me show you why nobody likes this design. Let me take you to a place that explains why we can only ever have bland, abstract memorials here.'

So we left the parliament. We got in his car and drove out of the city – me, Ferenc, a journalist friend and my publisher. We travelled east, through Slovenia's beautiful countryside. To our left were rolling hills, with the Alps shining white in the distance; to our right was the River Sava.

After an hour or two we turned off the main road and travelled up a narrow track through the forest. Eventually we came to a place called Huda Jama – a lonely spot by the side of a mountain. Here, built into the cliff, was a giant concrete doorway with an iron door. We stopped the car and got out.

The place had once been a coal mine, Ferenc explained, but it had been sealed up ever since 1945. In the last days of the war, when the German army was fleeing Yugoslavia, the partisans under General Tito had rounded up tens of thousands of fascist collaborators and massacred them. This mine was one of dozens of mass graves all over Slovenia. Around 2,500 people had been brought here, where they had been forced to strip and were then shot and thrown down mine shafts. Mitja Ferenc knew all about this particular site because he had been in charge of the government team that had exhumed it a few years earlier.

Ferenc called up the caretaker, who came and unlocked the

gate for us. First we walked down a long tunnel, deep into the mountainside – some 400 metres into the darkness. At one point Ferenc stopped and pointed to a hollow in the tunnel wall. 'This is where we found the first body,' he said. Someone had apparently survived the massacre and had been trying to tunnel his way out. He had ripped up a fragment of metal from the railway line and had been using it to dig. Unfortunately for him, Tito's men had been extraordinarily thorough: they had plugged the tunnel not only with tons of earth and rubble, but also with a series of brick and concrete walls. This lone survivor had come up against the first concrete barrier and had been forced to give up. This was where he had died, alone in the darkness.

We carried on walking. Soon we came to a mine shaft. Ferenc made me climb down a ladder to the bottom of the pit and stand where the bodies had been thrown. 'They filled this shaft to the top with corpses,' he called down to me. 'We pulled out 346 bodies – there are probably another 1,500 people still down there, beneath your feet.'

It was a uniquely disturbing feeling, standing at the bottom of that pit. It crossed my mind that Ferenc and the others could quite easily abandon me here, switch the lights off and lock the door, and no one would have known. I quickly climbed back up the ladder.

Next Ferenc took me deeper into the tunnel, where another 432 bodies had been found. Once again, he explained what had happened here. First, the men had been made to undress – Ferenc and his team had found a heap of their clothes and shoes in the tunnel. Then they had been forced to lie flat on the tunnel floor, where they had been shot in the back of the head. The next group had then been told to lie down on top of their bodies so that they too could be shot. Then the next group, and the next, until the bodies were stacked eight high.

I hardly had time to take this in before Ferenc took me to another section of the tunnel, where there was another metal door. He unlocked it and led me inside. 'Here they are,' he said.

Before me were hundreds and hundreds of plastic crates, stacked on shelves along the tunnel. Sticking out of the crates were bones and skulls and bits of human hair.

'We wanted to give them a proper burial,' Ferenc told me, 'but none of our politicians was willing to do it.' These people had been victims of the Communists; but since they had themselves been fascists, nobody wanted to make a shrine to them. It was difficult to know how to remember them at all. So in the end the authorities had simply locked the doors and tried to forget about them. According to Ferenc, in the previous seven years, only a handful of people had bothered to come and see this place for themselves – a couple of journalists, the US ambassador, and now me. It remained a guilty memory: everybody knew it was here, but nobody wanted to acknowledge it.*

That night, in my hotel room, I found it difficult to sleep. It wasn't the image of all those dead bodies stacked up in crates that kept me awake. I have spent years researching war atrocities, and was well acquainted with the general story of what had happened at sites like this in the former Yugoslavia. What really disturbed me was the thought of the lone man who had survived the massacre and tried to dig his way out. I could not stop imagining what it must have been like for him, stepping out of the pit in the darkness, finding a chunk of metal, and desperately trying to scratch his way through

* Since I visited Huda Jama, the Slovenian government have interred the bones. They were buried in October 2017 at Dobrava memorial park near Maribor.

the earth and rubble. There was something heroic about it. But in the end, this man had not been a hero but just another victim. And perhaps worse than merely a victim: after all, he had himself been a fascist collaborator, and a soldier – perhaps he too had taken part in his own atrocities. I just couldn't work out how to feel about him.

This was precisely why Mitja Ferenc had taken me to Huda Jama. I realised now that the discomfort I was feeling was not so different from the discomfort I had sensed in that room full of politicians: how can one possibly remember a past like this *without* feeling uncomfortable? I also began to understand the antipathy expressed by some of those politicians about the proposed design for their monument to the war. What did this bland, abstract memorial say about the horrors I had just witnessed? How can one accept a monument built out of clean white stone when the reality is much more squalid, hidden at the bottom of a dark pit in the Slovenian hills?

For anyone who has studied the war in Yugoslavia, this kind of moral confusion is quite normal. British and American historians often characterise the Second World War as a relatively simple conflict between the Allies on the one hand and the Axis on the other – but in Yugoslavia things were never so simple. The country had only existed since 1918, when it was constructed out of the ruins of the First World War. It lay across the fault lines between the remnants of three great nineteenth-century powers – Russia, Austria-Hungary and the Ottoman Empire. It was therefore the meeting point of three great religions – Christian Orthodoxy, Catholicism and Islam (or indeed four, if one includes the small Jewish minority that was all but wiped out by the war). More than half a dozen large national and ethnic minorities lived here, all of whom had nursed petty rivalries and jealousies for generations. When the Germans and Italians invaded in 1941, all these tensions were unleashed at once.

It did not take long before the whole country had descended into chaos. Croats began massacring Serbs in the name of Catholicism; Serbs began torching Muslim villages in Bosnia and Hungarian villages in Vojvodina; monarchist Chetniks began fighting pitched battles against Communist Partisans. In order to hide their crimes, militias sometimes deliberately wore the uniforms of their rivals, so it is not always easy for historians to work out who was massacring whom. Presiding over this soup of violent conflicts were the German, Italian and other occupiers of the country, who not only committed their own war crimes but also encouraged in-fighting between the different groups.

After years of war, the various groups began to coalesce into two main camps. On the one hand there was the German army and its collaborators from each of the different ethnic groups in Yugoslavia: the Croatian Ustasha and its militias, the Slovenian Home Guard, the Serbia Volunteer Corps, and so on. These ultra-nationalist groups never trusted one another – but they each collaborated with the Germans, and as long as the Germans were in control, they were all effectively fighting on the same side.

Opposing them was the resistance. By 1945, Tito's Communist Partisans had already defeated the other main resistance groups and assimilated most of their members. This group was no longer the amateurish force it had been in 1941, but a full-blown army of some 800,000 men. It also had the backing of both London and Moscow, and so was relatively well equipped. Unlike the Slovenian or Croatian fascists, Tito had no intention of allowing separate nations to set themselves up after the war. His mantra, and the phrase he used in all his speeches at the end of the war, was 'brotherhood and unity'. He wanted to restore a single country called Yugoslavia which would encompass all the different nationalities, united under Communist rule.

Given everything that had happened before, the final showdown between these two groups was always going to have an apocalyptic flavour. In the dying days of the war, when it became obvious that the Partisans were going to win, the German army and its various fascist collaborators fled northwards. Their aim was to retreat to Austria where the British were waiting for them. If they could surrender to the British Army, they reasoned, they might be treated with a modicum of mercy. They knew that they would receive no mercy from Tito.

The first Slovenian troops fought their way through to Austria on 14 May, almost a week after the German army and its auxiliaries were supposed to have surrendered. They gave themselves up to the British in the town of Klagenfurt, just across the Austrian border. A day or so later, the first Croatian units also fought their way through to Austrian border, near the town of Bleiburg.

Unfortunately, the British had no intention of giving these troops and refugees asylum. They did not have the resources to look after so many people, and they were more interested in keeping good relations with Tito, whose massive army was already encroaching on British territory. And so British troops either turned them away at the border, or disarmed them and handed them back to the Partisans.

What happened next was no less than a bloodbath. Most of the atrocities committed over the following weeks occurred in the Yugoslavian Republic of Slovenia, which lay on the border with Austria. In the fields and forests near Maribor, some 15,000 Croatian fascists were lined up along an anti-tank trench and shot. At Kočevje Rog, and further west near the border with Italy, thousands of Slovenians and Croatians were thrown into deep ravines, whose sides were then blown up with dynamite to cover the bodies. And at Huda Jama, which I visited in 2015, thousands more were murdered and hidden away in the tunnels and mine shafts.

It is tempting to characterise these massacres as hot-blooded vengeance for the violence unleashed upon Yugoslavia by the Germans and their fascist collaborators, but the evidence suggests that this was not just about revenge. The men who died in the mine at Huda Jama are a good example: they were not killed in the heat of battle, but were kept for three weeks in a prisoner-of-war camp before being taken off to be executed. During this time, the officers were separated from the rank and file, and long-serving members of the Slovenian Home Guard were separated from those who had only been drafted in the dying days of the war. This implies not merely an element of selection but a great deal of organisation. The massacres were obviously taking place on orders from above, and quite possibly from the very top.

The reality is that the massacres were carried out for cynical, political motives. Killing all these people solved a lot of problems – at least in the short term. Tito wanted to create a unified, Communist Yugoslavia after the war. It would be much easier to do so without tens of thousands of ultra-nationalist Croats and Slovenians undermining his idea of 'brotherhood and unity'.

Years later Tito's right-hand man, Milovan Djilas, looked back on the days of May 1945 and admitted that the massacres had been carried out for purely practical reasons. 'Yugoslavia was in a state of chaos and destruction,' he told a British interviewer in 1979. 'There was hardly any civil administration. There were no properly constituted courts. There was no way in which the cases of 20–30,000 people could have been reliably investigated. So the easy way out was to have them all shot, and have done with the problem.'

This was the bloody foundation upon which Tito's new Yugoslavia was built. Over the next forty-five years or so, an uneasy peace settled across the country. While Tito lived, nobody dared question his vision of brotherhood and unity – but in truth, the spectre of darker, nationalist sentiments never entirely went away. After Tito's death in 1980, an unhealthy rivalry between different republics and ethnic groups started up again. Conflict finally erupted at the beginning of the 1990s, when Yugoslavia descended once more into bloody civil war.

Slovenia was the first republic formally to break away from the Yugoslavian federation in 1991. It escaped the worst of the violence that engulfed Serbia, Croatia, Bosnia and Kosovo; nevertheless, tensions between Slovenia's former Communists, its new democrats, and hard-line nationalists remained high. Meanwhile, the terrible things that were taking place in other parts of the region reawakened painful memories of the past.

The idea of a monument to the events of the war was first mooted in the Slovenian parliament in 2009. From the beginning, it was conceived as a way to promote reconciliation between groups of different political persuasions, whose memories of the past clashed so painfully with one another.

In 2013 a competition was held, and thirty-nine proposals were received. The winning design, by a group of architects headed by Rok Žnidaršič, was the one that I saw unveiled in 2015. The monument was finally built two years later, and inaugurated on 13 June 2017.

The very blandness of the memorial is probably its greatest selling point. It has been designed to be sensitive – in other words, to offend no one, to avoid resurrecting the destructive passions of the war. If it says nothing about heroes, or martyrs, or perpetrators, then this is a deliberate choice. Even its title is purposely vague: despite the fact that everyone knows it to be a Second World War memorial, it is dedicated to the victims of *all* wars.

Most monuments are designed to stimulate and direct national memories; this one, by contrast, seems designed to disperse them. What struck me when I first saw it is that there is nothing for either one's eyes or one's mind to grab hold of. There are no figures, no carvings, no details of any sort. There are just a couple of smooth, empty walls. Its blankness is like a sheet thrown over a crime scene: it hides away something that is simply too painful for most people to look at.

If you can bear to look beyond this, however, and peel away the other layers of obfuscation that cloak the monument, you will see that it poses some very difficult questions. The most important of these is the most fundamental: what does the monument really *say*?

The official line, promoted by both the architects who built the memorial and the president who championed it, is that it symbolises the Slovenian people and the ideas by which they live: they may be opposed to one another, but they are made of the same material, and built on the same foundations. It is supposed to be a gesture of reconciliation. But if we follow this line to its logical conclusion, it leads us to a dangerous place. If each of these giant slabs of stone represents a different side of the people, what *are* the two opposing sides? The state against the people? The military against the civilian? Left against right?

Since this is a war memorial, and it is focused mainly on the Second World War, only one interpretation makes any sense. The two main blocs that faced one another here in 1945 were the fascists on one side (with their local collaborators, such as the Slovenian Home Guard) and the Communist Partisans on the other. In other words, the two blocks of stone don't represent the majority of Slovenians at all, but the extremes.

In order to genuinely represent the Slovenian people during the war, something should have been placed between the two blocks – the victim, oppressed from both sides by two vast and pitiless ideologies. Of course, visitors to the monument can, if they wish, put *themselves* in this position. Today, when you stand between the monoliths you can feel the weight of them on either side, and the sensation is quite claustrophobic. But if you stand back and look at the blocks from any distance, they say nothing about victimhood at all. All you can see is the monoliths themselves – fascism and Communism. An installation supposedly dedicated to the victims has inadvertently become a monument to the perpetrators.

This is certainly the conclusion that some people in Ljubljana have come to. In the summer after I first visited, vandals attacked the site where the monument was due to be built. In mid-July it was spray-painted with swastikas. A week later Communist red stars were put up. Two months after that, chunks of slaughtered pigs were strewn across the site, along with printed notices reading 'Death to Fascism' and 'Freedom for the people'. One piece of graffiti seemed to say it all: '*Nehajte že se igrat partizane in domobrane*' – 'Stop playing Partisans and Home Guards'.

Few politicians or city administrators paid much attention to such protests. Some expressed outrage at the vandalism, others expressed concern, and President Borut Pahor, as always, tried to pour oil on troubled waters. But nobody was willing to tackle the fundamental problem that lay beneath the attacks, or ask the questions that still needed to be asked. What did the nation need to remember and what should it try to forget? Was it acceptable to acknowledge the presence of war criminals among the victims? What was the memorial's purpose: was it to heal wounds, or merely to acknowledge them? And, most important of all, how could Slovenia free itself from the darkest chapters of its history? Such questions were lost in the fog of emotion and denial, of calculation and compromise, that makes up Slovenian politics.

Today, the monument seems to have been swallowed up in a bubble of invisibility. It has already become a familiar part of the urban landscape – everyone knows it is there, but few give it any thought. Since its inauguration in July 2017 it has largely been left alone – not only by political activists, but by people in general. Hundreds walk past it every morning and every evening on their way to and from work, but none of them ever look up. Why should they? The monument represents a painful aspect of their history. Who wants to interrupt their day with uncomfortable thoughts about Communism or fascism or victimhood? And so they hurry on. At the very most they might shoot it a sideways glance, noticing but not noticing, remembering but not remembering.

14

Japan: Yasukuni Shrine, Tokyo

It is not only in Slovenia that the line between heroes, martyrs and monsters has become blurred. Many nations, including my own, shy away from looking too closely at some of their past deeds. This is simply human nature. Whenever it feels too difficult to draw a clear line between our guilty actions and our innocent ones, or when it risks making us too uncomfortable, every nation will take shelter in the grey areas between right and wrong.

Those grey areas are not there by chance. They provide a very useful function in society: they allow us to move towards the idea that we have done wrong, without forcing us to fully acknowledge our guilt. They are, in effect, a cushion which softens our fall.

Take for example the legacy of British colonialism. British people know, deep down, that the subjugation and exploitation of other nations was morally indefensible; but they salve their conscience with the thought that the empire also brought one or two benefits to Britain's colonies, such as the railways, and cricket, and western-style education. 'Perhaps we did wrong,' they can tell themselves, 'but we weren't *monsters*.'

Some nations do not have that luxury. In 1945, Japan and Germany were defeated so comprehensively that they had no opportunity to construct their own narrative about the crimes they had committed during the war. At the Nuremberg and Tokyo trials, those crimes were laid bare for all to see. They included some of the worst possible violations of humanity: mass enslavement, mass rape, mass murder, genocide. Both regimes routinely worked their prisoners to death. Both conducted medical experiments on live human beings. There was no hiding from the fact that the people who committed these crimes *did* behave like monsters.

What does this do to a country? How do you come to terms with the idea that you belong to a nation of perpetrators? In such a context is it possible to mourn your dead? How can you honour military sacrifice without also excusing military crime?

These are the questions that faced Japan in the years after 1945, and have plagued it ever since. How to remember the war has become one of the most problematic issues in Japanese society. Some organisations have tackled the matter head on: they have embraced Japan's guilt, tried to make amends, apologised. But one institution in particular has chosen a different path: that of denial. The Yasukuni Shrine in Tokyo has never accepted the version of history that every other nation accepts. It rejects the verdicts of the war crimes trials; indeed, it seems to reject any distinction at all between the innocent and the guilty. It has repeatedly tried to muddy the waters around the subject in an artificial attempt to recreate those moral grey areas that other nations are allowed to enjoy.

Unfortunately, things have not quite worked out like that. History is a prison that cannot be escaped. By trying to wriggle out of the country's responsibilities towards the past, the priests in charge of the Yasukuni Shrine have only succeeded in angering all of Japan's near neighbours, who have now begun to view it not as a place of mourning and respect, but rather as a sanctuary for monsters.

There are so many misconceptions about the Yasukuni Shrine, particularly in the West, that it is important to clear some of them up at the outset. First, the shrine is not devoted exclusively to those who died in the Second World War, as some people assume, but to all Japanese soldiers who have sacrificed their lives on the battlefield since the Meiji Restoration in 1868. Tens of thousands of souls were already enshrined here long before 1937: those who had died in the Russo-Japanese war of 1904–5, for example, or in the First World War, or in various wars against the Chinese, the Taiwanese or the Koreans. If the Second World War seems to dominate, it is only because that war was of a different order of magnitude. As a consequence of the Second World War, the number of souls enshrined here increased by a factor of *seventeen*. Today there are more than 2,466,000 names listed in the symbolic registry of deities; 94 per cent belong to people who died between 1937 and 1945.

Unlike most of the other places described in this book, the Yasukuni Shrine is not a memorial or a monument; strictly speaking it is a holy site, more akin to a church or a temple. Ordinary Japanese people come here to pay their respects to their ancestors, much as Americans might honour their fathers at Arlington Cemetery, or British people might honour their grandfathers at the Thiepval memorial in France. However, no one is buried here. Rather, the souls of the dead are enshrined here: their names and other details are hand-written on rolls of paper, which are stored in a repository behind the main sanctuary of the shrine. Visitors who wish to pay their respects will stand before the shrine, bow deeply, clap their hands twice in order to draw the attention of the deities, and pray.

For the casual tourist passing through, it must be difficult to see why there is so much fuss about this place. The atmosphere that presides is one not of drama or conflict, but of tranquillity, beauty and harmony. As you enter the site from the east, you walk down a long, paved boulevard lined with mature trees. There are exquisitely carved stone lions, and monoliths decorated with carved inscriptions. There is a statue of the founder of the Japanese army, standing on a pillar, a little like Nelson's Column in London. Through the main gate to the shrine are dozens of cherry trees, which burst into a spectacular display of blooms every April. Beyond the shrine is a shady walkway through a series of monuments, and a sacred pond garden, whose mirror-like surface is broken only by the occasional rise of one of the giant koi carp that swim within it.

On the face of it, there is nothing offensive about this place. Every nation must mourn its war dead, and Japan is no different. It is only right that Japanese people should be allowed to honour the memory of those who died for a greater cause, regardless of whether or not that cause eventually proved to be misguided. Their sacrifice must be acknowledged, and this haven of peace in an otherwise overwhelming city seems like a fitting place to do so.

If this were the only message of the Yasukuni Shrine, there would be no controversy. Unfortunately, however, other messages hidden among the pines and cherry trees are not nearly so straightforward.

Take, for example, the many monuments that scatter the

site. Few people would have a problem with the memorials dedicated to war widows, or animals, or patrol boat crews, or even the one to kamikaze pilots. But tucked away behind the shrine is a memorial to the Kenpeitai – the military police that terrorised civilians not only in the countries conquered by Japan, but also within Japan itself. There is a vast and undisputed literature listing the human rights abuses that were carried out by this much-feared organisation. It was responsible for operating prison camps where hundreds of thousands of civilians and prisoners of war were worked and starved to death. It was responsible for running military brothels, where tens of thousands of women were forced into a life of sexual slavery. It was responsible for rooting out and terrorising Japanese citizens who expressed any kind of anti-war sentiments. Its closest equivalents in the West would be the Nazi SS or the Soviet NKVD. Why on earth, then, is it memorialised with such respect here?

More prominent is another memorial, which stands out in the open, closer to the shrine – it is a monument to Dr Radhabinod Pal, a judge in the Tokyo war crimes trials in 1946. Pal was the only one of eleven judges to insist that all the Japanese defendants should have been found not guilty. He had some important and valid points to make about victor's justice, and also about judging Japan's leaders harshly for acts that the Allies had themselves committed. Nevertheless, all the other judges agreed, more or less, that the Japanese leadership should be held accountable for the war. Furthermore, the Japanese government itself accepted the judgements of the war crimes tribunals when it signed the San Francisco Treaty in 1951. To erect a memorial to Pal, while ignoring the judgement of the vast majority, is not only a distortion of history, but it also sends out a strong political message: what the shrine authorities are effectively saying is that Japan did no wrong, and needs to take no responsibility for its actions.

To muddy the waters still further, there is also a war museum on the site, whose entrance lies just 30 or 40 metres (approximately 115 feet) from the shrine itself. I spent several hours in this museum, determined to view it with an open mind, but by the time I left I felt utterly sickened. The museum blamed the Chinese for Japan's invasion of China. It blamed the Americans for Japan's attack on Pearl Harbor. It suggested that the only reason Japan invaded south-east Asia was out of a selfless desire to liberate Asian people from European rule, rather than an entirely selfish desire to colonise these places for itself. I have spent much of my career trying to coax Europeans to face up to the terrible things that they have done in the past, including some of the crimes committed in the name of colonialism, but the scale of denial in this museum was beyond anything I'd ever come across before. There was not a glimmer of acceptance that Japan might have been even partly responsible for the war.

Perhaps even worse than these historical distortions were the museum's omissions. In the lobby of the museum stands a locomotive that was used on the infamous Burma railway. I have personally spoken to prisoners of war who were almost starved to death as they built this railway: around 100,000 people are supposed to have died during its construction. After the war was over, more than a hundred Japanese military officials were tried for their brutality during the project, and thirty-two of them were sentenced to death. *None* of these facts are mentioned in the display. As far as the museum is concerned, this is simply a locomotive – a symbol of modernity – proudly built by a Japanese company, Nippon Sharyo Ltd.

This was just one omission among many. The Rape of Nanking (or the 'Nanking incident', as it is euphemistically called here) was portrayed as a straightforward operation that involved the killing of no civilians, only Chinese soldiers hiding in civilian clothes. There was no mention of comfort women. There were no medical experiments on Chinese civilians, no torture of dissenters, no starvation of people in Indonesia, no massacre of women and children in Manila. These events are well known all over the world, and have been repeatedly proven – not only by foreign historians, but by Japanese ones. But they are entirely absent from the museum.

All these issues are problematic, but they are not the main reason why the Yasukuni Shrine has become so controversial. They do not explain why a Chinese man tried to set fire to the gates of the shrine in 2011. They do not explain why a South Korean man threw a bottle of paint thinners into the main hall in 2013, or why another set off a bomb in 2015. Those attacks were not directed at the museum, or the monuments, but at something far more fundamental: the shrine itself, and the very souls who are housed here.

The Yasukuni Shrine is hated by Japan's neighbours because it is not merely an institution that honours ordinary Japanese soldiers who died while doing their duty: since the late 1950s, it has also been an institution that openly and explicitly honours the souls of convicted war criminals.

The problem began in 1959. Until this point, convicted war criminals had always been excluded from the shrine. However, the families of some war criminals had long been lobbying for the enshrinement of their relatives, and they eventually succeeded in enlisting the support of the Ministry of Health and Welfare. In 1956, the ministry began passing on the names of Class B and C war criminals to the Yasukuni Shrine, and three years later the enshrinement of their souls began.

Between April 1959 and October 1967, some 984 Class B and C war criminals were enshrined. These were men who had been personally involved in the mass killing, exploitation and torture of prisoners and innocent civilians around Asia. The process took place quietly, without fanfare, partly in order to avoid any kind of public backlash, but also to avoid any accusations of a merging of religious and governmental affairs – something that was banned under the new Japanese constitution. It seems that the shrine did not even seek permission from the families of those they enshrined, some of whom were deeply ashamed of what their relatives had done, and did not want them to be given such an honour.

In 1969, the Ministry of Health and Welfare and the Yasukuni Shrine also agreed on a plan to enshrine fourteen of Japan's Class A war criminals. These were not men who had personally conducted atrocities, but rather the top brass: those who had masterminded and initiated an aggressive war. From the very beginning, the plan to enshrine these people was ideologically driven. Several members of the ministry and priests at the shrine were themselves ex-military men, and had never accepted the verdicts of the Tokyo trials. The process was stalled for a few years by the head priest, Tsukuba Fujimaro, but after his death his successor, Matsudaira Nagayoshi, proceeded quickly. In a secret ceremony on 17 October 1978, he enshrined all fourteen Class A criminals.

None of these steps was necessary. In the 1960s and 1970s there were far more people in Japan who opposed the enshrinements than there were those who supported them.

Unsurprisingly so: these people had broken all codes of morality and had brought shame upon Japan. The reason why so much secrecy surrounded the events is that the Yasukuni Shrine wanted to avoid provoking public opinion against them.

It appears that the emperor did not approve the enshrinement either. Between 1945 and 1975, he visited the Yasukuni Shrine eight times, but after the Class A war criminals were enshrined he never visited again. After he died, his son followed suit, and has never visited the shrine.

Japan's prime ministers, however, have not been quite so diplomatic. In August 1985, Prime Minister Yasuhiro Nakasone paid his respects at the shrine, as part of the fortieth anniversary commemoration of the end of the war. His visit, which implied a level of official approval for the shrine and everything it had done, caused a storm of criticism from the Chinese for the first time. In 2001, Prime Minister Junichiro Koizumi, who was running for the presidency of the Liberal Democratic Party, made a campaign pledge to visit the shrine every year regardless of the criticism it would cause. He claimed to be visiting in a private capacity, but the fact that he made it a campaign pledge speaks otherwise. Once again, his visits caused outrage in China and South Korea. In 2013 Prime Minister Shinzo Abe also paid his respects at the shrine, despite knowing that it would only cause further damage to international relations.

It is difficult to know what can be done to salvage the situation now. Some people have suggested 'de-enshrining' the spirits of Japan's war criminals or moving them to another location – but the priests at the shrine insist that this is impossible for theological reasons. What they forget to mention is that it would also go against the political ethos pursued by the shrine authorities ever since the 1950s. It suits the priests to have the guilty mixed up with the innocent, just as it suits them to allow monuments to the secret police to remain on their grounds, along with a museum full of misdirection and denial. It is all part of the same attempt to muddy the waters regarding Japan's responsibility for the Second World War.

Supporters of the shrine point out that British and American institutions are often guilty of similar evasions and moral equivocations, particularly regarding their bombing campaigns and their colonial record in south-east Asia. They also point the finger at China, which is much happier to cry foul on Japanese war crimes than it is to own up to its own questionable human rights record. They have a point. Why should Japan be held to a different standard from everyone else? But there is a qualitative difference that these people are failing to take into account. Western nations have at least been moving in the right direction: their denials are generally becoming weaker as, year by year, they swallow just a little more of their pride and admit to greater responsibility. The Yasukuni Shrine is moving in the opposite direction, increasing their denial rather than diminishing it.

Along the way, it has caused a great deal of distress, not only to the families of those who died at Japanese hands during the war, but also to the Japanese people. Had it not been for the actions of the authorities at the shrine, Japanese families would have been able to come here in peace, without ever having to think about the actions of war criminals. They might have been able to pay their respects to their ancestors without being harangued by ultra-nationalists waving banners or shouting at them through loudspeakers, and without having to worry about the possibility of an arson attack or a bomb.

The ordinary Japanese people who come here already had to shoulder the burden of history. Now, because of this toxic power play, every act of worship has also become a political act that threatens to poison the future as much as the past.

15

Italy: Mussolini's Tomb, Predappio

It is 28 April 2018, and a long procession is making its way out of the village of Predappio in central Italy. There are several hundred people here, almost all of them dressed in black, as if for a funeral. They walk slowly, solemnly, along the Viale della Libertà in the direction of the church of San Cassiano and its cemetery. Many wear strange black hats – sometimes a fez, sometimes a beret, sometimes even an old-fashioned military helmet adorned with black feathers. Some carry Italian flags decorated with eagles; others carry banners bearing the names of military organisations and marching bands. One holds a placard reading *Gli hanno sparato, ma non sono riusciti a ucciderlo* ('They shot him, but they didn't manage to kill him').

Anyone unacquainted with Italy and its history would be forgiven for thinking that the participants were here to attend the burial of a recent murder victim, but in fact they were here to commemorate a man who had died seventy-three years earlier. Benito Mussolini, the wartime dictator of Fascist Italy, was born in this village, and is also buried here. His body lies in the family crypt, and these people have come to honour his memory. They do this three times a year – on the anniversaries of his birth (29 July) and death (28 April), and on the anniversary of the day he and his followers marched on Rome to seize power (28 October).

There is something slightly spooky about the gathering. Very few people here are from the village itself, whose inhabitants generally frown upon the processions. Their black shirts are reminiscent of the uniforms worn by Mussolini's notorious Fascist militia, as are some of the slogans on their banners: *Onore e fedeltà* ('Honour and loyalty'), for example, or *Boia chi molla* ('Death to cowards'). The symbols they carry all come from a bygone era: eagles, daggers, Celtic crosses; and everywhere the symbol of the fasces – a bundle of sticks tied together with an axe. These symbols, still taboo, are carried openly and brazenly.

But most unnerving of all is the quasi-religious atmosphere that pervades. Italy is a country where processions like this happen every year in every village – but they usually take place in honour of the Madonna, or of a local saint. Today they are taking place in honour of a man that most of the world considers a monster. These people are making a pilgrimage not to the tomb of a Catholic saint or apostle, but to that of a Fascist dictator.

When the procession arrives at the cemetery, Edda Negri Mussolini stands on the steps to make a short speech. 'We are here to commemorate my grandfather,' she says, 'to pay our respects in this sacred place.' It is not entirely clear that she regards the place as sacred because it is attached to a church, or because Mussolini is buried here.

If the Yasukuni Shrine is guilty of blurring the line between the guilty and the innocent, the shrine to Mussolini blurs nothing. It is abundantly clear what this place represents, and there is no apology about it.

* * *

Mussolini did not spring from nowhere. In the early 1920s he was just one of many people promising to bring an end to the months of turmoil and civil unrest that had followed the First World War. The difference between Mussolini and most of his rivals was that he was not afraid to use violence to achieve his aims. His followers broke up strikes and demonstrations, and mercilessly hunted down Communist leaders and trade union representatives. Such methods proved so effective that he quickly won a great deal of support from business owners, military leaders and Italian aristocrats.

Unfortunately, Mussolini did not stop with breaking workers' strikes. In October 1922, 30,000 of his followers marched on Rome and demanded the resignation of the prime minister. Fearing further violence, the king simply handed power to Mussolini. In the following years, he and his followers used this power to terrorise his political rivals, assassinate those who stood in his way, remove the rights of the people to choose any other leader, and set up a police state. Mussolini provided the template for other fascist dictators like Hitler and Franco. Among his other faults, therefore, he is guilty of paving the way for years of ethnic cleansing, political violence and eventually a world war.

Mussolini repeatedly stated that his aim was to return Italy to its ancient imperial splendour through war and conquest. In 1923 he invaded Corfu, and refused to withdraw his troops until Greece paid a ransom. In 1935 he invaded Ethiopia, and gave his commanders written instructions to use poison gas on civilian populations, kill all prisoners and 'systematically conduct a politics of terror and extermination on the rebels and the complicit population' – all of which were war crimes, even at the time. In 1937 he sent thousands of troops to Spain to 'terrorise Valencia and Barcelona' for Franco. In 1939 he invaded Albania, and in 1940 he tried to invade Greece and Egypt. All this was done in complete independence of Hitler. His support of Nazi Germany in its even more murderous campaigns was merely the icing on the cake.

There are dozens of myths about Mussolini that survive to this day. The first is that he was not racist, on the grounds that his regime did not pursue Jews in the same way that the Nazis did. Anyone who has studied the ethnic cleansing of Libya in the 1920s and 1930s might take issue with that. Mussolini himself instructed the governor of Libya, Pietro Badoglio, to make intermarriage between Italians and Libyans a crime, for fear that the Italian race might become polluted with foreign blood. Though he repeatedly claimed that he bore no ill-will towards Jews or Muslims, his actions spoke louder than his words. In 1938, when he was at the height of his powers, he introduced race laws to Italy that were little different from Hitler's Nuremberg Laws.

Another dictum has it that, whatever his faults, Mussolini at least made the trains run on time – as if institutional violence and the loss of personal freedom were a price worth paying for getting to work promptly. Like many other tales that are told about him, this myth is the result of Mussolini's own propaganda. One needs only read the travel diaries of journalists in the 1930s to see that Italian trains remained pretty awful during the dictator's reign. According to the American journalist Bergen Evans, who worked as a courier in Italy in 1930, it was not just a matter of a few trains: '*most* Italian trains,' he wrote, 'were not on schedule – or near it'. When it came to public infrastructure projects, Mussolini was no more successful than many other European leaders, even those who did not feel the need to strip their populations of their rights.

It was the Second World War that caused Mussolini's down-fall. As defeat followed defeat in the middle of the war, his popularity among his own people began to wane. By 1943, even his own government were getting tired of him. In July that year, the Grand Council voted to strip him of his dicta-torial powers: he was arrested and held in a luxury resort in Abruzzo while his successor, Pietro Badoglio, made peace overtures towards the Allies.

Mussolini was famously rescued that autumn, not by his own people, but by German special forces. It was the Germans, too, who set him up again as their puppet leader in the north of the country. Italy's far right nationalists choose to forget this fact: between 1943 and 1945 Mussolini did not fight for Italy, but for Germany.

Now, at last, the viciousness that Mussolini had sanctioned against Ethiopians and Libyans was turned upon his own people. With German help, he organised the executions of some of the government members who had turned against him, including his own son-in-law, Count Ciano. With German help, his followers brutally suppressed any hint of resistance among the Italian population. Many of the portraits displayed in Bologna's Piazza del Nettuno (see Chapter 6) are of people tortured and executed not by Germans, but by their fellow Italians.

Some of the most notorious German atrocities were carried out with enthusiastic Italian collaboration. In Sant'Anna di Stazzema, for example, around 560 villagers were massacred in reprisal for resistance activity in the area. The victims included old people, pregnant women and around 100 chil-dren. It was the German SS who were responsible; but they were helped by the Italian XXXVI Black Brigade. It is worth noting that each of the Black Brigades was named after a prominent Fascist leader: this particular unit bore the name 'Benito Mussolini'.

This is the man who is honoured three times a year with processions in Predappio. The cruelty that gripped northern Italy in the last two years of the war was a direct consequence of his ultra-nationalist ideology, his glorification of brute force, and his utter disregard of the rule of law – qualities celebrated every time one of his modern-day disciples lays a wreath at his tomb.

Mussolini eventually reaped what he had sown. In the spring of 1945, German control of northern Italy collapsed under Allied pressure, and a widespread insurrection against Fascist rule broke out. Mussolini was captured by partisans as he tried to flee the country. He and his mistress, Clara Petacci, were executed by the side of the road, and their bodies were taken back to Milan and dumped in Piazzale Loreto – a site deliberately chosen because fifteen partisans had been executed here by Fascists the previous year.

The bodies soon attracted a large crowd, some of whom exercised their disgust by kicking and beating them. One woman tried to shove a dead mouse in Mussolini's mouth; others put a hunk of cheap, low-grade black bread in his hands, as if to say that he was now as poor and contemptible as he had made them. Another woman reportedly fired a gun into his body several times – once for each of her dead sons. In the end, it was the partisans themselves who stepped in to spare the bodies further indignity. To carry on displaying them to the crowd, as proof that the Fascist leader was indeed dead, the bodies were suspended by their feet from the roof of a petrol station. Clara Petacci's skirt was tied round her legs to preserve her modesty. Photographs were taken, and appeared in newspapers all over the country.

What happened next is both bizarre and quite gruesome. Mussolini was buried in an unmarked grave in a Milanese cemetery, but about a year later was dug up by a journalist named Domenico Leccisi and two other former Fascists. For several months his body was moved from place to place, before the authorities finally traced it to a monastery outside Pavia, where it had been concealed by two Franciscan monks.

Had the body been cremated, or disposed of at sea, then perhaps that might have been the end of the matter, but instead the authorities dithered. For over ten years the body was hidden at another monastery, in the small town of Cerro Maggiore, while a succession of governments tried to work out what to do with it. Eventually, in 1957, newly appointed Prime Minister Adone Zoli agreed to give the body back to the Mussolini family and allow it to be interred in the family crypt in Predappio. It is probably no coincidence that the minority Christian Democratic government led by Zoli was embarrassingly dependent on neo-Fascist votes.

Mussolini was finally reinterred on 1 September 1957, in a stone sarcophagus decorated with Fascist symbols. Above the sarcophagus, a larger-than-life white marble bust of Mussolini sits in an alcove, with carved stone fasces on either side. The whole space is lit from above, as if the light of God is shining down upon him.

In the years since, the town of Predappio has become something of a pilgrimage site for neo-Fascists the world over. The house where Mussolini was born has long been a tourist destination. In the centre of town are souvenir shops which sell everything from T-shirts and keyrings with Fascist slogans on them, to swastika flags and life-sized busts of *Il Duce* himself. Technically, these shops are breaking the law – ever since 1952 it has been illegal to glorify the 'exponents, principles, facts and methods' of Fascism – but the authorities here simply turn a blind eye. Prosecuting shop owners for peddling the trinkets of far right nostalgia is simply not seen as a priority.

For most neo-Fascist visitors, however, the spiritual heart of the place has always been Mussolini's tomb. Over the years the site has become a real object of worship. According to the Italian newspaper *Il Giornale*, it sees up to 200,000 visitors each year, many of whom seem to have formed a cult-like attachment to Mussolini. 'This place is our Bethlehem,' one visitor told a reporter for the *Washington Post* in 2018, before confessing that he visits Predappio several times a year 'to pay thanks for what he did for the world'. He is not the only one who seems to regard Mussolini as a kind of religious or mythical saviour. The visitors' book, which lies on an altar in front of the tomb, contains several messages exhorting the former dictator to 'rise again and save Italy'.

The sense of history here is so potent as to be almost palpable. It is impossible to enter the crypt where Mussolini is interred without feeling chills down your spine. And yet, in an academic sense, there is no proper history here at all. There is no weighing up of Mussolini's legacy; no documentation balancing his achievements against his crimes; no mention of the overwhelming evidence against him as a war criminal. This is a shrine, not a museum: local memories of this Fascist dictator have not been curated, but simply left to the shameless nostalgia of his apologists.

When I last visited in 2018, the town authorities were planning to fill the void by building a proper museum in the heart of town. They insisted that this was the only way to reclaim their town from those who were misusing it. Predappio is a prisoner of its history, whether it likes it or not: its only sensible course of action is to embrace that history and take charge of it. A proper museum, they hope, might at least attract tourists who are interested in what *really* happened in Italy's past, rather than mere worshippers of a Mussolini personality cult.

Critics of the plan, however, were worried that building a Mussolini museum might simply entrench the town's reputation, and make it an even more attractive destination for neo-Fascists. A handful of historians have opposed the project. While I was there, the president of the National Association of Italian Partisans, Carla Nespolo, also voiced her concern that any Predappio museum would simply become another 'place of pilgrimage for Fascists'. There are no easy answers to this problem.

Many people in Predappio wish that Mussolini's body had never been discovered. They say that if it had remained in its unmarked grave, far away, then they might have been spared the neo-Fascist processions that have made their town notorious throughout Italy. But there is no guarantee that the absence of Mussolini's body would have been any better, either for Predappio or for Italy as a whole. The problem with absence is that it can itself become a kind of presence. Or, to put it another way, a corpse that is nowhere is everywhere.

In the next chapter I will take a look at a country that has never discovered where the body of its fascist dictator is buried. Germany's treatment of its wartime past is, in many ways, a model of good practice. Its bans on Nazi symbols and the glorification of Hitler are strictly enforced. There is nothing in Germany that resembles a shrine to Hitler in the same way that Predappio has become a shrine to Mussolini, and the idea of any site tolerating quasi-religious processions every year in Hitler's honour is unthinkable.

But this does not mean that Germans can sleep easy in their beds. Their history is just as inescapable as Italy's. If not more so – because in parts of Germany, particularly in Berlin, history is everywhere you turn.

The noticeboard at the site of Hitler's bunker

The Topography of Terror

16

Germany: Hitler's Bunker and the Topography of Terror, Berlin

Adolf Hitler has no tomb. In the last days of the war, when Berlin was surrounded and under constant bombardment, Hitler retreated to the bunker beneath the gardens of the Reich Chancellery. Since it was obvious that his reign was over, this man – who has come to be known as the greatest monster of the twentieth century – decided to take his own life. It seems that his decision was made partly to deny anyone else the satisfaction of killing him, but mostly so that he could control what happened to his body. He had heard what had happened to Mussolini's corpse in Milan and didn't want to be subjected to the same indignities.

So, on 30 April, two days after the death of Mussolini, Hitler shot himself. His long-term mistress, now wife, Eva Braun, committed suicide at the same time by biting on a cyanide capsule. Then, in accordance with Hitler's written instructions, their bodies were carried to a bomb crater outside, doused with petrol, and burned. After the bodies had been consumed, the crater was covered over with earth and rubble.

When Berlin fell to the Soviets a few days later, a team of SMERSH counter-intelligence agents went in search of Hitler's body. They found his and Eva Braun's remains in their shallow grave, along with those of Hitler's propaganda minister Josef Goebbels and his wife (who had killed themselves and their children shortly after their leader's suicide). Their bodies were taken away to be examined, and Hitler was soon identified by his dental records.

The Soviet authorities were then presented with a problem: what should they do with the bodies? At first they buried them in a forest in Brandenburg, but this was considered insufficiently secure. So a few months later they were exhumed and moved to a SMERSH facility in Magdeburg. In 1970, to put an end to any possibility of Hitler's burial site becoming a shrine, all the bodies were exhumed one final time: they were thoroughly burned and crushed, and the ashes were dumped into a nearby river to be flushed away to the sea.

Without a body, there could be no tomb; but there remained the worry that Hitler's bunker might become a shrine instead. After all, this was the place where he had committed suicide, which gave it a kind of totemic power. The last thing the Soviets wanted was for it to become a symbol around which neo-Nazis could regroup.

Accordingly, they went about destroying the site as comprehensively as they had destroyed Hitler's body. This was no easy task. The bunker had been built to withstand the biggest bombs in the Allied arsenal. Its ceiling was made of reinforced concrete 3.5 metres (11.5 feet) thick, and its walls were even thicker. When Red Army pioneers tried to blow the place up in 1947, they succeeded in destroying the entrance and the ventilation towers, and many of the interior walls, but the main structure remained largely intact.

In 1959 they tried again. Further blasts were carried out,

the entrances were filled in, and a mound of earth was piled over the top of the reinforced concrete. But various tunnels still existed, and the East German secret police were able to open the bunker up again in 1967 to photograph it.

In the 1980s, the East Berlin authorities decided to remove all outward signs of what lay beneath the ground. They erected an apartment complex on the site of the old Reich Chancellery: while they were digging the foundations, they also removed the concrete roof of the bunker and filled the entire structure with gravel, sand and other debris. The area was levelled and a car park planned on top of it. As far as the eye could see, all traces of the bunker had gone.

There is still no shrine here, even today. There is no museum, or tourist recreation of Hitler's bunker. There is not even a plaque or a stone to mark where the bunker once stood, just a rather shabby information board at the side of the road with some dry text in German and English describing the history of the building.

I have been to this place, but only once, and only for ten minutes. This was not out of any scruples about 'paying homage' to Hitler, but because there is really nothing to see. That's exactly as it is intended to be: it is not a place to visit if you want to feel chills down your spine, or to daydream about the Führer and his legacy. There isn't even a bench to sit down on.

And yet there is still something slightly disturbing about the place. The attempt to erase all traces of Hitler in this way is reminiscent of some of the totalitarian actions carried out by the Nazis themselves: the annihilation of Lidice, for example, or the razing of Warsaw. Perhaps this is appropriate. Nevertheless, it feels like an exercise in denial. Berlin might like to pretend that this place is just an ordinary block of flats with an ordinary car park in front of it, but it is not, and never can be. Hitler's bunker will always be there, just beneath the surface.

In the aftermath of the war there was a tremendous desire in Germany for the nation to put the past behind it. Germans began to call 1945 'Year Zero', as if the war had swept away everything that had gone before and the whole country had been given the opportunity to start again from the beginning. A purge of sorts took place. Nazi officials were arrested and replaced. Nazi laws were repealed. Nazi symbols were banned, statues of Hitler were taken down and streets were renamed. The embarrassments of the past were hastily buried, and the whole country tried to focus its attention on the future.

Hitler's bunker was not the only historically significant building to be destroyed after the war. Nearby, on Wilhelmstrasse and Prinz Albrecht Strasse, stood the headquarters of the SS, the Reich Security Main Office and the other major organs of state terror. These buildings had been notorious during the Nazi era, particularly the Gestapo headquarters at No. 8 Prinz Albrecht Strasse, where 'enemies of the state' had been interrogated and tortured. Despite some bomb damage, there is no reason why this building could not have been rebuilt after the war. Instead, parts of it were pulled down in the early 1950s, and the rest was finally blown up in 1956. No attempt was made to commemorate what had once stood here.

Had it not been for the Cold War, it is quite possible that the place might have ended up much the same as Hitler's bunker – the site of a nondescript post-war apartment block. But in 1961 the Berlin Wall was built right through this area, and the ground was left vacant.

By the 1980s, the atmosphere in West Berlin had changed considerably. There was a new desire to confront the past, to acknowledge its inescapable shadow and to commemorate it. When plans were drawn up to build a new street through the site where the Gestapo headquarters had once stood, a group of western architects and civil rights organisations protested. Instead the site was partially excavated. A series of information boards were erected, explaining what had once existed here. It was opened to the public in 1987 as part of Berlin's 750th anniversary celebrations, and eventually given a new name, the 'Topography of Terror'.

After the reunification of Germany in 1990, the Berlin parliament decided to make this into a permanent memorial site. There were a couple of false starts, but at the beginning of the new century a research centre was erected on the ground where the Gestapo headquarters had once stood. Since 2010 a permanent exhibition has been on display, documenting the crimes of the Nazi state. It is now one of the most popular remembrance sites in Berlin, attracting around 1.3 million visitors each year.

And yet, at the heart of the project there is still a feeling of absence. It is a much more positive absence than that of Hitler's bunker, but an absence nevertheless: 'Look what Germany once was,' it says; but also, 'This is not what we are today.' To drive the point home, the rest of the site has been left deliberately and ostentatiously empty. Where once stood the offices devoted to terrorising the people, there is now a field of rubble. Nothing is allowed to grow here. There is not a single plant or blade of grass: it is completely barren. This is the legacy of Nazism: death, emptiness, nothingness.

* * *

These two places – Hitler's bunker and the Topography of
Terror – are excellent metaphors for the legacy of Nazism in
Germany today.

The first is an attempt to free Germany from its history.
The Soviet authorities in East Berlin thought they could bury
the past, just as they had buried Hitler's bunker. In the West,
too, there was a strong belief that if Germans simply focused
their energies on building a new, brighter future, then the
shame of their recent past could be put behind them. But no
matter how well they thought it was buried, their history was
always just beneath the surface.

Ever since then a new scandal has hit the newspapers
every couple of years, in which the past breaks through the
shallow topsoil. Sometimes a German police chief, or
company boss, or Nobel Prize winner is revealed to have
had a Nazi past. Sometimes historians weigh in, as they did
in the 1980s, to say that the Nazis were not so bad, or that
their crimes originated elsewhere, or that only a few people
were ever genuinely guilty. Or, as is happening today, a new
political group starts up, espousing racist or nationalistic
views that everyone thought were long dead. And each time
this happens the whole nation is shocked, because it has
told itself that the monsters of the past have been vanquished.
It seems that every generation must learn the hard way that
history is not merely what happened to another people in
another time, but still has an irresistible power over us
today.

The second site, the Topography of Terror, comes at history
from the opposite direction: it is an attempt to defeat the past
by confronting it head on. Here, the crimes of Nazism are
put under the spotlight to be examined in forensic detail.
Denial is almost impossible. Like a frightened animal on the

memorial site's vast field of rubble, the past lies entirely exposed, and there is nowhere for it to hide.

The Topography of Terror is not the only such location in Berlin. There are dozens of similar sites, all within a short walking distance: the Holocaust Memorial (see Chapter 19), the Jewish Museum, the memorial to murdered Sinti and Roma, the memorial to persecuted homosexuals, the Neue Wache memorial, the book-burning memorial in Bebelplatz, the memorial to the German resistance, the 'Stolpersteine' placed in the ground outside the houses of Jews who were taken away – the list goes on. Almost every building on Wilhelmstrasse has an information board outside it explaining its history and how it was used during the Second World War. Sometimes it seems as if the whole of central Berlin is an open air museum dedicated to its troubled wartime and Cold War past.

This overwhelming wealth of information, and the sense of universal guilt that comes with it, can feel stifling even to outsiders. When I first brought my children to see Berlin, their initial enthusiasm for the city's history was gradually crushed beneath the sheer weight of depressing detail: they felt compelled to turn away and concentrate their efforts on Berlin's more contemporary delights. If this is the way that English teenagers experience Germany's history, how must German teenagers feel, who are obliged to live with that history every day?

And yet, what is the alternative? Either we acknowledge our history or we don't: there is nothing we can do to change it.

Germans, just like everyone else, switch between these two positions – acknowledgement and denial – depending on their own shifting circumstances and the political atmosphere of the times in which they live. When they are feeling brave, they will face up to their history. They will grimly admit that most institutions, most corporations, most buildings and most families have some kind of Nazi past; and they will gird their loins for the perennial battle to prevent that past from reasserting itself in the present day. There is a little piece of Hitler, they will say, in everything we do; and we forget this at our peril.

But every now and then the uncompromising bleakness of the past will be too much for them, and they will turn away. They begin to look for excuses that will free them of their historic burden. On such occasions the omnipresence of Hitler becomes a kind of comfort. If all the evils of National Socialism can be gathered together and placed at Hitler's door, if this one monster can shoulder all the responsibility for the past, then everyone else is free to breathe once more. In this way, Hitler has become a kind of dark Messiah, whose evil presence absolves the rest of society of guilt for the sins of the past.

It is perhaps for this reason that the image of Hitler, though purged from German society in 1945, is still so prevalent in the country today. He appears in bestselling books by Joachim Fest or Volker Ullrich, and in history documentaries by Guido Knopp or Ullrich Kasten. He appears in award-winning movies such as Oliver Hirschbiegel's *Downfall*, which recreates the scenes in Hitler's bunker more vividly than any tourist attraction could ever manage. He appears in debates between journalists and between politicians. And in all internet discussions, according to Godwin's Law, it is only a matter of time before his memory is invoked by one party or the other.

I sometimes wonder what the victorious Allies of 1945 would have made of all this. When they tore down the statues and busts of Hitler, and changed the name of the streets and squares named after him, they must have imagined that they had dispensed with this monstrous warmonger for good. When they watched the people hurriedly destroying the portraits of Hitler that used to hang on their walls, and burning their copies of the once omnipresent *Mein Kampf*, they must have hoped that Germans would be too ashamed ever to invoke his memory again. The comprehensive annihilation of his body was supposed to symbolise all this and mark a definitive ending.

And yet today, in the twenty-first century, Hitler's memory seems to be stronger than ever. All it takes to bring him back to life is an outstretched arm, or a sketch of a slanting fringe above a black toothbrush moustache. In 2012, when Timur Vermes published his fantastically successful novel *Er ist wieder da* ('He's Back Again' or 'Look Who's Back'), there was no need to explain who 'He' was. The central message of the book, that his presence is still alive and thriving in Germany, is one that seemed to resonate with almost everyone.

This is something that does not come across at the site of Hitler's bunker or at the Topography of Terror. The sense of absence promoted by both sites is, at best, only half true.

Hitler has no tomb, but he doesn't need one. Even without a physical body, or a shrine in his honour, his memory continues to live alongside us whether we like it or not.

17

Lithuania: Statue of Stalin, Grūtas Park

No matter how much we might wish to, there is no escaping the monsters of our past. We might try to ignore them, or bury them, but sooner or later they always burrow their way back up to the surface. We might be tempted to rehabilitate them or excuse them; but that only makes us complicit in their crimes. Or we might try to annihilate them; but then their absence itself becomes a sort of presence. As the memorials described in the last few chapters demonstrate, monsters will always remain, whether we like it or not.

There is one final course open to us: ridicule. If we cannot escape our history, perhaps we can thumb our noses at it.

I recently attended a conference on public memorials, and one of the questions that came up was about the name of a lecture hall in London dedicated to Francis Galton. Some delegates insisted that, since Galton is the father of eugenics, the name of the hall should be changed immediately. Others insisted that Galton should not be judged by today's standards, and that the name should be retained. Others still sought a compromise: the name might stay, but some plaque or display should be added outlining the toxic side of Galton's legacy. The debate was quite heated, and very earnest on all sides.

Afterwards, in private, one delegate told me about a piece of graffiti that she had once seen scrawled beneath a statue of Galton: it read, simply, 'What a nob'. She suggested, somewhat tongue-in-cheek, that the building be renamed the Francis Galton 'What a Nob' Lecture Hall.

This is not the place to debate whether or not Francis Galton deserves to be vilified. My point is that there are all kinds of ways to protest against those we regard as monsters without tearing down their memorials. Ridicule is perhaps our most important weapon.

Before I move on to some of the more apocalyptic visions bequeathed us by the Second World War, I want to describe a place that has become one of my favourite memorial sites in all of Europe. Grūtas Park in Lithuania contains a collection of monuments dedicated to some of the greatest monsters of the twentieth century, including a statue of Joseph Stalin. It is a bizarre place, which breaks almost all the rules followed by conventional museums and monuments. What makes it work – perhaps the *only* thing that makes it work – is the way that it ridicules its subjects. Somehow this memorial park has stumbled upon an innovative way to acknowledge some of the darkest corners of our history.

Lithuania has had a very troubled past. Like several of its Baltic neighbours, it began the twentieth century as part of Russia, and only gained its independence in the chaotic aftermath of the First World War. Twenty years later, at the beginning of the Second World War, it was invaded by Soviet troops all over again. Then came the Nazis, followed once more by the Soviets three years later; and with each new invasion came new brutality.

In 1945 the country was swallowed whole into the Soviet Union. Anyone who refused to accept the nation's new Stalinist rulers was arrested, deported to Siberia, imprisoned or executed. Lithuania suffered terribly over the coming years. According to the Museum of Genocide Victims in Vilnius, around 300,000 Lithuanians were sent to Soviet gulags in the 1940s and 1950s. Between a third and a half of these people never came back.

Given such a history, it is not surprising that the symbols of Soviet power are regarded with universal horror in Lithuania. When the country finally regained its independence in 1990, almost all the monuments to Lenin and other Communist figures were torn down. Countless statues were decapitated, cut into pieces with blow-torches or crushed into rubble. Some were even dynamited. In an attempt to save some of these sculptures for posterity, the new Lithuanian government carted many of them away for storage in state-owned warehouses and salvage yards; but since no one had much love for them they simply sat there, for years, gathering dust.

Storing monuments costs money. In 1998, the government decided to spare itself the expense by loaning out forty or so of the best-known statues. A competition was announced, and proposals started to come in from municipal museums, such as the KGB Museum in Vilnius. But it was not clear that the government would save much money this way: most of the proposals insisted that they would require state funding to put the monuments on display.

There was one bid, however, that did not ask for any state funding at all. An entrepreneur named Viliumas Malinauskas offered to display the monuments in a specially constructed sculpture park, which he promised to build on his own land near Druskininkai, in the south of the country. He would pay all the transport and maintenance costs out of his own pocket. He would even pay the restoration costs. He asked for nothing but the statues. He was duly awarded the contract.

This was where the controversy began. Malinauskas was not a historian, an art critic or a museum professional – or indeed anyone who had any background in this kind of work. In fact he was a former wrestling champion who made his living as a mushroom farmer: he now has a multi-million-dollar business exporting his mushrooms all over the world. Some of his proposals for the sculpture park were quite bizarre. He wanted to build a special railway line, so that tourists from Vilnius could be brought here on cattle trucks, as if they were being deported to a Soviet-era gulag. He wanted to hire actors who would pretend to be soldiers, herding the tourists onto the trains. For the full gulag experience, Grūtas Park itself would be surrounded by barbed wire and guard towers, and the monuments would be displayed as if they were part of a Siberian prison camp. Unsurprisingly, critics began to call Malinauskas's project a 'Stalin theme park'.

It did not take long for the complaints to come rolling in. Local politicians opposed the building of the park. National politicians opposed the building of the rail line. A petition drawn up denouncing the whole idea of his sculpture park was signed by Catholic Church officials, national NGOs, prominent academics, art professors and over a million other people around the world. 'This part of history is full of suffering,' said one member of parliament, Juozas Galdikas, in 2000. 'It should not be used for show business.'

There were other controversies too. One of the statues due

to go on display was that of a schoolteacher called Ona
Sukackienė, a local martyr said to have been killed by Lithuanian
'bandits' (the term that the Soviets always used to describe
partisans and freedom fighters). In 1975 a statue had been
erected in her honour in the nearby town of Lazdijai. After
independence, however, the newly opened archives revealed
that she had actually been killed in a staged attack by the KGB.
Her two sons wanted the monument to be destroyed, and were
appalled that it was going to be displayed in Grūtas Park as a
tourist attraction. In a letter to parliament they wrote, 'Nobody
asked our permission when they created the monument.
Nobody asked us when it was taken down. And now nobody
is asking our permission for it to be re-established.'

Perhaps the strongest voice of opposition came from
former victims of the regime. More than thirty groups
of former partisans and political prisoners banded together
to protest about the sculptures going on display. They accused
Malinauskas of trying to profit from their misery, and
described the statues as 'monsters from a horror film'. Some
of them even went on hunger strike. 'Imagine yourself as a
resident in a small village,' said one former independence
fighter named Leonas Kerosierius, 'and someone came and
attacked your village, killed your brother and raped your
daughter. Would you allow your neighbour to build a park
for these executioners and rapists, or make money off these
crimes?'

MPs pushed for a vote in parliament to take back the statues
and keep them in state hands, and the resolution was accepted
by a majority. But their victory was short-lived, because it
was overturned by the constitutional court: Malinauskas had
won the government contract fair and square, and parliament
had no right to take it away from him simply on a matter of

taste. The most they could do was create a government watchdog to oversee the construction of the sculpture park.

The controversy quickly became international news. It featured not only in newspapers throughout the Baltic countries, but also in other parts of Europe. It even made the newspapers in America, parts of Asia and Australia. 'Miss the Soviet Era? Come to Stalin World' ran the headline in the *Sydney Morning Herald*.

Grūtas Park officially opened to the public in 2001, and immediately proved a hit with visitors from all over Lithuania and beyond. Even before the official opening it had already seen around 100,000 visitors. Since then it has added to its collection and become a well-established tourist destination.

I first came here on a sunny September afternoon in 2018. From the moment I arrived, it was plain to me that this was unlike any of the other memorial sites I've visited. Malinauskas's original vision of a bespoke railway line with cattle trucks for tourists was never given the go-ahead, but he has still placed a train carriage at the entrance of the park, as if it is just arriving at a gulag. Beyond the train carriage is a barbed-wire enclosure overlooked by guard towers. The towers are manned by mannequins in Soviet army uniforms, but there is no attempt to make the soldiers look realistic: they are obviously shop dummies. And what are they guarding? Beneath them, in the enclosure, is a row of plinths, displaying several huge busts of Lenin and other prominent Communists. The message is fairly clear: today it is not Lithuanian dissidents who have been sent to the gulag, but the architects of the gulag themselves. To add to their humiliation, they share this enclosure with half a dozen llamas.

The atmosphere only gets weirder once you enter the park.

One of the first places you come to after paying your entrance fee is a children's play area with brightly painted swings and slides. It is surrounded by engines, armoured cars, pieces of artillery and a huge monument to the Soviet wartime partisans. On the day I was there, the children did not seem to discriminate much between the sculptures, the guns and the slides – they were happy to climb on everything. The jolly atmosphere was enhanced by rousing Soviet-era anthems, blaring from nearby loudspeakers.

This place can't seem to make up its mind whether it is a museum or a toddlers' day out. On one side is a handful of huts, built in the style of gulag barracks, housing a nostalgic array of Soviet posters, flags and copies of *Tiesa*, the old Communist Party newspaper. On another side is a zoo, containing baboons, emus and a rather shabby, depressed-looking brown bear. Dozens of species of birds sing to you from aviaries as you pass by.

However, the real attraction lies beyond, in the forest. A wooden walkway takes you on a journey through pines and birch trees to a procession of socialist realist art. There are allegorical representations of Mother Russia, and stained-glass windows depicting soldiers and workers and farmers. There are statues of Lenin, busts of Felix Dzerzhinsky, and depictions of Lithuanian Communist leaders like Vincas Mickievičius-Kapsukas and Karolis Didžiulis, all displayed among the trees as if they had sprouted here like one of the proprietor's mushrooms.

At the time I visited there were eighty-six monuments in the park, some of them enormous. There was a bronze bust of Marx 4 metres in height (13 feet), and a statue of Lenin 6 metres high (19 feet) that once stood in the main square of Vilnius. There was a representation of a Lithuanian 'Mother'

8 metres high (26 feet) and weighing around 12 metric tonnes: she used to stand beside a highway until someone tried to blow her up shortly after independence. While visitors contemplate the sculptures they are never far away from one of the Disney-style guard towers, an ominous stretch of barbed wire, or a loudspeaker blaring out Soviet propaganda.

People still occasionally call this place 'Stalin World', but in fact there is only one full-size statue of Stalin in the whole park. I found him just beyond the zoo, peeping out between the trees like some fairy-tale troll. (The comparison to a fairy tale is not random: in a nearby glade, closer to the children's playground, is a set of sculptures representing Snow White and the seven dwarves. The difference between folk tale and reality is not always scrupulously delineated here.)

This particular statue used to stand outside a station in Vilnius, until it was taken down in 1960. It is one of hundreds of Stalin statues, some of them truly vast, that used to adorn streets and squares all over eastern and central Europe. After Stalin's death in 1953, however, even the Soviets began to recognise him as a monster. In the following years he was universally denounced and discredited. Statues of him everywhere were taken down and destroyed. This is one of the very few survivors.

It is easy to see why so many people became upset when the park's creation was first announced. Many dissidents had spent their lives struggling against the Soviet system. In 1991 they had torn down these icons of Soviet power with great joy: it must have been deeply painful to see them so lovingly restored and put back on their pedestals, regardless of the setting.

The resurrection of Stalin's statue was perhaps the most

painful of all. This man had been responsible for tens of millions of deaths across eastern Europe, and for the enslavement of hundreds of thousands of Lithuanians. He had not been on public display for decades. And yet here he was, standing in a sunny glade, waiting for tourists to come and take selfies with him. Critics pointed to a worrying trend in contemporary Russia for the rehabilitation of Stalin's memory, with brand new memorials to him being raised in Pskov, Lipetsk, Novosibirsk and several other places. What if the trend were to spread to Lithuania and beyond? What if Grūtas Park, too, were to become a twenty-first-century shrine to this monstrous dictator?

Had this statue, and all the others, been given to another bidder, perhaps there would have been less controversy. Europos Parkas, in Vilnius, wanted to exhibit the statues purely as works of art alongside a range of avant-garde creations by artists from all over the world. Here, perhaps, the aesthetic qualities of a Stalin statue might have been divorced from its political meaning.

The KGB Museum in Vilnius also applied for the contract. It would have displayed the monuments in its main hall and courtyard. Had Stalin's statue been placed here, it would have been seen alongside an extensive exhibition dedicated to his crimes. Many of those who protested against Grūtas Park wanted the KGB Museum to win the bid precisely because it would have put the benign-looking statues of figures like Stalin in a much, much grimmer context.

But there is something about the way that Grūtas Park displays its statues that is enormously refreshing. Seeing Stalin with a squirrel on his head takes away some of the nightmarish power he continues to exercise over us from beyond the grave. When birds are nesting in Lenin's fingers, and children are climbing over the guns that were once aimed at Lithuanian partisans, these symbols of state power no longer seem as frightening as they once did.

This seems to be exactly what Viliumas Malinauskas is trying to achieve. In an interview with the *Guardian* in 2000, the proprietor was unapologetic about his peculiar approach to Lithuania's troubled history. 'People can come here and joke about the sculptures,' he said. 'And that will mean Lithuania is no longer afraid of Communism.'

Grūtas Park is bizarre mix of playground, zoo and atrocity museum. It trivialises the past in the most appalling ways, especially with its Disneyfied guard towers and barbed wire. Some of the displays in its barrack-style huts are more nostalgic than critical of the regime, and its commercial exploitation of Lithuania's painful past is questionable to say the least: I managed to buy myself a Stalin mug and a Stalin key ring in the gift shop on my way out. In fact, so many aspects of Grūtas Park could be considered offensive that I hardly know where to start; and yet somehow, through its sheer banality, it comes closer to freeing us from our history than any of the more serious and thoughtful monuments that have been so carefully produced in other parts of Europe.

The magic ingredient is ridicule. I'm not sure how much this was ever intended by the park's founder and owner, and how much is just a function of a ridiculous set-up. Nevertheless, it is there, and it is a powerful antidote to the atmosphere of fear that plagued this country for so many years.

Josef Stalin, eh? What a nob.

Coda: The Value of Monsters

There is no good way to commemorate the criminals of the Second World War. If we portray them as devils, we give them far more power over us than they deserve. If we ridicule them, we risk making light of a history that is unbearably painful for huge numbers of people. If we try to be nuanced, if we portray the undoubted historical reality that such criminals were mere human beings, and probably not so different from ourselves, then we lose all moral power. Any memorial that acknowledges their humanity opens the door to apologists whose only wish is to rehabilitate our war criminals, deny their crimes, and pretend that they were never monsters but merely misunderstood heroes.

Our solution to the problem is, generally speaking, to avoid commemorating them at all. Commemoration of any sort is an honour, and such men deserve no place in our public spaces. But this too has consequences. The memory of figures like Hitler and Stalin has been dispersed throughout society: they continue to exercise a hold over our imagination even when they are not present. This has profoundly affected our memorial landscape. Our memory of our Second World War criminals is much more widespread than we ever give it credit for.

It is our memory of these people – these monsters – that makes the monuments to our heroes and martyrs possible. When we honour figures like Churchill or Douglas MacArthur, we are also remembering the evils that they faced and fought. When we mourn our dead and our damaged, we are also remembering the monsters who victimised them. Our heroes become more heroic, and our martyrs more tragic, because of the contrast with these monsters. Without the monsters, they would not be nearly so revered.

I began this book with a look at the numerous monuments around the world that have been taken down in recent years. Why, I asked, should our Second World War monuments have been comparatively immune to this wave of iconoclasm?

The answer lies partly not in what these monuments represent, but in what they oppose. The reason why Winston Churchill is still revered as a hero is not because of his grit and determination, but because he was the man who stood up to Hitler. Had his adversary been less monstrous, we might be more inclined to remember Churchill's many, many faults – his pompous grandiosity, for example, his permanent drunkenness, or his Victorian attitudes towards race and empire. It was Hitler who made Churchill.

What is true of our heroes is also true of our martyrs. The victims of any war will always be mourned; but what makes the victims of this war so tragic – what transforms them into symbols of such purity and innocence – is the nature of the people who persecuted them. It is one thing for a Korean woman to be raped in wartime; quite another for her to be consumed by a system of organised sexual slavery. The death of a Polish officer in battle is not the same as the wholesale massacre of Polish officers after they have surrendered. The reason why these victims hold such an important place in our communal memory is not only the fact that they suffered, but because they suffered at the hands of such monsters.

This highlights another important fact about our Second World War monuments: our memories of our heroes, martyrs and monsters do not stand alone, they reinforce one another. The monuments we have created to these people are part of a much bigger memorial framework. This is not just history, but mythology. We have built a story not only of war and suffering, but also of an epic struggle between the forces of good and the forces of evil.

This is precisely what our monuments are for. They transform the ordinary, everyday stories into timeless archetypes that tell us important truths about the human condition.

In the next part I shall explore another category of Second World War monuments that also taps into our need to express our memories in mythological terms. Only this time it is not the people who fought the war that are being transformed into legendary figures – but the war itself.

Part IV

Apocalypse

If the Second World War was a titanic struggle between good and evil, then we can be rightly satisfied that, in the end, good won. But at what cost?

In America, the war is generally remembered as a glorious event – one that transformed the nation into a global superpower and a champion of peace and democracy around the world. In Britain, too, it is often remembered in the words of Winston Churchill as 'our finest hour'. But in other parts of the world very different memories take priority. The wholesale destruction of cities like Manila, Warsaw, Tokyo or Berlin allowed little scope for glorification. Instead the war is remembered as uniquely destructive: a twentieth-century Armageddon.

In the following chapters I will describe some of the world's most moving monuments to the devastation caused by monsters and heroes alike. They each have the same motto, which is in some cases literally inscribed on the monuments themselves: 'Never Again'.

18

France: Oradour-sur-Glane

In west-central France, about 20 kilometres (around 12 miles) north-west of Limoges, there is a village unlike any other in Europe. From a distance it looks like a typical French village, nestling among the trees and fields, but as you come closer you discover that none of the houses have roofs. There are no doors on the buildings, and the windows are empty spaces through which the wind blows freely. Nothing moves in the streets. The only vehicle is a decaying old car which lies abandoned near the empty market place: from its make and model, it looks as if it was parked here three-quarters of a century ago and has not been moved since. At the western end of the village, not far from the abandoned post office and the vacant town hall, is a tram station; but from the rusted state of the tracks that run down the centre of the main street, it is quite clear that no tram has passed through here in decades.

This was obviously once a busy place, thronging with rural life. All the houses and shop fronts along the main street have plaques on them bearing the names and professions of people who once lived and worked here. If you put your head through any of the windows you can still see small indications of their lives: the remains of an old bicycle, pots and pans hanging on the wall, a rusting sewing machine sitting on a window sill.

The whole village has the atmosphere of having been abandoned in a hurry, as if in response to a natural disaster: it is like a modern-day Pompeii. In a way, that is exactly what happened, although there was nothing natural about the disaster that engulfed this place. A clue to what occurred lies in the abandoned church at the south-eastern end of the village. Beside the altar lie the charred remains of a baby carriage. Behind it, the stone wall is pockmarked with bullet holes.

Life in the small market town of Oradour-sur-Glane came to an end quite suddenly on the afternoon of 10 June 1944. It was a Saturday, and the place was busy with people going about their daily business. Some of the local men had taken time out from their tasks in the farms and fields – Saturday was the day when their tobacco rations were distributed. It was also a school day. Parents from the surrounding hamlets had made a particular effort to get their children to school today, because a medical check had been scheduled for that afternoon.

The calm of this perfectly ordinary day was shattered at around 2 p.m., when a regiment from the infamous 'Das Reich' division of the Waffen-SS suddenly drove into town. Unbeknownst to the residents of Oradour, the soldiers were in a vengeful mood. In the wake of the Normandy landings there had been a sudden surge in resistance activity all over France, particularly in this region: the Germans had come to take reprisals.

Soldiers quickly surrounded the town, and then went from house to house, summoning everyone to gather in the market place. Thinking that they were simply going to have their identity papers checked, most of Oradour's residents willingly complied. A few young men hid in basements or attics, afraid that the Germans might be here to round them up as forced labourers. One schoolchild, eight-year-old Roger Godfrin, fled through the back door of his school and ran towards the river. He was the only schoolchild in Oradour that afternoon who would survive.

Once everyone was assembled, the SS troops separated the women and children from the men and herded them off to the church. Then a German officer stepped forward to address the remaining men. Speaking through an interpreter, he told them that he knew there was a cache of arms in the town, and demanded that all those who owned firearms should step forward. When no one responded, he turned to the mayor and instructed him to select hostages from among the town's men. The mayor refused, offering up himself and his sons as hostages instead. After a brief pause and more discussion, the officer appeared to change his mind about taking hostages and announced instead that he was going to search the town. The men were divided into six groups and taken off to various barns and garages around the market place.

What happened next would transform the village of Oradour-sur-Glane for ever. As the men were herded into the barns, the soldiers were already setting up machine guns outside. At a signal from their officer, they opened fire. Within a few moments more than two hundred villagers had been shot. Various German soldiers then stepped forward to finish off what they had started: they walked among the bodies killing anyone they found still alive, before covering them with straw and fuel and setting fire to both the bodies and the buildings that held them.

The only people to survive the massacre were six young men in one of the larger groups, who had fallen to the floor during the initial round of firing and had been buried beneath the bodies of fifty-six others. As smoke and flames filled the barn where they lay, they crawled out from underneath their dead friends and neighbours and scrambled out of a small back door. Five men managed somehow to slip to safety through the back gardens of the town; the sixth was spotted by one of the German soldiers and shot.

After all the men were dead, the SS turned their attention to the town's women and children, who were still huddling, terrified, in the church. At around 5 p.m., two soldiers entered the church. Placing a large chest on the altar, they laid out a long fuse, lit it, and shut the door. After a huge explosion filled the church with smoke and noise, the soldiers threw open the doors and sprayed the surviving women and children with gunfire. They then piled up church pews around the bodies and set fire to them. The only woman to survive was forty-seven-year-old Marguerite Rouffanche, who had hidden behind the sacristy while the soldiers were firing. When the church was alight she found a stool and climbed up to one of the windows blown out by the blast. As she dropped to the ground, a woman and her baby who tried to follow were shot with machine guns.

Over the next few hours, SS troops combed the rest of the town pillaging the houses and shops, shooting anyone they found, and systematically setting everything on fire. Anyone who emerged from the smoke was immediately shot. Several bodies were thrown down a well.

By the time they had finished, the Waffen-SS had burned down 123 houses, 4 schools, 22 stores, 26 workshops, 19 garages, 40 barns, 35 agricultural sheds, 58 hangars and the tram station. These are the ruins that stand in the deserted town of Oradour-sur-Glane today. Piled up among the ruins, both individually and in large groups, were the bodies of 642 people.

Oradour-sur-Glane was just one village of many in France that suffered such atrocities towards the end of the German occupation. Eleven days after Oradour was put to the torch, Mouleydier in the Dordogne suffered a similar fate, albeit without quite so many deaths. A month later the same happened to the town of Dortan near the border with Switzerland; and a month after that SS troops surrounded the village of Maillé in the Touraine and massacred 124 men, women and children with machine guns and hand grenades. One of the most gruesome massacres occurred in the town of Tulle, around 100 kilometres from Oradour, where a German garrison had come under attack from members of the resistance. In reprisal, the Waffen-SS seized ninety-nine men from the town and hanged them from the balconies, trees and bridges all along the main street.

Other nations have similar tales to tell. In Czechoslovakia, the village of Lidice was literally levelled in reprisal for the assassination of Reinhard Heydrich in nearby Prague. Its menfolk were massacred and its women and children imprisoned or taken away to be murdered elsewhere. In Norway the coastal village of Telavåg was razed in reprisal for the killing of two German Gestapo officers. In Italy 770 people were massacred in Marzabotto in reprisal for local resistance activity. In Greece, the infamous massacre of more than 200 civilians in the village of Distomo took place on 10 June 1944, exactly the same day as that at Oradour-sur-Glane. Perhaps the worst destruction took place in Warsaw, the capital of

Poland, which was systematically destroyed by German soldiers at the end of 1944. They went from house to house with explosives and flame throwers, trying to wipe the entire city from the face of the earth.

Some of these places were rebuilt after the war, as local people tried to move on and put the past behind them. Oradour-sur-Glane is unique in that the entire town has been preserved as a ruin, exactly as it was on the day after the massacre.

The decision to turn the ruins of Oradour into a national monument was made very early on. In October 1944, just four months after the town had been burned down, various local notables were already making plans. They were aware that Oradour symbolised something of enormous importance, not only to the local community but to the whole of France. Their view was endorsed by President Charles de Gaulle when he visited the village in March 1945. 'Oradour is the symbol of what happened to the country itself,' he said in a short speech. 'A place like this remains something shared by all. Never again; a similar thing must never happen anywhere in France.'

In the following months the ruins would indeed become an official monument – but a monument to what? In the victorious atmosphere of 1945, it was tempting to portray them as a monument to the Resistance – after all, it had been destroyed in reprisal for Resistance activity in the area. Newspapers like *Ce Soir* often listed the people of Oradour alongside a litany of Resistance heroes, and others spoke proudly of the village's 'halo of glory'. But this begged uncomfortable questions: if the Resistance were indeed so active in this backwater area of France, do they not bear at least some of the responsibility for the reprisals that took place here?

Others wanted to emphasise the purity and innocence of those who had died in the village, especially the children. Many of the survivors have always denied that there was any real Resistance activity in Oradour in 1944 – there was no need to resist, since none of them had ever seen a German soldier anywhere near the village until that tragic day in June. For these people the village was, and will always be, a pure symbol of French martyrdom.

Then there were those who saw Oradour as a monument to the evil inflicted upon France by a nation of monsters. For Pierre Masfrand, the driving force behind the creation of the monument, its purpose was to 'symbolise heinous Nazi barbarism'. According to Pierre Pacquet, the architect charged with conserving the ruins in 1945, Oradour was a 'sacred place', devoted not only to the victims but to 'the savagery of the German race'.

In the following years, however, this comforting story of French martyrdom and German atrocity turned out not to be quite as clear cut as everyone wanted to believe. When a war crimes trial was held in 1953, German citizens were not the only people to appear. Fourteen of the twenty-one men who stood in the dock were from Alsace, a border region of France. Alsace had been annexed to Germany during the war, and its young men had been conscripted into the German army, most of them unwillingly. Nevertheless, these men – these *French* men – had been in Oradour, and had taken part in the massacre. Their trial was a painful reminder of the divisions within France itself, and of the painful legacy of French collaboration with the Nazis during the war.

In the end the ruins of Oradour-sur-Glane did not become a simple memorial to heroes, or to martyrs, or to monsters, because they were reminiscent of all these things at once.

More than anything else, they became a symbol of negation. The apocalypse that took place here in June 1944 was merely the tip of something much bigger: the old France – a nation untainted by collaboration, sure of its strength, its purity and its virtue – had effectively ceased to exist.

We are all prisoners of our history in one way or another, but Oradour-sur-Glane is more of a prisoner than most. Each place I have mentioned so far in this book has been trapped in a vision of its past. Some have been trying to live up to an ideal of past greatness; others have been struggling to come to terms with past suffering or atone for past sins; and in each case, the history of the Second World War threatens to poison both the present and the future. But Oradour has no present and no future: the entire village has been frozen at the exact moment of its destruction. It exists in a state of perpetual apocalypse.

Unlike Oradour, other places in Europe refused to be bowed by the devastation they faced. All the hundreds of European cities that were reduced to rubble by bombardment have since been rebuilt: from Glasgow to Odessa, from Leningrad to Marseille, they are now thriving once again. The centre of Warsaw has been lovingly reconstructed so that it now looks almost identical to the city as it was before the war. The centre of Dresden has likewise been reconstructed. But not Oradour. This devastated French village acknowledges what none of these other places is prepared to face: a whole world was destroyed in the Second World War, and no amount of reconstruction can ever bring it back.

Nobody understands this better than the survivors of the massacre themselves. After the war, many of them settled in a brand new town that was built next door to the old one and given the same name. Living here was inevitably both a comfort and a curse. On the one hand, being within sight of the ruins made it easier to mourn; on the other hand, the old town cast a constant shadow over the new one.

For years, mourning was strictly enforced, especially during the month of June. For example, when a new hotel opened in the town in 1952, its owner wanted to host a ball to celebrate – but a group of families came with rifles to stop the ball going ahead: celebrations like this were not to be permitted in a town so devoted to mourning. In her excellent book about the legacy of Oradour, *Martyred Village*, Sarah Farmer describes how gloomy it was for local teenagers to grow up in a town where they were only ever allowed to wear dark colours. The anniversary was always a particularly sombre time. It was not until 1988 that the association of the families of the martyrs lifted its blanket ban on June weddings.

Even today the memory of what happened in June 1944 makes it hard for residents of Oradour to move on. This is particularly the case for the survivors of the massacre itself. 'It's always difficult for me to come here,' said Robert Hébras, one of the men who survived the mass shooting in the barn by falling beneath the bodies of his neighbours, in an interview in 2013. 'I relive my village in my head,' he said, 'hear its old sounds, put faces to the ruins.'

But the old village of his memories no longer exists. The ruins are all that is left.

19

Germany: Memorial to the Murdered Jews of Europe, Berlin

What if the apocalypse were not something that affected the entire community of a nation, but just one strand of that community? What if it were a very selective kind of apocalypse?

Like the national monument at Oradour-sur-Glane, most memorials devoted to the apocalyptic destruction of the war highlight its random, indiscriminate nature: the violence claimed everyone and everything, without distinction. But the genocide of the Jews was different. There was nothing indiscriminate about it at all: it targeted a specific group of people, plucking them out of their communities and concentrating them in large groups, far from home, so that they could be killed more efficiently. In some places whole villages were wiped out. In other places it might have been just a handful of people – few enough for non-Jews to be able to tell themselves that nothing much out of the ordinary had happened. But make no mistake, the Holocaust was completely extraordinary. Collectively it added up to a wartime catastrophe far greater than any other: a true apocalypse.

Today there are monuments to this archetypal genocide all over the world, but perhaps the most important is in central

Berlin. There is nothing modest or retiring about the Memorial to the Murdered Jews of Europe. It is easily the biggest single, purpose-built monument in this book. Covering an area of 19,000 square metres, it is one hundred times the size of the Marine Corps memorial in Washington, DC, and twenty times as big as the site of the Bomber Command Memorial in London. Even America's National World War II Memorial is less than half its size.

The huge chunk of land that the monument occupies is not some obscure field in rural Germany: it stands right in the centre of Berlin, less than two minutes' walk from the Brandenburg Gate. The monetary value of the land runs into hundreds of millions of euros. The historical value is perhaps greater still. During the Second World War the site was surrounded by the offices and ministries where the war in general, and the Holocaust in particular, was planned. Goebbels' bunker lies directly beneath. During the Cold War it lay in the no-man's-land between Communist East Berlin and democratic West Berlin – indeed, the only reason why it was still vacant at the end of the twentieth century was that the Berlin Wall itself had run right through it. For decades, the area lay not only at the centre of Berlin, but at the centre of world events.

To sacrifice such a large and important piece of land shows how determined Germany is to atone for its past sins. It is supposed to be the mother of all grand gestures – a national act of contrition. But ever since it was first inaugurated in May 2005 I have always thought that there is something not quite right about the memorial. Like many of the other monuments in this book, it is not entirely honest about its intentions.

* * *

The Memorial to the Murdered Jews of Europe was designed at the end of the 1990s by the American architect Peter Eisenman. It consists of 2,711 rectangular concrete blocks, laid out in a grid pattern across the whole of the site. Each block is identical in width and length, but they are all of slightly different heights: those at the edges are less than a metre high, while those in the middle are much taller – some are almost 5 metres (16 feet) high.

The designer himself gave no specific meaning to the blocks except to say that they represented the dehumanisation that occurs when a rigid system is imposed upon the landscape without compromise. There is no significance in the number of blocks, and the blocks themselves do not represent anything. In fact, there is nothing symbolic in the memorial at all.

From the edge of the memorial, the play of light and shadow on the vast field of cuboid blocks is quite beautiful. It looks like some huge, satisfyingly geometrical pattern. Many people have commented that, from the outside at least, the memorial resembles a giant field of rectangular tombstones. Eisenman strenuously denies that this was ever his intention. He deliberately added no names or symbols to any of the blocks, as one would in a graveyard. Nevertheless, this was also my own reaction to the memorial when I first saw it: it looks as if this important location in central Berlin has been turned into a vast, symbolic cemetery for Europe's Jews.

When you walk into the memorial, however, and wander among the blocks, a different perspective emerges. As the ground dips down and the blocks become taller, you become immersed inside a series of claustrophobic concrete canyons, with only distant glimpses of the trees and buildings beyond. It can be quite disorienting. Being surrounded on all sides by identical concrete surfaces gives you the feeling of being inside some kind of maze: you turn down one avenue, then another and another, but they all look the same, and very soon you lose all understanding of where you are. Whenever I come here with anyone I always lose them within moments. Sometimes we don't find one another again until half an hour later on the opposite side of the memorial.

There are disturbing echoes here. The barrenness, the claustrophobia and the shadowy light inside the memorial all hint at some dark experience in our communal memory. But since that memory is never explicitly spelled out, it is worth reminding ourselves for a moment exactly what happened to the Jews during the war in Europe, and how their genocide was finally revealed to the world.

The Holocaust was not dreamed up halfway through the Second World War; it was implicit from the very moment that Germany began to view the existence of the Jews as a problem. Even before the war began, the Nazis had singled out Jews, isolated them and removed them from public life. After the invasion of Poland, when Germany found itself in control of the largest population of Jews anywhere in the world, the 'problem' became much greater. To isolate Jews more effectively, they were forced into ghettos. There was much talk of removing them from Europe altogether, to Siberia perhaps, or to Madagascar. But since this was always impossible, there was only ever one logical, final solution: they should all be killed.

The first large-scale massacres took place soon after the invasion of the Soviet Union in 1941. The massacre at Oradour looks insignificant by comparison. At Babi Yar, a deep ravine in central Ukraine, some 33,000 Jews from nearby Kiev were shot in an orgy of killing that lasted two days. There were so many bodies that their killers had to dynamite the sides of the ravine in order to bury them all.

In the following year, the *Einsatzgruppen* (SS death squads) murdered over a million Jews across eastern Europe, mostly in mass shootings. Canyons and quarries were filled with bodies. Vast fields and entire forests became mass graveyards. Eventually the Nazis set up specialised extermination centres at places like Treblinka, Sobibor, Belzec and Auschwitz, where the slaughter could be industrialised. By the end of the war they had murdered almost six million Jews, and caused hundreds of thousands more to flee their homelands.

Though the Allies had received reports of what was happening across Europe, the extent of the genocide was not revealed until the Allied armies began to take back territory from the Germans. As the Red Army advanced into Ukraine and Poland they discovered village after village whose population had been utterly wiped out. The Soviet journalist Vasily Grossman described his anguish as he passed through these empty communities. 'There are no Jews in the Ukraine,' he wrote in *Einikeit*, the journal of the Soviet Union's Jewish Anti-Fascist Committee:

Nowhere – Poltava, Kharkov, Kremenchug, Borispol, Yagutin – in none of the cities, hundreds of towns, or thousands of villages will you see the black, tear-filled eyes of little girls; you will not hear the pained voice of an old woman; you will not see the dark face of a hungry baby. All is silence. Everything is still. A whole people has been brutally murdered.

When the Red Army overran Majdanek concentration camp in July 1944 they discovered the first of a series of vast warehouses filled with hundreds of thousands of pairs of shoes stolen from the dead. At Treblinka, which they reached shortly afterwards, they captured former camp guards, who described it as a 'hell' where 900,000 Jews had been roasted in furnaces 'reminiscent of gigantic volcanoes'. The largest death camp, at Auschwitz, was discovered six months later.

In western Europe, the British and Americans soon began to uncover similar scenes at other concentration camps. War crimes investigators who entered Buchenwald, Dachau, Mauthausen and Bergen-Belsen found the same scenes of atrocity repeated again and again. When I interviewed one of these investigators, Ben Ferencz, in 2016, he told me that it was the sheer repetition that was hardest to take. 'They were all basically similar,' he said; 'dead bodies strewn across the camp grounds, piles of skin and bones, cadavers piled up like cordwood before the burning crematoria, helpless skeletons with diarrhoea, dysentery, typhus, TB, pneumonia, and other ailments, retching in their louse-ridden bunks or on the ground with only their pathetic eyes pleading for help.'

These scenes were caught on camera and played on news-reels in cinemas all over the world. In western Europe especially, they have formed our collective memories of 1945 as a vision of hell. But for Jewish communities all over the continent, this was more than mere hell – it seemed like the end of the world. Centuries of Jewish tradition, learning and craftsmanship had been snuffed out in an instant. Yiddish, the unique language of the Jews in eastern Europe, was all but dead. An entire culture, it seemed, had been eradicated.

The statistics at the end of the war do not make happy reading. Of 140,000 Dutch Jews, only around 20,000 survived the war: in most areas of the Netherlands, this effectively brought an end to more than eight hundred years of Jewish history. In Greece only 12,000 Jews were left in 1945: a culture that had survived here for over two thousand years was now on the brink of total extinction. And in Poland and Ukraine, once home to the world's largest community of Jews, there was nothing but a wasteland. Three million Polish Jews were killed during the Holocaust. The vast majority of those who survived fled the country in the following years – partly because they no longer felt safe, but partly because there was nothing left to stay for. Everything they had known before the war was gone.

The story told by one Jew speaks volumes. Eleven-year-old Celina Lieberman was the only member of her family to survive. In Ukraine in 1942 she was taken in by a Christian woman who promised to protect her. She quickly grew used to attending church like a good Catholic; but every now and then, in private, she would pray to her Jewish god. Years later, when interviewed by the Holocaust Education Centre in Vancouver, she confessed that this was her way of apologising to all the other Jews who had died. 'I was fourteen at the end of the war,' she said, 'and believed that I was the only surviving Jew left on earth.'

The Memorial to the Murdered Jews of Europe is supposed to commemorate this apocalypse. The rigid sense of order in the field of concrete blocks is intended to call to mind the rigidity of the Nazi system. The feeling of alienation we experience when we enter this field is supposed to remind us of the feeling of isolation that Jews like Celina Lieberman experienced at the end of the war.

I visit the memorial whenever I am in Berlin; however,

while I appreciate this remarkable space I can't help feeling that there is something distinctly odd about it. If it is supposed to be a memorial to Jews, it certainly does a good job of hiding the fact. Nothing here calls to mind the mass shootings at Babi Yar or the gas chambers at Auschwitz. There are no urns containing ash or earth from Holocaust sites. Neither is there any sense of nostalgia or lamentation for the Jewish worlds that were lost. (According to the designer, this is quite deliberate: nostalgia was the one emotion he insisted he was trying to avoid.) There are no symbols of Judaism here, nor of individual Jews, nor of the regime that organised their genocide. In fact, there is not even a sign bearing the title of the memorial. When I first brought my twelve-year-old daughter here she had no idea what the place was. Her first thought was that it must be some kind of gigantic playground: she was about to climb up onto one of the blocks and begin leaping from one to the next, and was mortified when I explained to her why this was inappropriate.

So what's really going on here? Why does this memorial seemingly not invite us to *remember* anything specific at all? And if it is supposed to be a memorial to *Jews*, why does it fail to make any reference to those Jews?

According to Peter Eisenman, there is a certain logic behind his design. Traditional monuments often take a single view of history and try to freeze it forever in stone – and this is precisely what Eisenman was trying to avoid. 'The enormity and horror of the Holocaust are such that any attempt to represent it by traditional means is inevitably inadequate,' he explained in his original proposal. 'In this monument there is no goal, no end, no working one's way in or out.' By making his memorial entirely abstract, and

Is this a cemetery? Or a playground? Without guidance from its designer, visitors to the memorial are free to interpret it as they choose

leaving absolutely everything open to interpretation, he wanted to allow visitors space for their own memories to arise spontaneously. Eisenman doesn't want to tell you what to remember. That is up to you.

It's a noble sentiment, but in the real world it runs into one problem after another. To begin with, is it really possible to create a monument that people can experience without preconceptions? Anyone familiar with the events of the Holocaust will come here with certain images already in mind. And anyone familiar with the language of memorials will immediately see parallels with other similar places they have seen: perhaps this is why so many visitors to Berlin instinctively liken this particular monument to a vast graveyard. I myself could not help noticing similarities between this memorial and one in the nearby Jewish Museum, called the 'Garden of Exile', which also consists of tall concrete blocks on a sloping ground. There is no such thing as a completely abstract monument – knowingly or not, viewers will always impose upon it the language of commemoration that they have picked up from other, less esoteric places.

For those who know little about monuments, and even less about the Holocaust, there is the opposite problem. Since there are no symbols and no signposts, this landscape of boxes could mean virtually anything. Perhaps the concrete blocks are a comment on environmental issues. Perhaps the grid-like pattern is symbolic of our grid-like modern cities, and the alienation we feel when we walk down into it is symbolic of social isolation. Or perhaps it is not alienating at all. Perhaps it is somewhere joyous, like a place to play hide-and-seek or a gigantic children's playground. Without any direction from the designer, any of these things could be true: who is to say that it is a monument about the Holocaust?

The first people to point out these problems were the German government, who were not entirely comfortable with Eisenman's abstractions. They were quite clear about the kind of monument they expected in this prime location in the centre of the capital: it should honour the dead, and keep alive 'the memory of these inconceivable events in German history'. When they voted on whether or not to approve the monument, they specified that their main motive was to 'admonish all future generations never again to violate human rights . . . and to resist all forms of dictatorship and regimes based on violence'.

It was not enough for the monument to imply rigidity and uncompromising order – what the government required was good, hard facts about the evils of Nazism. They therefore insisted that Eisenman's abstract monument should have an information centre next to it, with a permanent exhibition about the events of the Holocaust.

At first Eisenman fought hard against this idea. What was the point of building an abstract monument, designed to set the mind free, if he then attached an information centre which told visitors exactly what to remember and how to feel about it? In the end, however, he was forced to back down. An information centre was indeed built in a kind of underground bunker beneath the memorial. It contains a chronology of the genocide, an exhibition detailing the stories of fifteen individual families, and a 'Room of Names', where the details of all those known to have been murdered are read out, one by one, in a cycle that lasts over six and a half years. The only consolation for the designer was that he was allowed to keep the entrance to the centre inconspicuous. (Indeed, it was so inconspicuous that when a survey was carried out shortly after the memorial's opening in 2005, many respondents claimed that they had failed to notice that there was a museum here at all.)

The next group to criticise the monument was Germany's Jewish population, along with Jews from other countries. As a symbol of the apocalypse, they complained, it was wholly inadequate. There was nothing here to remind them of the world that had been destroyed or the suffering that they had been forced to endure. The monument, they said, had nothing to do with them: it was a monument for Germans, not Jews. Stephan Kramer, Secretary-General of the Central Council of Jews in Germany, was particularly vocal: 'We did not ask for it. We do not need it.' Other critics claimed that the monument was nothing more than an ostentatious display of German virtue, an attempt by Germany to 'wash its hands clean' of the past.

That sounds harsh, but when one considers the other memorials that surround this one – memorials that I have already described in Chapter 16 – it is hard to deny that they have a point. The real intention of most Second World War memorials in Berlin is to remind us not that the Jews are all gone, but that the Nazis are all gone. That is something to be celebrated, for sure. But perhaps not in *this* memorial, which is supposed to commemorate something quite different, and much, much darker.

There are a couple of lessons to be learned from the controversy that surrounded Peter Eisenman's memorial. The first is that, regardless of the benefits of abstract design, some areas of history are simply too sensitive to leave open to interpretation. Societies develop rituals for a reason, and the rituals around death are particularly sacred. What else is a memorial, if not a ritual cast in stone?

A certain language about the Holocaust has developed over the decades. All the major Holocaust museums across the world tend to follow the same basic patterns in the way they narrate their history; and memorials to the Holocaust have likewise developed certain conventions. They often carry the names of villages, towns or national communities that were wiped out. They often include statistics regarding the number of Jews killed. They often contain earth or ashes taken from Auschwitz or other main killing sites; and they are almost always inscribed with Jewish symbols, such as stars or menorahs. There are lots of obelisks and monoliths, lots of off-kilter walls and floors, and lots of images of barbed wire, or cattle trucks, or chimneys. Over the years, Jews have become familiar with such symbols. Sometimes they can seem inescapable and quite stifling – but at least there is a certain comfort in the ritual of them. So when Peter Eisenman dropped them all from his memorial, it is not surprising that so many people hated the idea.

Germans, meanwhile, are also prisoners of this history,

although the emphasis is not on crimes suffered, but on crimes committed. German children go on school trips to former concentration camps to learn about the sins of their grandfathers and great-grandfathers. There are memorials everywhere, from the brass cobbles that mark the pavements outside the houses of Jews who were taken away, to plaques and statues devoted to larger, more communal crimes. Berlin's Memorial to the Murdered Jews of Europe is just one item in a whole landscape of guilt. As I shall show in the next chapter, in Germany, even those Second World War memorials that have nothing to do with the Holocaust are nevertheless tainted by it. Whether they like it or not, Germans and Jews cannot escape this history, and they cannot escape each other. The Holocaust has bound them together in an endless embrace.

It is a link that not even the most abstract of memorials could ever break.

20

Germany: Monument to the Victims of the Firestorm, Hamburg

One of the monuments that has most fascinated me over the years stands in Ohlsdorf Cemetery, in the German city of Hamburg. Unlike most of the monuments in this book, it is not particularly controversial; but it has a strange, other-worldly beauty that I find utterly compelling. Of every memorial I have visited over the past twenty years, this is the one that draws me back again and again; and each time I see it I find new layers of meaning.

I first came across this place in 2005, while I was researching a book about the Allied bombing raids on the city. I had just spent a week interviewing survivors and combing through eyewitness testimonies in various local history archives. The effort of struggling through endless documents in German, which I do not speak at all fluently, had been exhausting, and some of the stories I had uncovered were quite harrowing; so I had come to the cemetery to give myself a break. This was where most of the victims of the bombing were buried, and it seemed an apt place to gather my thoughts.

The monument to the bombing victims stands at the centre of four huge communal graves at the eastern end of the cemetery. One can only approach it by walking past the mass graves, which hold the bodies of 36,918 people. At regular intervals an oak beam stretches across each grave, marked with the name of an entire suburb that was destroyed in the bombing. Rothenburgsort, Veddel, Horn, Hamm, Hammerbook . . . eighteen districts of Hamburg are named here.

From a distance the monument itself looks like a mausoleum – rectangular, austere, made from large blocks of solid sandstone. As you come closer, however, you can see that it has no roof: it is, in fact, just four stone walls enclosing a paved courtyard. A wrought-iron gate in the front wall invites you to step up and peer inside. Through the gateway you can see a sculpture set into one of the internal walls: it is a scene from Greek mythology of the god Charon ferrying the souls of the dead to the underworld.

This sculpture forms the most important element of the monument. It is entitled *Fahrt über den Styx* ('Journey over the Styx'). What first struck me about the sculpture when I finally came face to face with it that April afternoon was how extraordinarily emotionless it seemed. All week long I had been uncovering stories of astonishing violence and terror – but there was nothing of that here. The characters on the boat looked sorrowful, but there was no suggestion of the fear that the victims must have experienced at the moment of their death; nor of the pain and anguish suffered by those left behind in a shattered city. It seemed to me that this was a memorial designed to soothe, not to evoke.

Aside from Charon, the deathly boatman, there are four other sets of characters here. On the prow of the boat is an old man: he is the only one who faces his destination, apparently resigned to his fate. Behind him is a sombre-looking mother, comforting a child who is too frightened to behold the reality of what is happening. Next is a young couple, holding one another for support; and at the stern, next to Charon himself, is a man in his prime.

Each character is very stylised, and it is clear that they represent not real people but archetypes. In other words, there is a figure representing every kind of individual who died in the bombing. Anyone coming to the cemetery to mourn a loved one would be able to find a representation of him or her in the sculpture.

For mourners this might be comforting, but there is also something terribly bleak about the idea. The old man in the sculpture does not represent a single old man but thousands of old men. The mother represents not one but thousands of mothers. An entire community was destroyed in 1943: the young and the old, men and women, the married and the single – all gone.

As I stood at the gates to the memorial, the stories of witnesses to the bombing still ringing in my ears, I suddenly understood the scale of what was being depicted here. It is not a group of individuals that is being ferried to the underworld by Charon, but the whole of Hamburg. This sculpture is not merely a portrayal of death and mourning; it is a portrayal of Armageddon.

What happened in Hamburg at the end of July 1943 was unlike anything the world had ever experienced before. Military theorists had long been speculating about the destruction of major cities through bombing, but this was the first time that it was ever carried out on a large scale. It remains, even today, the most destructive set of bombing raids in European history.

Operation Gomorrah, as it was aptly called, was a combined

attack by the British and American air forces: the Royal Air
Force bombed Hamburg by night, and the US Army Air Force
attacked specific targets in the Hamburg docks by day. During
the course of just a week and a half, they dropped 9,785 metric
tonnes of bombs on the city. That is equivalent to almost a
quarter of the bombs dropped on the *whole* of Britain during
the *whole* of the Blitz.

One of these attacks in particular was to become infamous.
On the night of 27 July, 722 RAF bombers appeared over the
city and dropped their bombs in a concentrated mass over
the working-class suburbs to the east of the city centre. The
majority of these bombs were incendiaries. Within minutes,
tens of thousands of fires had been started. The fires quickly
joined up to create a single conflagration more than four
square miles in area.

What happened next was so horrific that even those who
were used to dealing with large fires struggled to understand
it. It seems that the fire was so intense that it set off a kind
of chain reaction. As superheated air rose rapidly above the
city, more air was sucked in from the surrounding areas to
fill the vacuum. This air brought fresh oxygen, which in turn
made the fires burn even more fiercely. As the fire became
hotter and hotter, the winds became stronger and stronger,
until the whole city was like a furnace with a hurricane-force
wind blowing through it. A new phenomenon had been born:
the 'firestorm'.

According to the chronological record kept by the chief
engineer at the main fire station that night, the Hamburg
firestorm took hold even before the bombing itself had
finished. Within an hour the hurricane was so powerful that
firemen emerging from the station could only crawl on their
hands and knees against the force of the wind. Those who

made it out into the street were helpless against the wind and the blaze, and many were forced to abandon their vehicles to take cover in bomb craters.

One fireman reported seeing 'No smoke on the streets, only flames and flying sparks as thick as a snowstorm'. Other eyewitnesses also claimed that the hurricane was 'a blizzard of sparks', which set fire to people's hair and clothes as they tried to flee. Many survived only by throwing themselves into the canals, or by struggling on towards the open space of the city's parks. There are countless eyewitness accounts of people bursting into flames as they ran, of children being sucked into the fire by the wind, and of people fleeing across roads, becoming stuck in the boiling asphalt which had turned to liquid in the intense heat, and dying 'like flies in the hot wax of a candle'. Those who stayed in their basements and shelters were often no better off. According to a report by the Hamburg chief of police, those who were too afraid to run for it often baked to death, or died from smoke inhalation and carbon monoxide poisoning.

It is impossible to tell precisely how many people died during the catastrophe, but the best estimates from the various police reports, census data and post-war bombing surveys suggest that more than 30,000 people succumbed on this one night alone, and between 37,000 and 45,000 in total during the sequence of raids. In just ten days, the entire eastern quarter of the city had been utterly destroyed, and much of the western quarter too. Roughly 61 per cent of Hamburg's total living accommodation – more than 40,000 residential buildings in total – had been obliterated. In the following days, around a million refugees fled the city. To all intents and purposes, Hamburg had ceased to exist.

Those who ventured back into the city in the following

months described a scene of utter devastation. One eyewitness said she saw nothing but 'Ruins everywhere, as far as the eye could see. Debris on the streets, collapsed house fronts, far-flung stones on kerbs, charred trees and devastated gardens . . . One was without words.' The novelist Hans Erich Nossack was so alienated by the ruins that he found it difficult to believe he was in Hamburg at all. 'What surrounded us did not remind us in any way of what was lost,' he wrote. 'It had nothing to do with it. It was something else, it was strangeness itself, it was the essentially not possible.' He entitled his memoir of the destruction *Der Untergang* – 'The End' – as if what he were witnessing was the apocalypse itself.

Given the sheer scale of what happened in Hamburg, one would expect it to be commemorated in an impressive way, with memorials as large and ambitious as those in Berlin, Hiroshima and Oradour-sur-Glane. But there is no 'Peace Park' here, no gigantic monument taking up several blocks of the city centre. For decades nothing existed but this small, taciturn sculpture in a quiet corner of the cemetery, which hides itself inside an enclosed courtyard, almost as if it is ashamed.

It is worth remembering that no monument at all existed here until nine years after the firestorm devastated the city. The Nazis did not build one in 1943 because they were already hopelessly overstretched; and besides, they had little incentive to draw attention to how badly they were losing the war. When the British took over the city in 1945, they did not build a monument either: again, resources were scarce, and they were not keen to encourage local people to dwell on the traumas of the past (especially since the British themselves bore much of the responsibility for those traumas). The

Ohlsdorf memorial was only planned after 1949, when democratic power was finally handed back to local people. But the Germans, too, were desperate to look forward, not back. Nobody wanted a huge, grandiose memorial. The past was something that almost everyone wanted to forget.

It is difficult for people today to fully appreciate the sense of shame that engulfed Germany in the aftermath of the war. The apocalypse that overcame the country was not only physical but spiritual. Germans were ashamed of losing the war; they were ashamed of having to grovel at the feet of those who had defeated them; but more than anything else they were ashamed of what the Nazis had done in their name. They knew that, as far as other nations were concerned, they were now pariahs.

Worse still, they were pariahs in their own eyes. In the aftermath of the war, the German people were forced to question almost every aspect of their society. All their institutions had been revealed to be corrupt and exploitative – not only the government, which was rotten to the core, but also the army, the judiciary, big business and even the medical profession, which, during the Nuremberg trials, had been implicated in the crimes of the Holocaust. Nazism seemed to have left its taint on everything. Even the mass graves at Ohlsdorf had been dug and filled by forced labourers from the local concentration camps. Nothing seemed sacred any more, not even the burial of the dead.

There are traces of this sense of shame in the memorial itself. I have always been curious as to why this monument expresses nothing of the outrage that I have seen in so many other memorials around the world. There is no sense of martyrdom here, as there is in places like Oradour or Hiroshima. There is no indignation, as expressed by the Katyn

Memorial in New Jersey or the 'comfort woman' statue in Seoul. The characters depicted are not protesting in any way: they seem to be going willingly to their deaths. Is this not quite a chilling thought?

Perhaps there is a silent acknowledgement here that the violence and destruction suffered at the end of the war was simply the price that Germany had to pay for its crimes; perhaps there is even a suggestion that, since the violence ultimately led to the defeat of the Nazis, it was a price *worth* paying. The artist who created the memorial, Gerhard Marcks, was himself fervently anti-Nazi. Before the war he had been blacklisted for opposing the regime, and his sculptures had been declared 'degenerate art'. Perhaps this was his way of showing the people of Hamburg that, according to some kind of divine justice, they had only reaped what they had sown.

This was certainly the main message at the inauguration ceremony for the monument in August 1952. In a speech to the assembled crowd, the first post-war mayor of Hamburg, Max Brauer, asked the mourners to take a good long look at themselves. 'Have the courage to see the real reason for the deaths of your fathers, mothers, brothers and sisters!' he said. 'They did not have to be sacrificed. It was only because they put themselves in the hands of violent criminals that violence overcame our families and our peaceful cities.'

With this in mind, it is worth taking one last look at the monument in Ohlsdorf cemetery. In later years it was criticised for not openly condemning the Nazis and their crimes. Subsequent memorials to the firestorm have certainly been much more explicit. The ruined Nikolaikirche in central Hamburg, which was converted into a memorial space in the 1970s and 1980s, now has a sculpture in its grounds dedicated to the victims of a nearby concentration camp. And the monument to the firestorm victims in Hamburger Strasse, in the north-eastern suburb of Barmbek, has the words 'Never again Fascism' and 'Never again war' carved into its base. But anyone who thinks that these sentiments are not expressed in the Ohlsdorf monument needs to look again.

Gerhard Marcks's sculpture shows a series of archetypal characters on the way to the underworld. Each is emblematic of a particular virtue: the old man represents wisdom, the woman represents motherhood and femininity, the young couple represents love and loyalty. In other times, these virtues might have been considered sacred, but during the war they too had been twisted into the service of the regime. Wisdom had been replaced by propaganda. Mothers had been conscripted to churn out soldiers for the Reich. Even concepts like loyalty had been co-opted and exploited. The disturbing implication is that these virtues, so tainted by the past, have now lost their sacred qualities: the underworld is the best place for them.

Perhaps the most fascinating character in this respect is the one that sits towards the back of Charon's boat: the man in his prime. Of all the virtues worshipped in Nazi Germany during the war, those represented in this figure – strength, virility, power – were the most cherished. And yet he does not stand like the other passengers; instead, he sits with his head in his hands, as if in utter despair. This is what has become of the martial glory of the war years. He, like the Thousand Year Reich that the German people were promised, is on his way to oblivion.

The apocalypse took everything from the people of Hamburg. It killed their families and their friends. It destroyed their homes and businesses, and devastated their city. But worse than this, it took away their pride in who they were.

If the monument that stands in Ohlsdorf cemetery is only a modest one, it is because the people of Hamburg did not want anything bigger. They were tired of the past and its troubles.

In this they were not so different from the people of Dresden and Berlin, of Hiroshima and Nagasaki, or of countless other people in cities all over the world that had been affected by the war. After all the years of destruction and death, they were no longer interested in building monuments to the apocalypse. They were more interested in building something to celebrate the possibilities of the future.

A-Bomb Dome, Hiroshima

21

Japan: A-Bomb Dome, Hiroshima, and Peace Statue, Nagasaki

In the immediate aftermath of the war, the urge to mourn had to compete everywhere with the urge to forget. Some places, like Hamburg, tried to move on from the war as quickly as possible. Others, like Oradour, found the process of coming to terms with the past almost impossibly painful. But there are one or two locations, like Hiroshima and Nagasaki, that seem to have embraced the devastation that they experienced, and tried to use it as an opportunity for change.

Of all the cataclysms described in this book, none was quite so apocalyptic or so total as the one that struck Japan at the beginning of August 1945. The hot blast that ripped through the city of Hiroshima on 6 August was unlike anything the world had ever seen. It was the result of a single explosion, about 600 metres (nearly 2000 feet) above the city centre. Within moments, 90 per cent of the city was obliterated, and tens of thousands of people lay dead. The destruction was so complete, and so sudden, that witnesses had no rational way of explaining it. 'I thought it might have been something which had nothing to do with the war,' wrote novelist Ota Yoko, who survived the bombing, 'the collapse of the earth, which it was said would take place at the end of the world'. Other survivors said that 'it felt like the sun had fallen from the sky', or that they had suddenly been transported to a parallel world, 'the world of the dead'.

Three days later, at 11.02 a.m. on 9 August, a second atomic explosion destroyed Nagasaki. Once again, witnesses had no way of understanding what was happening to them. At the university hospital, doctors cowered in their shattered building, asking one another if the sun had just exploded. One of their colleagues, Nurse Hashimoto, described walking through the streets outside and seeing naked bodies lying everywhere surrounded by large trees torn up by the roots: for a while, she said, she truly believed that she was 'the only person left alive in the whole world'.

Unlike any of the other events I have described so far, these intimations of Armageddon were not confined to those who directly experienced the violence: they rapidly spread all around the world. People everywhere began to speculate about what future wars might look like if such weapons ever became widely available. 'One forgets the effect on Japan . . .' wrote the *New York Herald Tribune* directly after the Hiroshima bombing, 'as one senses the foundations of one's own universe trembling.' According to *Time* magazine, the war itself had suddenly shrunk to 'minor significance'; compared to the revelation of atomic power, the prospect of victory was nothing but 'the shout of a child in the street'. The French philosopher Jean-Paul Sartre called the atom bomb 'the negation of man'; while Albert Einstein considered the new situation 'the most terrible danger in which man has ever found himself'. All of a sudden, annihilation was not merely something that might strike a single village or a single people. Compared to other apocalyptic events, the devastation of

Hiroshima and Nagasaki had implications for the future of mankind as a whole.

How on earth does one commemorate events like this? In the immediate aftermath of the explosions, the Japanese people did not even try. Individual grave stones were erected by some survivors to mark where their relatives had died. In Nagasaki a single monolith was placed in the rubble to mark the hypo-centre – the spot directly beneath where the bomb had exploded. But otherwise very little was done. Both cities, still reeling under the shock, were simply too busy trying to survive.

In the absence of any formal memorial, the ruins themselves began to take on a special meaning. In Hiroshima, where virtually every building had been swept away by the blast, the charred remains of the Hiroshima Prefecture Industrial Promotion Hall became symbolic of the apocalypse that had so suddenly engulfed the city. Its dome, now reduced to a skeleton, was the tallest structure for miles around – everything around it was just ash.

Both cities struggled for years to get back on their feet. It was not until 1949, when the Japanese Diet passed specific laws allowing for their reconstruction, that the people of Hiroshima and Nagasaki were able to think properly about how to commemorate what they had been through.

In Hiroshima, a new plan was drawn up which included a significant memorial space in the former Nakajima district, once the commercial heart of the city. There was to be a museum devoted to the history of the bombing; a 'peace park' for the quiet contemplation of the apocalypse that had taken place; and monuments to the destruction, to the dead, and to hopes of rebirth. A design competition was held, and of the 145 proposals submitted, the city chose one by the modernist architect Kenzo Tange.

From the very beginning, the ruins of the Industrial Promotion Hall – now known as the 'A-Bomb Dome' – were central to Tange's design. His Peace Memorial Park was deliberately constructed with a museum at one end, the A-Bomb Dome at the other, and an arch-shaped Cenotaph in between. Wherever you stand on the central axis that links these three points, the A-Bomb Dome is always ahead of you. Furthermore, if you stand before the Cenotaph to pray for the dead, as the city's representatives do each August in their annual Peace Ceremony, you automatically find yourself gazing directly through its arch towards the A-Bomb Dome, which forms the main focal point of the memorial space.

As Japanese designers and historians often point out, the overall effect is similar to that in a Shinto shrine. The main entrance at the south end of the Peace Memorial Park is through the museum, which is built on pillars or pilotis: you pass beneath it, just as you would pass beneath a shrine's ceremonial gateway. The central path through the park is like a shrine's ceremonial path. It leads up to the Cenotaph, which is like the oratory, or *haiden*, where worshippers come to pray. Beyond this, the A-Bomb Dome stands like a shrine's most sacred building, the *honden*. By building the park in this way, Tange elevated the A-Bomb Dome from a mere ruin to an object of sacred significance: it is as if the souls of all of Hiroshima's 140,000 atomic bomb victims are enshrined here.

Even for those who know nothing of Shinto architecture, there is something darkly compelling about this building. While the rest of central Hiroshima has been redesigned and rebuilt from scratch, the dome alone remains to remind us of the city that used to exist before the apocalypse. That it survived at all seems something of a miracle. It is just 160 metres (525 feet) from the hypocentre, and therefore received the full force of the blast. Like the relics preserved in the museum – the melted watches and the charred children's tricycles – the building is forever marked by the divine force that obliterated so much else.

For twenty years after the war, many of the city's residents wanted the A-Bomb Dome torn down. Its presence was a constant reminder of the horror they had suffered and now wished to put behind them. But school children in the city's Paper Crane Club repeatedly petitioned the city council to make the ruins into an official memorial, and in 1966 they got their way: the council voted unanimously to preserve the ruins 'forever'. Contributions began to pour in to pay for the reinforcement work, which was completed the following year.

Thirty years later, in 1996, the dome was declared a UNESCO World Heritage Site. It has become a place of pilgrimage for people from all over the world: over a million tourists come here each year. While the vast majority only pause beside the ruins for a few moments in order to take photos and selfies, there is still an air of almost religious solemnity here. Most people seem to have taken on board the primary message of the monument, written on a plaque at the front of the ruin, that it stands as a 'lesson for mankind'.

In Nagasaki, commemoration of the bomb that destroyed the city has taken a different form. In the months directly after the war, the ruins were just as symbolic as those in Hiroshima, and perhaps even more so. Urakami Cathedral, like Hiroshima's A-Bomb Dome, was very close to the hypocentre, and was extremely badly damaged. To Nagasaki's Christian population the ruins began to seem symbolic of the huge sacrifice that the city had been made to suffer. However, unlike the A-Bomb Dome, the cathedral was rebuilt after the war, and only a few small fragments of the ruined original were preserved. Instead, the city invested its emotional energy in a new, purpose-built monument – the Peace Statue.

The statue stands in its own space, separate from most of the city. Unlike in Hiroshima, the memorial landscape in Nagasaki is not in the central, downtown area, but in the suburb of Urakami, a few kilometres north of the main harbour. It is spread out across three different sites. First are the A-Bomb Museum and the Peace Memorial Hall, which stand next to one another, connected by a subterranean corridor. Second, a short walk away, is the A-bomb hypo-centre, now a small park scattered with various monuments and relics. Further away still, and out of sight of the other two places, is the Peace Park. It is here, at the northern end of the park, that the Peace Statue stands.

This is easily Nagasaki's most important monument to the bombing. At the base of the statue is a black marble vault containing the names of the atomic bomb victims. Just as Hiroshima's city representatives hold their Peace Ceremony in front of the Cenotaph facing the A-Bomb Dome, Nagasaki's representatives stand each year before this statue. Like the dome, it is, symbolically, a shrine to the dead.

The Peace Statue was designed by the sculptor Seibo Kitamura, and was inaugurated by the city of Nagasaki on the tenth anniversary of the bombing in August 1955. It shows a virile, god-like figure, 10 metres (32 feet) high, seated on a rock. One huge, muscular leg is folded beneath him in a symbol of quiet meditation, but the other leg is poised for action in case he is called to spring forward to assist humanity. With his right hand he points towards heaven, to the threat

Peace Statue, Nagasaki

of nuclear weapons. His outstretched left hand, however, symbolises tranquillity and world peace. His eyes are closed 'in a solemn prayer for the victims of the war'. According to the artist, the statue is supposed to symbolise the desire for global harmony, and the turning away from war.

Far fewer tourists come here than visit the much larger and more central Peace Park in Hiroshima; but the same atmosphere of pious pilgrimage is evident. I first visited this place on a rainy Monday afternoon in March, and yet there were still dozens of visitors standing solemnly before the statue, umbrellas in hand. Some were speaking Chinese, others Korean, and still others English – this may not be a UNESCO World Heritage Site, but it nevertheless attracts visitors from all over the world.

It has to be said that among local residents the statue is not universally loved. One local language scholar has called it 'a clumsy approximation of a Greco-Roman deity', which thus pays tribute 'to the civilisation that deliberately dropped atomic bombs on two cities populated mostly by non-combatants'. Others have drawn attention to its Buddhist symbolism – hardly appropriate, they say, considering that the community most devastated by the bomb was Nagasaki's long-persecuted Christian minority. In an interview with the *Japan Times*, local historian Shigeyuki Anan pointed out that the statue was built at a time when the Japanese government should have had other priorities. 'It cost ¥40 million to build, at a time when there was no legal protection at all yet for *hibakusha* [atomic bomb survivors]'. All these people bemoan the fact that Nagasaki did not preserve the ruins of the Urakami Cathedral as the city's main memorial to the destruction.

According to the sculptor himself, however, such critics are missing the point. Seibo Kitamura deliberately fused eastern and western styles in order to evoke 'the qualities of both Buddha and God'. His intention was always to transcend the barriers of race and religion, and try to build a sense of harmony between the two cultures that had spent so many years fighting one another. He wanted to create a monument that would be more than simply a lament to what had been lost. 'After experiencing that nightmarish war, that blood-curdling carnage, that unendurable horror,' he wrote, 'who could walk away without praying for peace?'

Today, when visiting the various monuments in Hiroshima and Nagasaki, it is possible to pick out certain themes in the commemoration. The first and most important is exactly the theme that Kitamura highlighted: 'praying for peace' is the leitmotif that dominates the memorial landscape in both cities.

In Hiroshima, the A-Bomb Dome stands among dozens of other monuments, almost all of them dedicated to the idea of peace. For example, there is a Children's Peace Monument, a Peace Cairn, a Flame of Peace, a Peace Bell, a Peace Clock Tower and a Pond of Peace. There is even a statue directly representing a Prayer for Peace. Near the middle of the park is a Peace Memorial Hall containing the names, photographs and stories of atomic bomb victims. Beyond the Peace Memorial Museum is an installation called the Gates of Peace. In case the point has not been driven home strongly enough, the main road that connects the park to the rest of the city is called Peace Boulevard. The A-Bomb Dome presides over this landscape as a chilling example of what lies in store for any nation that abandons the path of peace.

In Nagasaki, meanwhile, the Peace Statue represents something similar. It too stands inside a Peace Park, near a Peace Fountain, a Monument of Peace, a Maiden of Peace, several Cranes of Peace, and many other sculptures devoted to the concepts of peace, love, friendship and life.

All this is significant. Japan today still has one of the

strongest peace movements anywhere in the world – indeed, a commitment to peace is enshrined in the Japanese constitution. The experience of the war, and the phenomenal destruction it brought upon Japan, and especially upon Hiroshima and Nagasaki, taught it a lesson that it has never forgotten.

The second major theme that arises from the fate of the two cities is a message of victimhood. Hiroshima and Nagasaki unquestioningly mark out Japan as a victim rather than a perpetrator of the war. Nowadays the Japanese government and the Japanese newspapers routinely portray Japan as 'the only A-bombed nation', and they have been doing so since at least the 1970s. The A-Bomb Dome, especially, plays an important role in this sense of victimhood: it is the greatest symbol of Japan's atomic martyrdom.

The idea has angered many of Japan's former enemies because it automatically implies a kind of absolution for the whole country. Today Japanese people do not always take responsibility for their past, partly because they do not feel they need to: they regard Hiroshima and Nagasaki as proof that they have already paid the price.

It is easy to be indignant about this, but there is a rather more praiseworthy flip side to such an idea of victimhood: at least the memorials in Hiroshima and Nagasaki say nothing about blame.

The ruins of the A-Bomb Dome have not been preserved, as the ruins of Oradour have, to show the barbarism of the enemy. In fact, there is almost no mention of any enemy at all. The plaque in front of the A-Bomb Dome makes mention of the 'single bomb' that turned the city 'into ashes' – it says nothing of the American airmen who dropped that bomb. The nearby museum does exactly the same: it is dedicated to 'the horrors and the inhuman nature of nuclear weapons', not to any vilification of the American leaders who dared to use them.

Similarly, at Nagasaki's Peace Statue, the only enemies mentioned are 'the atomic bomb' and the abstract concept of 'war'. As you walk around the park, you will find no references to America, or President Truman, or the US Army Air Force. Furthermore, as Hiroko Okuda of Nanzan University has pointed out, the Japanese word for 'victim' used in Nagasaki commemorations is not *higaisha*, implying a victim who has suffered at the hands of another person, but *giseisha*, implying merely someone who suffers. It is almost as if the A-bomb was not perpetrated by an enemy at all, but was rather the result of some natural disaster, like an earthquake or a tsunami.

Thus Japan not only evades its own responsibility for the war, but allows its former enemies to evade their responsibilities too. This is not quite the same as forgiveness and reconciliation – nevertheless, it forms the basis of a new friendship that has served Japan and the USA well ever since 1945.

The final major theme on display at Hiroshima and Nagasaki is slightly more subtle. It involves the idea of national rebirth.

In Nagasaki's Peace Park, a short distance from the colossal Peace Statue, is a 'World Peace Symbols Zone'. This was established in 1978 by the city authorities, who invited donations of monuments from other nations around the world. There are sculptures here from several European countries, as well as from China, the Soviet Union, Argentina, Brazil, the USA, Australia, New Zealand and many others. If each sculpture represents a different nation, then that begs the question: what nation does the *main* Peace Statue represent? Is it possible that it doesn't symbolise international harmony after all, as its sculptor claimed? Does it perhaps represent Japan itself?

In the aftermath of the war, Japan knew that it had to change its ways, and do so rapidly. Less than two weeks after its historic surrender, before the Americans had even had the chance to occupy the country, the head of the Japanese government's Information Bureau was touting the experience of the atom bomb as the key to changing Japan's image in the world. In an article in one of Japan's national newspapers, *Asahi Shimbun*, he announced that the best way of showing 'repentance' was to wholeheartedly embrace the concept of peace. He suggested that by taking a lead role in a movement to prohibit the future use of nuclear weapons, the Japanese might be able to turn themselves from the 'losers of the war' into the 'winners of the peace'.

When I look at Nagasaki's colossal Peace Statue, I can't help remembering these words. It seems to me that this giant muscular figure does not in some ways represent 'peace' at all, but rather the might of the nation. Its obvious physical power seems to reflect the martial virtues that Japan had always strived for before and during the war. When the statue was inaugurated, the country was already on the path back to its former economic and national health. As the nation grew in strength during the 1950s and 1960s, statues like this were surely an effective way of reassuring Japan's neighbours that this new-found power was nothing to worry about. And perhaps not only Japan's neighbours, but also the people of Japan itself. As long as the nation's most iconic war monuments were devoted to the concept of peace, and not martial glory, there was no reason for Japan to be afraid of its own strength.

Even the A-Bomb Dome in Hiroshima flirts with this idea. The contrast between the ruins and the shiny new buildings that have risen out of the ashes has always been a part of the dome's emotional power. It is only by remembering how completely the city was destroyed that we can fully appreciate the miracle of Hiroshima's rebirth. The A-Bomb Dome is a measuring stick, which allows the people of Japan – and indeed the world – to see how far the nation has come in the years since 1945.

Hiroshima and Nagasaki will forever be tied to the events of August 1945. Rightly or wrongly, many people have come to regard them as the sacrifice that Japan had to make in order to bring an end to the war. Even some Japanese people occasionally refer to them this way. One of Nagasaki's most famous *hibakushas*, Takashi Nagai, called his city 'a whole-burnt offering on an altar of sacrifice, atoning for the sins of all the nations during World War II'.

The example of Hiroshima and Nagasaki has since served as a lesson to the rest of Japan – to modernise, to reinvent itself, and to embrace its former enemies. Like so many other places I have described so far, they have become prisoners of their history. But in the process, to a certain degree, they have also set their nation free.

Today, Hiroshima's A-Bomb Dome and Nagasaki's Peace Statue are symbols that resonate not only in Japan, but on the world stage. They represent a new danger that threatened the world for the first time after 1945 – the threat of nuclear war. But they also represent something more hopeful: a new age, and a new world order that was born out of the ashes of war. As such, perhaps they are not symbols of the apocalypse at all, but rather symbols of rebirth – not just on a national scale, but on an international one too.

This is the concept I will explore in the final part of this book.

Part V

Rebirth

The end of the Second World War in 1945 unleashed a wave of hope around the world. After years of conflict and destruction, the possibility of a lasting peace finally seemed within reach. The bombs would stop falling. The killing would stop. And the men and women who had devoted their lives to fighting would now be allowed to go home.

The atmosphere of hope inspired by the end of the hostilities was universal, and spread even to those parts that had suffered little or no violence during the war. The rhetoric of freedom, which had inspired the world to fight the forces of fascism, now inspired it to throw off other forms of oppression. In South America, for example, the years between 1945 and 1948 saw nations across the continent toppling their dictators at an unprecedented pace: a new age of democracy seemed to be dawning. Likewise, national leaders in Africa and Asia began to talk of a new era of self-determination: it was time for colonial peoples to throw off the yoke of imperialism and start governing their own affairs. In Europe, where the war had destroyed so much of the physical and institutional infrastructure, people everywhere saw the opportunity to build a kinder, fairer society, untainted by the old traditions that had led them to war in the first place: 1945 saw the birth of social security, social housing projects and health-care systems across the continent.

Some of our most moving Second World War monuments celebrate not the war itself, but the dawn of this new era of hope and peace. Many traditional monuments are worth mentioning. The Joy of Life Fountain in Rostock, Germany, and the Tree of Life Memorial in Birmingham in the UK both depict new life rising from the rubble of cities destroyed by bombing during the war. Numerous statues around the world depict wartime parents holding up babies – a symbol duplicated in real life by the baby boom that happened after the war ended. In the Hiroshima Peace Memorial Park, for example, there is a statue of a mother and her baby standing upon a crescent moon: the baby blows a trumpet to signify the beginning of a new, more peaceful era. Even some of the memorials dedicated to tragedy and destruction have room for a similar idea of rebirth. In the garden of the Nanjing Memorial Hall, for example, a goddess of peace stands upon a tall column. She too holds up a smiling child.

Such statues can be quite moving, but for the sake of variety I would like once again to widen our understanding of what constitutes a monument. In the last few chapters I will explore some of our less traditional memorial spaces. They include a painting, a balcony, a church and a hiking trail. Sometimes monuments can be all the more powerful for the fact that they appear to us in unexpected guises.

UN Security Council chamber, New York

22

United Nations: UN Security Council Chamber Mural, New York

In New York City stands one of the great icons of the post-war world – the United Nations headquarters. This complex of buildings was created by architects from every part of the globe, working in collaboration. It was built out of concrete, steel and glass – the materials of the new age. Like so many other buildings raised in the years after 1945, it was designed to be symbolic of everything that had been won during the war: freedom, hope, modernity, international cooperation and, most of all, rebirth.

If you walk around the UN headquarters today, you will find plenty of monumental works of art that represent the end of war and the birth of a new age of peace. There is a giant sculpture of a sword being beaten into a ploughshare, and another of a gun whose barrel has been tied in a knot. In front of the Secretariat building is a sculpture of St George slaying a dragon, entitled 'Good Defeats Evil': the dragon is made from pieces of scrapped nuclear missiles.

However, perhaps the most eloquent expression of what the UN is supposed to stand for is not in the architecture, or in the sculptures that litter the grounds, but in the decoration

of the most important room in the organisation. At the back of
the UN complex, in the Conference Building, is a large
chamber reserved for meetings of the UN's most powerful
organ, the Security Council. It is here that the world's leading
powers gather to discuss global peace and security. On the
wall above the circular debating table is a huge mural, some
9 metres (29 feet) wide and 5 metres (16 feet) high: it
completely dominates the room. It was painted by the
Norwegian artist Per Krohg in the aftermath of the Second
World War, and depicts a world coming back to life after years
of conflict. If you are looking for a single work of art that
sums up the United Nations and all it represents, then this
surely is it.

There are two parts to the mural. The lower part is painted
in dark, sombre colours, and shows a devastated landscape
full of shell holes and abandoned weapons. This world is very
much in the foreground. In the centre, curled around the
pillars of a subterranean bunker, a dragon plunges a sword
through its own body. On either side of this dying beast are
human figures in dire circumstances: some of them cower in
caves, others struggle to climb out of a dark abyss, others still
stagger, zombie-like, in chains.

The upper part of the painting depicts the world to which
all these figures are heading. This world is painted in bright
colours, and is full of happy, healthy-looking people in a
prosperous environment of order and plenty. Some of the
characters reach down to help those who are struggling up
from the lower region of the painting. On the left-hand side,
for example, a man has lowered a rope to a woman climbing
out of the abyss. On the right, an Asian man and a western
woman reach down to embrace some of the slaves in chains.

Everything about this brighter world speaks of freedom,

A close-up view of Per Krohg's mural

happiness and peace. On the left-hand side a woman throws open a pair of windows to let the light come flooding in. Closer to the centre, in a pair of rectangular panels, a community festival is going on: children of different races frolic, play drums and strew flowers, while their parents dance behind them in a line. One of the revellers holds up a UN flag. Along the top of the mural are scenes of peaceful activity: people on the left-hand side measure out grain, scientists on the right gaze through telescopes and microscopes, and between them are various artists, architects and musicians.

In the centre of the painting can be seen the figure of a phoenix rising from the chaos of the old, dying world beneath it. Behind this classical symbol of rebirth is an almond-shaped panel depicting the ideals that all nations are striving towards: a peaceful life of love and kindness. In Christian religious painting, particularly in church frescoes, the holiest images are always placed in a panel shaped exactly like this – it is called the 'mandorla'. For Per Krohg, who was very much influenced by Christian religious art, this is the most important part of his painting. It shows an idealised image of a loving family. A man and woman kneel together, surrounded by their children, clasping each other's arms in companionship. One child reaches down from a tree to hand a piece of fruit to his sister in a symbol of charity; while the youngest child reclines at his parents' feet, cradling a dove of peace.

These important, central images stand directly above the chair occupied by the president of the Security Council. They depict everything that the Council is supposed to be striving for: rebirth, charity, prosperity, brotherhood between peoples and, above all, peace.

As the Second World War entered its final stages in 1944 and 1945, these were the images that the whole world was crying out for. The creation of an organisation devoted to promoting world peace seemed to be an appropriate answer to all the years of hardship and violence. At a conference in Dumbarton Oaks in Washington, DC, representatives from Britain, China, the USA and the USSR hammered out a blueprint for exactly such an organisation. The spirit of their mission was probably best summed up by the head of the Chinese delegation, Dr Wellington Koo. 'The establishment of an effective international peace organisation,' he said, 'is the united hope and aspiration of all the freedom-loving peoples who have been making such heroic sacrifices in life, blood and toil. We owe it to them, as well as to humanity at large, to subordinate all other considerations to the achievement of our common object.'

Six months later, in April 1945, delegates from fifty nations gathered together in San Francisco in an attempt to bring this mission to fruition. Over the course of the next nine weeks they worked together to draft the United Nations' founding document, the UN Charter. Their success was greeted with universal enthusiasm. Newspapers across the world hailed it as 'a great historical act' (the *Gazette de Lausanne*), a 'great coalition for peace' (the *Times of India*), even a 'utopian garden' (*Straits Times*). 'Never before,' said the Nigerian campaigner Eyo Ita in the *West African Pilot*, 'has the human race seen a greater and better opportunity for a world community of free and equal peoples.'

Some of the most enthusiastic champions of the UN were from the one nation that had always previously tried to keep itself out of global affairs: the USA. American politicians from both parties seemed determined to outdo each other with their praise. Senator Tom Connally, a Democrat from Texas, called the UN Charter 'the most important document in the history of world statesmanship'. Republican Congressman Charles Eaton claimed it would lead to 'a golden age of freedom, justice, peace and social well-being'. The general public seemed to agree: in a Gallup poll taken in July 1945, those in favour of the United Nations Charter outnumbered those against by twenty to one. The whole world seemed to be imagining the same images that Per Krohg would soon be painting on the wall of the UN Security Council chamber.

It would be easy to dismiss all this as mere rhetoric, but in a world that was still being torn apart by war the prospect of future peace and harmony awoke deep longings to which it is difficult to do justice today. Some were almost religious in their intensity. One story, told by a French soldier, demonstrates exactly how desperate people were for an organisation like the United Nations. Jean Richardot was on the battlefield in northern France when he first heard about the UN. He was sheltering in a foxhole when a torn and muddy fragment of newspaper blew past. He grabbed it to distract himself from his predicament. It carried a story about how the Allies were attempting to set up a new world organisation whose aim was 'to banish war forever from the face of the globe'. The news, he later confessed in his memoirs, 'had a tremendous impact on me – like a message sent by God. Right then and there I prayed for peace and the success of this great enterprise and, solemnly, in my foxhole, promised myself that I would do everything in my power to join this new organization if I came through the war alive.' After the war, true to his word, Richardot applied for a job at the UN. He was one of 20,000 applicants.

* * *

Unfortunately the UN was never quite able to live up to such ideals. Regardless of its aspirations, it simply is not set up in a way that promotes peace and harmony.

To begin with, the organisation was closely modelled on its predecessor, the pre-war League of Nations. Given that the League had been such an utter failure at preventing war in the 1930s, it was unclear why anyone believed that the UN would fare any better.

The most powerful organ of the UN was to be the one that would soon be meeting beneath Per Krohg's mural: the Security Council. This was effectively the heart and brains of the organisation. It was the only body with the power to make binding decisions that all member states were obliged to carry out. But it was not a council of equals. Five members were to have special privileges and responsibilities: Britain, China, France, the USA and the USSR. Unlike the other council members, the Big Five would not be elected to their seats every two years – they would have a permanent place at the table whether the rest of the world liked it or not. Furthermore, since the UN Charter states that all decisions of the Security Council must be unanimous, each of these five nations effectively had a permanent veto on any proposal they disagreed with.

In 1945, with the Second World War still raging, this made a certain amount of sense. These were the five nations that were doing most of the fighting in the war; and they were also the nations most likely to end up acting as the world's policemen once the war was over. It therefore seemed only fair that they should have a greater say than other nations in how their manpower and resources were to be deployed. However, structuring the Security Council like this also meant that power was entrenched in the hands of the very nations who were most capable of threatening world peace. As several smaller nations pointed out at the time, it was all very well to appoint the Big Five as policemen, but who was going to police the Big Five?

By the time Per Krohg's painting was unveiled in August 1952, the UN Security Council was already failing at its job. In the previous seven years it had presided over a catalogue of disappointments, largely because the veto powers of the Big Five had left it powerless to act. In the 1940s it had stood by as the Soviet Union enslaved much of eastern and central Europe. It had allowed France to reimpose colonial rule upon Algeria and Indochina, with disastrous consequences for both countries in the years to come. It had remained mute while Britain pursued its catastrophic policy of partition in India in 1947, and had likewise allowed the ethnic cleansing of Germans and other minorities from eastern Europe. The only time it had acted decisively was when it had intervened in the Korean War in 1950. But even this had not brought much cause for celebration: the war had been a bloodbath, and by the summer of 1952 it already looked as if it were going to end in stalemate.

Worst of all, the Security Council had proven powerless to end the increasingly bitter divide between the USA and the USSR.

The two superpowers disagreed on almost everything. By the time Per Krohg's painting was inaugurated, the Soviet Union had used its veto no fewer than forty-seven times, and the Security Council was virtually paralysed. A new Cold War had begun, fuelled by increasing paranoia on both sides, and backed up by nuclear weapons. (Nuclear proliferation was yet another dangerous development that the UN had failed to prevent.)

All this had taken place *before* Per Krohg painted his mural. If you look at the painting with this in mind, it begins to take on an entirely different meaning. It no longer seems like a depiction of the bright new world that was born out of the Second World War, because such a world demonstrably did not exist. Krohg himself never claimed it was a portrayal of the post-war world, saying only that he wanted to paint an ideal that lay somewhere in the future. '[T]he work of the UN and the Security Council [must] provide the seeds for a new and more valuable life,' he wrote; and, hopefully, his great mural would inspire them to strive towards this aim.

With this in mind, it seems painfully significant that the president of the Security Council always sits with his back to Krohg's painting. It is perhaps just as well, because the bright, harmonious world depicted in the top half of the picture is quite literally beyond the reach of anyone standing on the floor of the chamber. If the delegates were to look behind them, they would find themselves sitting among the forlorn figures at the bottom of the picture. In the summer of 1952, the foreground remained a place of darkness and struggle.

It is easy to be cynical about the United Nations from a distance; but cynicism is not something that the United Nations itself can afford. For the delegates who entered the gates of the organisation's headquarters in New York in the early 1950s, the expectations were huge, and the ensuing disappointments greater still. Such people needed ideals to strive for, otherwise where would they find the energy to keep up their endless struggle for compromise and consensus?

With this in mind, it is hardly surprising that idealism seems to be everywhere you look. Even for tourists coming here in the twenty-first century, the atmosphere of idealism is palpable. It is present in the art and the architecture. It is certainly present in Per Krohg's painting. It is hard to explain to someone who has never experienced the place for themselves, but there is an ambience of hope here every bit as tangible as that in the new Coventry Cathedral (see Chapter 24); and a feeling of earnestness at least as strong as that in Hiroshima Peace Memorial Park. But there is also a sense that, unlike those other places, here is a genuine chance for real change, if only the various delegates can muster the political will.

But if the United Nations is to make strides towards achieving world peace, then it must first make strides towards reforming itself. The first time I visited the UN Security Council chamber, what most struck me about it was how old-fashioned it looked. With its red leather chairs and dramatic lighting, the chamber itself looks like a time capsule left over from the 1950s. Krohg's painting, which dominates the eastern end of the room, looks hopelessly dated. It is not only a matter of the clothes, hats and hair-styles, which all belong to the 1940s and 1950s, but the bright colours themselves, which now look cartoonish. Some of the imagery also seems to belong to times gone by. For example, the clunky-looking telescope and microscope in the top right-hand corner no longer seem futuristic; and in an age dominated by social media, the old-fashioned idea of community portrayed here no longer feels quite real. If a complete overhaul of the chamber is out of the question, then surely at least some contemporary touches could be added to what is already there? A place of such symbolic importance needs to look relevant to our lives today.

The United Nations itself has also dated – and no organ more so than the one that sits in this particular chamber. The five great powers that still make up the core of the Security Council are no longer so powerful as they once were. Britain and France no longer command empires – they are today no greater than a dozen nations of similar size around the world. The Soviet Union is no more; and while Russia now holds the position that the USSR once held on the Security Council, it is a mere shadow of its predecessor. The only two nations that continue to dominate world affairs are the USA and China. In the meantime, nations that have grown in stature since 1945, such as Germany, Japan and India, have no greater say in UN affairs than do relative minnows like Liechtenstein or Micronesia.

Despite numerous attempts at reform, the Security Council has remained largely unchanged since its formation in 1945. Those who currently hold power are unwilling to relinquish it, regardless of their true position in global affairs; and no one can agree on whether, or how, to share power with the emerging world nations. Like Per Krohg's painting, it seems to be frozen in time.

In a curious way, therefore, the mural remains highly symbolic – although not, perhaps, in the way that Per Krohg intended it to be. The darkness of the foreground still feels unpleasantly close. The vision of Utopia in the background seems more out of reach than ever. And over it all hangs an atmosphere of paralysis that maintains us, like the characters inside the picture, as prisoners of history.

23

Israel: Balcony at Yad Vashem, Jerusalem

Not all monuments are statues or works of art. Not all monuments have plaques explaining what they represent. Sometimes our places of memory can come in surprising forms. A bridge, a gateway, a bunker, a ruin or a wall – even the simplest architectural feature can convey meaning, if viewed in the correct context.

This chapter is about exactly one such feature, the balcony at the end of the Holocaust museum at Yad Vashem in Jerusalem. Unlike every other architectural feature I have described so far, this one has never been the site of any particular historical event; indeed, it was only built in 2005. Despite this, it still carries a huge weight of historical meaning. It is a powerful symbol of rebirth – not only of a people, but of a political state – and as such it is as controversial as any of the other monuments in this book.

Yad Vashem is an unusual organisation. It was set up in 1953 after the Israeli Knesset voted unanimously to create a memorial site for the victims of the Holocaust. Over the following decades it developed in several different ways. It opened a research institute, a library, a publishing house and an International School for Holocaust Studies. It oversaw the creation of a complex of memorials, which are dotted around its grounds. And it opened a museum for the general public. Today Yad Vashem is one of the world's foremost remembrance sites: in the words of Nobel Peace Prize laureate Elie Wiesel, it is 'the heart and soul of Jewish memory'.

For the million or so people who visit each year, the Holocaust History Museum is by far the most important attraction. It was opened in 2005 to replace an older museum dating back to the 1960s, and its architecture is one of its most important elements. The museum building is a long, narrow structure, shaped like a triangular prism, which slices through Mount Herzl from one side to the other. Most of the building is buried in the mountainside, but the two ends stick out into the open air. One end is closed, like the box of a Toblerone chocolate bar. But the other end holds a large, open balcony which juts out over a forested valley below.

When you enter the museum, the balcony is one of the first things you see. It stands at the very end of the dark, austere walkway that forms the central axis of the museum: it is literally the light at the end of a long tunnel. Your automatic instinct is to head for this light, but you can't. The walkway is blocked, repeatedly, by wires and trenches cut into the concrete floor. There is no short cut to the balcony: it can only be reached by zigzagging your way back and forth through a series of dark rooms on either side of the central walkway.

These rooms contain an increasingly harrowing history of the attempted extermination of the Jews in Europe. The exhibition starts with a poignant depiction of Jewish life before the Holocaust, and proceeds through persecution, imprisonment, massacre, ghettoisation, heroic resistance, and the horror of the concentration camps, to final liberation. Each time you cross the central walkway your eye is drawn towards the balcony at the end, but it remains out of reach.

The rooms grow progressively darker and more claustrophobic as you proceed. Videos, photos and information boards are all displayed against the grey, undecorated concrete of the museum walls. It is not until you are nearing the end of the exhibition, which shows the Jewish exodus from Europe towards Israel after the war, that the rooms open out again.

The final room is the Hall of Names: a circular vault where the biographical details of the millions of victims are stored.

It is only after you have left this final room that you are at last able to walk up a steep concrete slope towards the balcony at the end of the museum. As you step out through the doors into a flood of light, you are greeted with a panoramic view of the Judean hills. The effect is remarkably soothing. After the darkness, the concrete walls, the enclosed spaces and the terrible, terrible history, to stand here for a while looking at the sun shining on the trees below is an enormous relief.

The museum's architecture transforms it from an educational experience into a deeply emotional one. It takes you on a journey through the darkness and into the light, from the horrors of Europe to deliverance in Israel, out of apocalypse and into rebirth. The view from the balcony is the final exhibit in the museum. This is the reward that was granted to the survivors of the Holocaust as consolation for their suffering: the land of Israel, where they might at last find a safe home.

* * *

The message conveyed by the balcony is broadly similar to the message of Yad Vashem as a whole. The very existence of the memorial site is itself a symbol of rebirth and redemption. Yad Vashem was set up in 1953 by the Israeli government, but half of its initial funding came from the Conference on Jewish Material Claims against Germany. In other words, reparations payments from the former persecutor of the Jews were, aptly, used to create a permanent memorial to that persecution. The Claims Conference has continued to finance Yad Vashem ever since.

Yad Vashem was built on Mount Herzl, a site that was also highly symbolic. Unlike so many other places in and around Jerusalem, Mount Herzl is not associated with any aspect of ancient or biblical history. In other words, the location could not be placed within a long history of death and destruction, like Jerusalem's other Holocaust museum, the Chamber of the Holocaust: it was a fresh start. The founders of the memorial were effectively saying that this was where the historic persecution of the Jews would stop and finally be replaced with something new.

But that is not all. Mount Herzl is also a symbol of Israeli nationalism. It is named after Theodor Herzl, one of the founders of Zionism and the 'spiritual father of the Jewish State'. The body of Herzl himself was moved from his grave in Vienna and reinterred here in 1949. The hill is where Israel buries its national leaders, as well as its soldiers who have died in the line of duty. By the time Yad Vashem was instituted here, such traditions were already well established.

Today, Yad Vashem is intimately connected to the nearby sites belonging to the Israeli state. There is even a commemorative pathway joining them together. In case the message were not clear enough, a noticeboard spells it out explicitly.

The path, it states, links Yad Vashem to the national military cemetery, the national leaders' burial site and Herzl's grave: 'Passage along it is a symbolic voyage in time from catastrophe to rebirth. It represents the journey from the Diaspora to the homeland of the Jewish people, from exile and destruction to a life of endeavour and hope in the State of Israel.'

This is the official message that Israel preaches today. The Holocaust was a kind of apocalypse, but it was also the pathway to rebirth. Without the Holocaust, the state of Israel might never have come into being.

It is perhaps for this reason that visiting dignitaries to Israel are always given a tour of Yad Vashem before they embark upon official business. Foreign leaders first visit the Holocaust museum before laying a wreath in the nearby Hall of Remembrance. These visits are mandatory: according to one senior Israeli diplomat, Talya Lador-Fresher, any foreign leader who doesn't want to take part is politely told that they should not come to Israel at all. 'Yad Vashem is an important part of our history,' she told the *Times of Israel* in 2012. 'You cannot understand Israel, even today, without understanding the Holocaust.'

And so presidents and prime ministers from other countries are regularly taken to this long, prism-shaped building cut into the mountain outside Jerusalem. They must follow the route through the series of dark, claustrophobic rooms; and they must experience the relief of stepping out onto the balcony with its view of the Judean hills. They must see the history that Jews see. And they must feel it the way that Jews feel it. Yad Vashem, and its balcony, is an important diplomatic tool.

Like all nations, Israel is in thrall to its history. And like all nations, Israel strives hard to pay homage to the aspects of its history that illustrate a positive political message, and to avoid those that are not quite so attractive. It is what Israel ignores, and Yad Vashem omits, that makes this official message of redemption and rebirth so controversial.

First, it paints a rather rosy picture of the way that Holocaust survivors were treated when they arrived in Israel (or Palestine, as it was called until 1948) after the war. Many of the impoverished, bedraggled European Jews who disembarked from the ships at Haifa were given a chilly welcome by Palestinian-born Jews (or Sabras, as they had come to be known). Few Sabras properly understood quite how hopeless the situation in Europe had been during the war. Some regarded European Jews as weak and submissive people who had gone willingly 'like lambs to the slaughter'. As a consequence, while Holocaust survivors appreciated being given a new place to live away from Europe, they often did not feel at home here. It was not until the 1960s that Sabras and European Jews finally began to integrate more closely and accept one another more generally as brothers and sisters in the state of Israel.

Second, the idea that the new state of Israel was a safe haven for Jews is also hopelessly idealistic. At Yad Vashem, not far from the museum building, is a monument called the Memorial to the Last of Kin: it is dedicated to those Holocaust survivors who arrived in Israel as the final surviving members of their families, but who went on to die fighting for the new state. This indicates how dangerous Palestine was in the years immediately after the Second World War. In 1947, the country was already embroiled in a civil war between Jews and Arabs. The following year, when Israel declared its independence, it was invaded by several neighbouring states. If you had been able to stand on the balcony at Yad Vashem in 1948, the sight that greeted you would not have been one of peace and tranquillity at all. Israel was at war; and it would find itself at war again and again throughout the rest of the century.

The final point to make is perhaps the most controversial of all. The history on display at Yad Vashem is quite specifically *Jewish* history. Like national museums all over the world, it filters out the aspects of history that are not relevant to its immediate narrative. In this case, the most glaring silence involves the history of the Palestinian Arabs. I don't mean to criticise Yad Vashem for this: any museum must maintain its focus, and the purpose of this particular museum is to describe the horrors of the Holocaust, not the history of Arab–Jewish relations. Nevertheless, there is something faintly disingenuous about the way the architecture presents the land of Israel as a kind of divine gift to ease the suffering of the survivors of the Holocaust. Israel was not an empty land waiting to be colonised in 1948. Nor was it a kind of sanatorium, reserved for the rehabilitation of a traumatised people. It was a territory with a long and rich history of its own, much of which had nothing to do with Jews.

Jews undoubtedly have close spiritual and historical ties with this landscape, but in the 1940s that alone did not make it a Jewish land. Over the previous 1,500 years, the vast majority of the population had been Arab Palestinians, Bedouins and Christians. In all that time, the region had been ruled by a variety of Romans, Persians, Muslim caliphs, Mamluk sultans, Ottoman emperors and, since 1918, the British. Jews lived side by side with all these people over the centuries, but not in significant numbers. It was only towards the end of the nineteenth century, when immigrants started arriving from Europe, that the Jewish population began to grow once more. Successive waves of European Jews continued to move here in the 1920s and 1930s, often fleeing persecution elsewhere, but even by 1945 they made up less than a third of the population. Palestine was still an overwhelmingly Arab land.

In the early days of Zionist immigration Jews and Arabs generally lived side by side without too many problems. But inevitably there were Arabs who began to view the arrival of so many foreigners with resentment, particularly when they learned that Jews aimed not only to make this their homeland but eventually also to establish political control. In the early 1920s, riots broke out in Jerusalem and Jaffa and dozens of Jews were murdered. A few years later, after another riot, an Arab mob in Hebron massacred sixty-seven defenceless Jews, including women and children. A dangerous precedent had been set.

In retaliation, Jews set up their own militias. Most of these paramilitary groups were focused purely on protecting Jewish villages from attack, but some, including the infamous Irgun, were determined to be much more aggressive in their tactics. In retaliation for violence against Jews, they began terrorising Arab civilians. They targeted people in public locations such as buses, coffee shops and market places. On several occasions they threw hand grenades into Arab crowds in order to cause as much terror as possible. Another dangerous precedent had been set.

After the Second World War, tensions between the two sides increased still further; and both sides blamed the British for failing to bring the violence under control. Hardline Jewish organisations like the Irgun believed that the only way to properly protect themselves was to drive the British out of Palestine and take control of the country. They launched a series of terrorist attacks against the British, including the bombing of their headquarters in Jerusalem's King David

Hotel. Eventually, tired of mediating between the two sides, the British turned the problem over to the United Nations.

What happened next has been the subject of controversy ever since. When the UN voted to split Palestine into two parts – one for the Jews and one for the Arabs – Arab leaders refused to accept their decision. Attacks on Jews increased all over the country. In an effort to bring the matter to a close once and for all, Jewish troops simply seized the territory that they now regarded as their own, and drove away the Arabs who lived there. The only way to protect Jewish communities was to expel as many Arabs as possible – the innocent along with the guilty.

According to the official version of this violent chapter in Israel's early history, the Arabs were never formally expelled but fled of their own accord. But even the Jewish soldiers who took part in these operations acknowledge that Arabs were purposely driven away, and that an atmosphere of extreme violence encouraged them to go. Hundreds of villages were cleared in this way.

Inevitably there were atrocities. The most famous occurred in the village of Deir Yassin, not far from Jerusalem. In April 1948, just a month before Israel formally declared its independence, Jewish paramilitary forces entered the village and killed the majority of its inhabitants with guns and grenades. Once again, the Irgun played a central role in the action. At least a hundred people were massacred, including women and children. Just as the Hebron massacre of 1929 had become a symbol of Arab violence against Jews, so the Deir Yassin massacre would soon become a symbol of Jewish violence against Arabs.

A month later, the state of Israel was declared. After a brief but decisive war against its Arab neighbours, who tried to

destroy the new country even before it had a chance to establish itself, an uneasy peace descended. That uneasiness has
remained ever since.

None of this is mentioned in the exhibition at Yad Vashem.
And neither should it be: it is a subject for another institution,
not for a place dedicated to the memory of the Holocaust.
But foreign leaders who are brought to the museum for political reasons should remember that other stories about Israel's
past exist alongside the narrative presented here. The balcony
at the end of the exhibition, and its view over the Judean hills,
is not quite the happy ending that it seems.

Arabs have their own organisations devoted to ensuring
that the past is not forgotten. Many of them like to point out
that when one stands on the balcony at Yad Vashem and looks
north, one can see the hilltop where the village of Deir Yassin
used to stand.

To their great credit, certain Jewish organisations also strive
to remember this past. One of them, an organisation called
Deir Yassin Remembered, has this to say about Yad Vashem:

> The Holocaust museum is beautiful, and the message 'never
> to forget man's inhumanity to man' is timeless. The children's
> museum is particularly heart wrenching; in a dark room filled
> with candles and mirrors the names of Jewish children who
> perished in the Holocaust are read along with their places of
> birth. Even the most callous person is brought to tears. Upon
> exiting this portion of the museum a visitor is facing north
> and looking directly at Deir Yassin. There are no markers, no
> plaques, no memorials, and no mention from any tour guide.
> But for those who know what they are looking at, the irony
> is breathtaking.

Israelis cannot escape this history any more than they can escape the history of the events that took place during the Second World War. The rebirth of the Jewish people in Israel was indeed something tender and beautiful, but it was not nearly as straightforward as the iconic balcony at Yad Vashem implies. It was a messy, violent business, with winners and losers.

If Israelis really wish to come to terms with their past, they must remind themselves occasionally that for all the terrible power that the Holocaust still has over Israeli memory, it was not the only painful event that preceded the birth of their nation.

The ruins of Coventry Cathedral

24

UK: Coventry Cathedral and the Cross of Nails

Of all the cities that were bombed in Britain during the Second World War, one has always stood out. Coventry is a city that became internationally famous after it was attacked in 1940: in symbolic terms, it is the closest that Britain has to Dresden in Germany or Hiroshima in Japan.

At the centre of Coventry stands a monument to this great tragedy. The ruins of Coventry Cathedral are probably the city's most famous landmark, and stand as a permanent reminder of the effects of the Second World War. The remains of red sandstone walls jut out of the ground like jagged teeth. Gothic windows stand empty, their ancient glass long since shattered or removed. The space once enclosed within the chancel, the nave and the aisles now lies open to the elements, with tufts of grass sprouting between the exposed flagstones of what used to be the church floor. Broken stumps of pillars form an avenue down the centre and, a little to one side, the remains of a stone staircase mark where the pulpit used to be before, like the rest of the church, it was burned down.

The site might have ended up being a symbol of terror and apocalypse, much like the ruins of Oradour-sur-Glane in

France. But in fact this is not its main message: other, more religious sentiments have won through instead. The ruins of Coventry Cathedral are a much richer and more hopeful monument than almost any other I have covered so far.

To understand how this transformation came about, one needs to look much more closely at the catastrophe that took place here during the war, and the dramatic impact it has made on Coventry's subsequent history.

The bombing that took place here on the night of 14 November 1940 was easily the most sustained raid carried out on Britain until this point in the war. It began soon after 7 p.m. and continued all night. By the time the last bombs landed some ten hours later, more than four hundred German planes had dropped over 500 tonnes of explosives and incendiaries on the city. A fraction of the quantity later dropped on cities like Hamburg and Dresden, it was nevertheless an enormous amount by the standards of the time.

The bombers were guided to their target by a revolutionary system of radar beams, but by all accounts the majority of them did not need it: within a short time the city was burning so brightly that it was visible for miles around. 'I have never seen such a concentration of fire during a raid, not even on London,' claimed Günter Unger, one of the German pilots who flew that night. 'Usually in our target cities the area of fires was dispersed, but not this time. There was no chance of missing the target.'

The Germans had good reason to bomb Coventry: the city contained some of the biggest and most important industrial complexes in the country. There were factories that produced aircraft engines, armoured cars, barrage balloons, electrical equipment, machine tools, VHF radios and many other items essential for the British war effort. But this was not the only reason to bomb the city. According to German propaganda, the bombing was carried out in retaliation for an earlier British raid on Munich. In other words, it was simply the latest victim in a cycle of reprisal and counter-reprisal that had been going on ever since the bomber war began.

Several of Coventry's factories were badly damaged by the German bombs, including the Triumph motor manufacturers and the General Electric Company's cable works, which were completely devastated. But alongside these military targets, thousands of civilian buildings were also destroyed. The Coventry City Library burned down, as did a brand new department store, a school and a hospital. Scores of shops, public buildings and offices were destroyed, along with 2,500 civilian houses. Another 20,000 houses were so badly damaged that they were considered uninhabitable.

Amid all this destruction stood the cathedral. The provost, Richard Howard, did his best to save it from the fires. He and three other volunteers braved the terror of the night in order to watch for incendiaries – but in the event, the bombs fell so thick and fast that the four of them were quickly overwhelmed. The fire brigade arrived after the fires had already taken hold, but when the water mains gave out even they were unable to save the building. In the end, firefighters and clergy alike were forced to stand and watch as the cathedral, along with the rest of the centre of Coventry, burned to the ground.

In the days that followed, the propaganda machines of both sides tried to make use of these events. The Nazis quickly proclaimed their bombing raid as a symbol of strength. The city, said one radio broadcast, had been 'smashed completely'. Another broadcast claimed that Coventry's factories had been damaged so badly that they would never work again: 'This was a total, not partial, destruction of Coventry.' Hitler's propaganda machine even coined a new word – *coventrieren*, 'to Coventrate' – with the implication that this was an act they could repeat again and again at will. It suggested that Britain would do well to capitulate sooner or later, because Germany was bound to win in the end.

The British newspapers, meanwhile, used Coventry as a potent emblem of Nazi brutality. In an editorial dated 16 November, *The Times* called Coventry 'A Martyred City' – a description that would define Coventry for the rest of the war. Almost every newspaper carried photographs of the ruined cathedral – partly because they were much more emotive than any picture of a ruined factory, but also because they made the German raid seem much more illegitimate and barbaric.

When these images made their way across the Atlantic, they became a useful tool in the recruitment of US support for Britain. A report in the *New York Herald Tribune* was typical: 'The gaunt ruins of St Michael's Cathedral, Coventry, stare from the photos,' it declared, 'the voiceless symbol of the insane, the unfathomable barbarity, which had been released on Western civilisation. No means of defense which the United States can place in British hands should be withheld.'

The pictures also made a rallying cry for those in Britain who wanted revenge. The front page of the *Sunday Express* on 17 November spoke volumes. It too showed a photograph of the ruined cathedral; and above it, running across the width of the paper, the headline read, 'Please God, you will avenge what was done to us that night'.

Both sides were attempting to use Coventry as a symbol of their respective causes. However, alongside the wartime propaganda, other voices were calling for a very different kind of symbolism. In Coventry itself, some of the city's most influential people appealed instead to a more spiritual set of values based on Christian tradition.

On the morning after the bombing, provost Richard Howard made a solemn declaration to his congregation. 'The cathedral will rise again,' he said, 'will be rebuilt, and it will be as great a pride to future generations as it has been to generations in the past.' To laymen this might have sounded like a straightforward statement of defiance: despite the destruction of his cathedral, he was refusing to admit defeat. However, there was more to it than that. Howard was expressing a vision of the doctrine that is central to Christianity: the resurrection. He was using the cathedral as a metaphor for Christ himself. It too would rise again from the dead.

Six weeks later, Provost Howard went a step further. In a Christmas message to the nation, broadcast by radio from the ruins of the cathedral, he spelt out his vision of what the future should look like. 'What we want to tell the world is this: that with Christ born again in our hearts today, we are trying, hard as it may be, to banish all thoughts of revenge . . . We are going to try to make a kinder, simpler, a more Christ-Child-like sort of world in the days beyond this strife.'

Many others in Coventry followed Howard's lead. In the weeks after the bombing, the cathedral's stonemason, Jock Forbes, gathered together some of the larger stones among the rubble and constructed a makeshift altar, so that services could continue to be held in the ruined church. He then picked up two charred oak roof beams and bound them together in the shape of a cross. This charred cross has been preserved, and remains on display inside the church to this day.

Meanwhile, a local priest named Arthur Wales made

another cross out of three medieval roof nails that he scavenged from the rubble. At first he tied them together with wire, but later he had them welded and plated. This 'Cross of Nails' was set upon the altar. It has been a potent symbol ever since of the cathedral and all it stands for.

Finally, after the war, the words 'Father Forgive' were inscribed on the stonework of the sanctuary. The words can still be seen today, written on the wall in gold lettering.

Unfortunately, in 1940 the world was not yet ready for this message of forgiveness. There was still a war to be won. Over the following months the bombing only intensified: Coventry ultimately proved to be just one target in a long list of British cities that were heavily damaged in the Blitz. In return, the RAF conducted devastating raids on Lübeck, Rostock, Cologne, Hamburg, Dresden, and a hundred other German towns and cities. The Second World War left cities all over Europe in ruins.

It was not until 1945, when the war finally came to an end, that anyone could seriously put their minds to rebuilding. In many places it took years just to clear the debris away. The rubble in Coventry Cathedral itself, for example, was not cleared until 1947, almost seven years after its destruction.

All over Europe, debates took place about how rebuilding should be carried out. Many people simply wanted their cities to be returned to the way they had been before the war; but there were others who saw the destruction as an opportunity to build something new, better, and more in tune with the needs of the post-war era. One of those people was Donald Gibson, Coventry's town planner. Gibson famously called the bombing 'a blessing in disguise': the Germans had 'cleared out the core of the city,' he said, 'and now we can start anew'.

In the years to come, Coventry would be regarded as a trail-blazer for modern city planning in Britain. It would be the first British city to make its town centre entirely car free: instead of driving into town, motorists would leave their cars in new, specially built parking garages and navigate their way around the shops on foot. With Gibson's new city plan, the old, historic streets, damaged and destroyed by the war, were swept away and replaced by a modern shopping centre with wide avenues and plazas free of noise and pollution.

Soon the city began to adopt a new symbol: the phoenix. When the 'Levelling Stone' was ceremonially laid in the centre of Coventry in 1946 to mark the start of the city's reconstruction, it was carved with an image of a phoenix. Phoenixes were added to the city's coat of arms, and to the logo of the city's Lanchester Polytechnic, now Coventry University. At the beginning of the 1960s, local artist George Wagstaffe was commissioned to erect a statue of a phoenix in the centre of Market Way. Today the mythical bird appears all over the city.

Perhaps the greatest phoenix of all was the cathedral itself. There had been plans to rebuild the historic building ever since Provost Howard made his famous declaration on the morning after the bombing, but progress had been slow because of a shortage of resources during and after the war.

Arguments raged back and forth about how the cathedral should be reconstructed, but eventually the decision was made to hold an open competition. In 1950 architects from all over the country were invited to submit plans. According to their brief, there was no reason to keep most of the ruins of the old cathedral – just the surviving tower and spire. Consequently, the vast majority of entrants envisaged either incorporating the ruins into a new building, or sweeping them away entirely.

The winning entry, by Basil Spence, was one of the few

designs that left the ruins of the old building as they were. Spence's idea was to build a brand new cathedral alongside the ruins, with a gigantic porch linking the two spaces together. The idea was, in his words, to build something 'that stood for the triumph of the resurrection' – in other words, to give concrete form to the religious image of Christ rising from the dead. In more secular terms, he was expressing the same as the city planners were doing elsewhere – the city of Coventry rising like a phoenix from the ashes.

And so the building of the new cathedral went ahead. The foundation stone was laid by Queen Elizabeth II in 1956. The building was completed six years later, a modernist master-piece of red sandstone, polished marble, reinforced concrete and a blaze of stained-glass windows. To this day, the original 'Cross of Nails' stands upon the high altar as a permanent reminder of the destruction of 1940, and of the resurrection that has been taking place ever since.

The new cathedral stands beside the ruins of the old.
They are linked by a huge, concrete porch

While the planning and rebuilding was taking place, Provost Howard also went about trying to live up to his wartime promise to try to create a kinder, 'more Christ-Child-like sort of world'. Now that the war was over, he was at last free to pursue his vision of forgiveness and reconciliation between nations. As early as 1946, he conducted a service in which the Bishop of Hamburg also took part via radio link. The following year he established a strong link with Kiel in northern Germany, and sent a 'Cross of Nails' to the city as a symbol of reconciliation. In the following months, more crosses were sent to Dresden, Berlin and several other German cities that had suffered from British bombing.

Over the years, Howard and his successors built up a community of fellow sufferers with ruined and rebuilt churches throughout Germany. These included the Kaiser Wilhelm Memorial Church in Berlin, which, much like Coventry Cathedral, was preserved as a ruin with a new, modernist church built alongside it. It also included the ruins of the Nikolaikirche in Hamburg, which has been preserved as a memorial to the firestorm; and St Katherine's church in the same city, which was rebuilt. And, perhaps most significantly of all, it included the Frauenkirche in Dresden. The Frauenkirche and Coventry Cathedral regularly hold exchange visits, especially on the anniversaries of each other's bombing raids.

Today, the idea of reconciliation is at the core of everything that Coventry Cathedral does. As one walks around the ruins of the old cathedral, it is not the symbols of destruction that dominate, but those of rebirth and reconciliation. In the north-west corner is a sculpture donated by the Frauenkirche in Dresden, which represents the survivors of bombing. Near it is another statue entitled 'Reconciliation', which is one of an identical pair – the other is in Hiroshima's Peace Memorial Park. The information board at the south side of the nave briefly describes the destruction of 1940 before giving a much lengthier description of the cathedral's reconciliation work around the world. Since 1945 the cathedral has formed links with more than 180 likeminded organisations in every continent, devoted to the idea of reconciliation between peoples. In recognition of its origins in Coventry, this worldwide partnership is called the 'Community of the Cross of Nails'.

Coventry as a city has embraced the same work. It officially styles itself the 'City of Peace and Reconciliation', and has been twinned with many other martyred cities around the world, including several already mentioned in this book: Volgograd, Warsaw, Dresden and Hiroshima. Its main theatre is named the Belgrade Theatre in honour of the Yugoslavian city destroyed by German bombers in 1941. It has streets named after the village of Lidice, which was razed to the ground by the Nazis in 1942; and the German town of Meschede, destroyed by the US Army Air Force in 1945.

I would love to be able to write that, through its reconciliation work, Coventry has managed to transcend the tragedies of the past – but of course things are never quite so simple. History is a prison from which no one escapes.

No matter how many symbols of reconciliation and rebirth are dotted around the ruins of Coventry Cathedral, it is still the ruins themselves that speak most eloquently. If the new cathedral next door is a symbol of the resurrection, then the ruins represent pure destruction. Their jagged outline against the sky is a permanent reminder of Coventry's martyrdom in November 1940.

Coventry today is Britain's closest equivalent to Dresden in Germany, or Hiroshima in Japan, and it is still regularly mentioned in the same breath as these other cities. This is not because the destruction that took place here was anywhere near as bad – 40 times as many people died in the bombing of Dresden, and around 250 times as many eventually died in Hiroshima. However, Coventry happened first, and thus was the harbinger of the devastation that was to come. In the British and American popular imagination, the destruction of Coventry and its famous cathedral has become a microcosm of the whole bombing war.

The resurrection that took place in this city is also partly a myth. Coventry's rebirth was never quite as glorious as the brochures and postcards of the 1950s and 1960s promised. The city centre boomed during those years, but in later decades began to look tired and grey. It was partially regenerated in the 1990s, and is undergoing a further round of regeneration even as I write. But no amount of modern planning will ever adequately replace the picturesque medieval city that was destroyed by both the German bombers and the British town planners of the 1930s, 1940s and 1950s. The ruins of the cathedral are a reminder of exactly what was lost.

The city is no longer the prosperous place that it was during the boom years of the mid-twentieth century. The dozens of factories that once attracted the ire of the Luftwaffe are long gone, much as they are across Britain. In recent decades Coventry has become a symbol of Britain's industrial decline. In the 1980s it had one of the highest unemployment rates in the country, and even today unemployment is far higher than the UK average. No matter how often the city's civic and religious institutions champion the idea of rebirth, there is still a feeling that the Second World War took a toll on the city, and that the post-war European consensus has let the people of Coventry down. This disillusionment was reflected in the 2016 Brexit referendum, when the majority of Coventry's voters elected to leave the European Union.

When you stand among the ruins of the old cathedral, it is difficult not to see these things as well as the story of rebirth towards which the church authorities so eagerly point you. The history of destruction necessarily precedes the history of reconciliation.

Like so many other places covered in this book, Coventry and its cathedral will always be defined by its Second World War history. Nevertheless, it has come closer than most to

Cross of Nails

rising above that history. The city continues to dream of rebirth, no matter how elusive that may be. The cathedral continues to pursue its work of reconciliation, both locally and in the wider world, regardless of its endless challenges.

Its people continue to do this, as they have done for more than eighty years, by harnessing the emotive power of the monument that still stands at the heart of their community: the cathedral ruins that remain one of the most richly complex monuments in the world today.

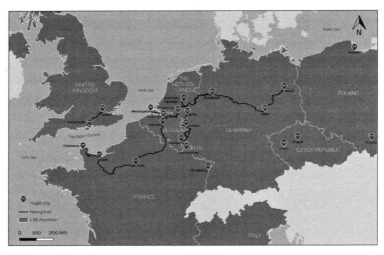

Liberation Route Europe's international hiking trail

25

European Union:
Liberation Route Europe

Monuments come in all shapes and sizes. During the course of this book I have explored the meanings and motivations behind a wide variety of memorials – not only conventional statues but also abstract sculptures, murals, architectural features, museums and memorial parks, ruined buildings and ruined villages, concentration camps, cemeteries, tombs and shrines. All these have become repositories for our memories of the Second World War. They are used to transmit those memories across the generations, so that even when there are no longer any veterans of the war left alive, we will continue to remember what they witnessed during the most tragic and dramatic events of the last century.

The final monument I would like to describe is different once again. It is a hiking trail that stretches for 2,000 kilo-metres (1240 miles) and spans several countries, following the route that the western Allies took during the liberation of Europe in 1944–5. As a transnational monument, it is by far the biggest memorial in this book. It is also the newest – in fact, at the time of writing, it does not yet even exist. It is due to be inaugurated in May 2020, the same month as the seventy-fifth anniversary of Germany's surrender and the end of the war in Europe.

The Liberation Route Europe bills itself as a hiking trail, but in fact it is a memory trail linking the main sites of the liberation of western Europe. It begins in London at the Churchill War Rooms, where the idea for an invasion of Europe was first discussed; and it ends in Berlin, where Nazism finally reached its bitter end. Along the way it travels through Normandy, Paris, Brussels, Arnhem and the sites of the Battle of the Bulge, before crossing into Germany. Strictly speaking it is not one route, but several, with numerous branches that reach out into other places where major battles took place.

Those who walk the trail will be following in the footsteps of the vast armies that fought their way through the continent in 1944–5. Their journey will therefore be a kind of homage to the memory of another, much tougher journey that took place so many decades ago. The route takes in hundreds of sites of memory along the way. Travellers will be able to visit the major memorials, cemeteries and museums that are scattered along the route. They will walk on the very battlefields where tens of thousands sacrificed their lives. And, all the while, they will accumulate stories not only of the profound events that took place in each location, but also of many of the individuals who took part.

Among the most important aspects of the trail will be the website and mobile app that accompany it, so that even in the remotest sections of the route, its followers will be able to download stories and descriptions of the events that took place exactly where they are standing. In other words, this is a monument that exists as much in the digital, virtual world as it does in the physical world.

According to Rémi Praud, the director of Liberation Route

Europe, the organisation that created the hiking trail, the digital aspect of the project is essential. 'This is a new way of doing things,' he told me. 'You don't have any transnational monuments like this one, with different locations and so on . . . We want to make it a bit more modern, a bit more appealing for young generations and all types of audience, like hikers, tourists, families – not just the people that come to commemorations every year.'

For those who have no time to walk the entire route, the journey will be available online. However, the real emotional power of the trail lies in the experience of visiting the physical locations of the war's historic events.

To signify that this is a walking trail with a single message and purpose that brings together all these stories and events, the route will be signposted by waymarkers built to a common design. Specially devised by the architect Daniel Libeskind, they each consist of a spiral of metal and concrete, enclosing a sharp, triangular fin called a 'vector'. Some will be placed on the ground and others mounted on walls; and at major points along the way there will be larger versions, forming monuments in their own right.

The message of these vectors is clear. The smaller versions consist of sharp metal spikes. The larger, monumental versions are like a blade rising out of the ground and both large and small will point at Berlin. There is an inherent sense of threat in these sharp metal objects. But there is also a singleness of purpose: they all point one way. The armies that passed along the route in 1944–5 were not on a pleasure trip: they were driving a spearhead through the continent towards the heart of the beast that had terrorised the people of Europe for years.

In June 2019 I interviewed Daniel Libeskind about the

Hypothetical design for a 'Vector' monument at Normandy, one of
the key points on the Liberation Route hiking trail

meaning behind his vectors, and what they were supposed to
represent. He told me that their blade-like appearance was an
important aspect of the design: 'Yes, it has a sharpness, defi-
nitely, that's part of it, because it's cutting through all the evils
of history towards something good.' But more important was
the fact that all the markers point the same way. 'They are all
of different sizes; and they play different roles . . . but all of
them are united in revealing the *direction* of the liberation.'

In some ways the most interesting stretch of the route is
the journey through Germany. Were this a nationalist monument, like so many of the other memorials I have described
so far, Germany might be portrayed as the monster, and
Germans as the enemy. But this is a transnational monument
that passes through Germany for over 600 kilometres (372
miles) and includes Germany in its narrative of liberation. In
other words, Germany had to be liberated from Nazism along
with every other country involved in the war.

The purpose of this monument is to portray the liberation

as the key moment of the twentieth century. This was the one event that finally brought an end to the terror and violence, and signified the rebirth of the whole of western Europe, including Germany, into a new era of peace and prosperity.

Like all the monuments in this book, the Liberation Route Europe says as much about the world we live in today as it does about history. There is a political message – or, at least, a political point of view – behind the walking trail that stands beside its historical message.

I first came across Liberation Route Europe as an organisation in 2014, when they asked me to make a speech at an event they had organised at the European Parliament in Brussels. They were launching a new Europe-wide exhibition, whose purpose was to describe the liberation not from any one national point of view, but from a multinational perspective. One of the other people who gave a speech at the launch was Martin Schultz, who was then president of the European Parliament. Schultz was, and still is, one of the most active supporters of Liberation Route Europe.

Since 2014, the organisation has grown and flourished. It has forged links with scores of museums, memorials and tourist sites all over the continent, and has turned itself into a kind of umbrella group, helping those museums and memorials to communicate and interact with one another. The hiking trail is a culmination of that work: it is a physical path that links all the various institutions and sites of memory together. The trail from London to Berlin is just the first stage in a project that is likely to take many more years, and which one day will involve many other walking trails from northern, eastern and central Europe, likewise culminating in Berlin.

It is no coincidence that the European Parliament should want to endorse such an organisation, or that the former president of that Parliament should be one of its greatest champions. In April 2019 the Council of Europe also formally endorsed the Liberation Route Europe by certifying it as an official European Cultural Route. The trail espouses many of the fundamental values that these institutions regard as sacred. It is a physical link between different countries in Europe. And it tells a narrative of freedom, of the triumph of democracy and, above all, of the importance of unity. It is the European Union in microcosm.

The EU has always mythologised the Second World War as the fire in which it was forged. The founding fathers of the EU were people with first-hand experience of the misery and chaos created by the war, and who saw the creation of what Churchill called 'a kind of United States of Europe' as the only long-term remedy. This is also the spirit that infuses the Liberation Route. The history that it commemorates is very much one of international cooperation. It speaks of a time when the western Allies arrived on the beaches of Normandy not to liberate individual countries, but the continent as a whole. The liberation, it reminds us, was not carried out by a single national force, but by an alliance of Americans, Brits, Canadians, Poles, Czechs, the forces of the Free French, and a dozen other nationalities. It was the very model of international cooperation.

According to Daniel Libeskind, this is the true message behind the Liberation Route. 'The aftermath of the liberation created a new sense of Europe, and a new sense of what it meant to *be* in Europe . . . The unity of an outlook of human beings towards peace and towards the past – and also looking hopefully towards the future – brought a new notion of what freedom means. That, at the core, is what this route means. It's not just looking backward at what happened, but at what was the gift that Europe received as a result of this conflict.'

One of the purposes of any monument is not simply to commemorate the events of the past, but to transform them into myth. In my conversations with Rémi Praud and Daniel Libeskind they both referred to the route as a 'pilgrimage'; Libeskind even compared his vectors to the kind of primeval route markers that Odysseus might have encountered on the road during ancient times. The Liberation Route is an attempt to create a mythological space somewhere between history and memory, where people walking the trail can begin to feel part of something much greater than their immediate environment. One does not need to walk the entire trail in order to feel an emotional connection to the vast undertaking that ended up in the liberation of Europe.

This is a message of hope and redemption that is difficult to resist: it is the happy ending to the war that makes all the suffering and heroism worthwhile. The only problem with this kind of mythology is that it must compete with other mythologies created by national or local groups, who are more interested in commemorating the things that make them unique than those that they have in common. A community that was once involved in a local triumph over the Nazis may not wish to share that glory with the wider Allied world. A community that has suffered may not wish to put aside its martyrdom for the sake of a greater story of redemption and rebirth.

The inauguration of the Liberation Route in 2020 coincides with a period of unprecedented tension between these two competing visions of the past. The success of this monumental hiking trail, much like that of the European Union itself, will depend on its ability to navigate the stormy waters that lie between the internationalist values that have sustained the continent ever since 1945, and the nationalist narratives that were also a part of the war, and which are still an important part of our heritage today.

The reason why I am optimistic about the future of this particular monument is that its sheer scale gives it the chance to pay homage to both visions of history at once. Indeed, it is big enough to incorporate all the ideas I have explored in this book. The trail passes through sites of heroism as well as sites of martyrdom and unforgivable atrocity. It encompasses stories of local triumph and national glory within its overall narrative of continental liberation. More than any other monument in this book, it has the potential for nuance and variety.

But, most of all, it has chained itself to a solid foundation of historical fact. Its long odyssey through a year of conflict and 2,000 kilometres of territory – mythological though it is – is anchored at every point along its route to the historic events that took place in each location.

The creators of the Liberation Route have realised that, if it is to survive in the long term, they had no other choice but to create it in this way. The old monuments, carved in metal and stone, are often torn down because they lose their relevance to later generations. History changes, and if monuments do not keep pace with that change they sometimes have to go.

Perhaps the best way to avoid future waves of iconoclasm is to embrace nuance, and cling as closely as possible to historical facts. Because monuments, just like peoples, will always be prisoners of history.

Conclusion

We live in an era when people question the symbols of the past with increasing frequency. Monuments representing ideas that are no longer palatable to us, or which seem too outdated or outlandish for modern sensibilities, are often taken down. I have watched the removal of some of these monuments in recent years – in the USA, in South Africa and in eastern Europe – and I must confess that, while I understand the intense emotions that the monuments can sometimes spark, and indeed share some of those emotions myself, I can't help mourning their loss when they're gone. Our monuments are valuable historical documents: they speak eloquently about the values of our ancestors, both good and bad. They are curiosities with the power to inspire and provoke all kinds of debate. They are often also great works of art, of astonishing craftsmanship and imagination. To tear all this down for the sake of contemporary politics seems like a great shame.

Monuments can indeed exert an oppressive power over our public spaces; but I hope I have shown that there are other ways to deal with the problem without tearing them down altogether. We can create counter-monuments, as the people of Budapest have done in protest at their government-sponsored symbols of Hungarian victimhood. We can build new monuments around the offending one, as they have in Amsterdam, where the National Monument now represents just one layer in a rich and nuanced memorial landscape. If worst comes to worst, we can move objectionable monuments to museums and sculpture parks, so that future generations can at least come to marvel at their artistic merit, even while they disagree with their politics. Should we really come to loathe our monuments, then we can always recast them as objects of ridicule. Nothing undermines the gravitas of a statue so well as putting it in an enclosure with a herd of llamas.

Tearing monuments down does not solve our history; it simply drives that history underground. While a monument still stands, it will always need to be confronted, discussed. In this way, our monuments hold us to account. They are objects that make sure we never forget our debt to history – or our enslavement to it.

So far, most of the monuments we have raised to the memory of the Second World War seem to have resisted this wave of iconoclasm. Unlike certain monuments to other eras, our Second World War memorials are still largely revered. This is in part because the war is still relatively recent – it's difficult to justify tearing down a monument when some of the people honoured by it are still alive.

On the whole, however, our war memorials have survived because they continue to say something important about who we are – or, at least, who we would like to believe ourselves to be. They speak to our present-day longings as much as to our memory of the past. They answer a need that is not being met by the contemporary world.

I have described five different categories of war monuments in this book, and each of them remains important to us in different ways. Our heroes offer up a vision of loyalty, bravery or moral fortitude that seems to be in short supply in our day-to-day lives: this is how we wish we could be. Our martyrs offer us something equally valuable: they remind us of the past sacrifices and traumas that have both scarred us and made us who we are. Our monsters remind us of everything we most reject in society, and that we were once willing to defend ourselves against, to the death. Our visions of Armageddon remind us of the vast destruction we once suffered; and our visions of rebirth celebrate our efforts to re-establish order after the chaos of the war.

None of these categories exists in isolation. Another major reason why our war monuments have proven more robust than those of other eras is that these five categories of memory not only support one another, but amplify one another. The idea of Armageddon provides the perfect backdrop for our folk memories of the war as a titanic struggle for the soul of mankind. Our heroes are made more heroic by the image of absolute evil against which they were fighting; and our monsters are made more monstrous by the innocence of the martyrs that they tortured. Tying all these images together is the final idea: our belief in a new world, born from the ashes of the old. This is the prize given to our heroes and martyrs. It's what ennobles their sacrifices and makes the suffering seem worthwhile. Without the resurrection, what was the point of all the heroism?

These five ideas form the mythological framework that underpins our collective memory of the Second World War. At a local level they allow us to mourn past traumas without becoming overwhelmed by them, because the forces that once victimised us were at least defeated and replaced with something new. At a national level they allow us to take pride in our communal values, which led us, eventually, to victory. And at an international level they have given us faith in our new, international institutions, and inspired hope for a future free from the scourge of war. These ideas form the bedrock upon which our international system is built.

But just because this mythological framework has been so robust until now, that does not mean that it will remain so in the future. The cracks are already beginning to show. In eastern Europe, monuments to the heroes of the war have already started to come down: it is easy to dismiss the heroism of the USSR when its soldiers came not only as liberators, but as conquerors. Attitudes to the other great Allies of 1945 are also beginning to change. The British and the Americans no longer command the gratitude or respect that they once did: other nations now prefer to raise monuments to their own home-grown heroes. The day might come when memorials to American heroes – men like Douglas MacArthur, who had great flaws as well as great qualities – are also forced to come down.

All kinds of political changes also threaten our monuments to the heroes of the Second World War. Some of these monuments were raised by people holding a particular political point of view. The Bomber Command Memorial in London, for example, was raised with overwhelming support from the political right; while the Shrine to the Fallen in Bologna was erected by those on the left. If the political atmosphere were to change substantially in either place, such monuments might one day be seen as a problem. Furthermore, since monuments like the Bomber Command Memorial were raised without adequately addressing the controversies of the past, there is every possibility that they will one day fall foul of those controversies again.

As with our heroes, so too with our martyrs and our monsters. I have written at length about how our monuments to people regarded as monsters have almost all been taken down. This has created a vacuum in our public memory which has been filled with something much more nebulous and difficult to destroy. Nevertheless, our inclination to erase any monument to fascism and Stalinism persists. We might never be able to destroy the spirit behind such monuments, but we can at least try to prevent that spirit from ever finding a physical home.

At first glance, monuments to our Second World War martyrs seem much more robust: what government or institution would ever dare take down a memorial to national suffering? But even these monuments are not immune to the pressures of an ever-changing world. The ruins of Oradour-sur-Glane cannot be preserved forever exactly as they were in 1945 – at some point they will either crumble, or will have to be reinforced, or even rebuilt. The Katyn Memorial in Jersey City was saved from relocation in 2018, but who is to say that the commercial pressures that threatened it might not one day become irresistible?

Much like our monuments to heroes, our monuments to martyrs can be vulnerable to political considerations. For example, the 'comfort woman' statue in Seoul was raised partly as a symbol of anti-Japanese sentiment; as such, the Japanese have been calling for its removal ever since. Should their diplomatic efforts prove fruitful, or should a new era of friendship ever break out between the two nations, it is conceivable that the statue might one day have to come down. In Budapest, where Hungary's status as a victim of the Germans is hotly contested, there has always been a strong and vocal opposition to its monument to national martyrdom.

Perhaps most vulnerable of all are our monuments to the rebirth in 1945. Here, the greatest threat is disillusionment. The brave new world that seemed within reach after the Second World War never quite materialised in the way that people all around the world hoped it would. Whatever happened to the haven of safety and security for Jews promised by Yad Vashem? What happened to the vision of world peace and harmony promised by Per Krohg's mural in the UN Security Council chamber; or to the vision of reconciliation promised by Coventry Cathedral's 'Cross of Nails'? Why should we commemorate a rebirth that never really happened? Most of these monuments are fairly inoffensive and seem unlikely to be torn down; but even if they remain, there is no guarantee that people will continue to come and see them.

Once again, changes in the political atmosphere can also pose a threat to such monuments, even those that might seem relatively innocuous. Some of them were raised by international institutions, such as the United Nations or the European Union, and this might also prove to be their undoing. Nationalists have always been suspicious of such institutions. In Europe, especially, nationalist politicians have come to regard the EU as a threat to their own sovereignty. It is for this reason that the continent's first transnational war monument, the Liberation Route Europe, tries to avoid any overt connection to the one institution that most supports and endorses it. Instead, it is at pains to incorporate nationalist stories into its wider message of cooperation and unity. Any monument that fails to do likewise will always be vulnerable to nationalist sentiment.

* * *

Despite these threats, however, our Second World War memorials continue to multiply. Almost a third of the monuments described in this book were created after the year 2000, and more are inaugurated every year. Our fascination with the war seems to be growing, not diminishing.

As I write, several new memorials are being planned in Britain alone. A major new Holocaust memorial and museum is scheduled to open in central London in 2021, right next to the Houses of Parliament. There are also campaigns to raise monuments in Liverpool (to the seamen who died during the war in the Atlantic), in Staffordshire (to Caribbean military personnel who fought in the war), and again in London (to the Sikhs who fought for Britain during the war). Other monuments are also being raised in other countries. For example, a major Holocaust memorial is due to be built in Croatia's capital, Zagreb; and in Germany a campaign is under way for a new memorial to the Polish victims of the war in Berlin.

If history is the basis of our identity, then *this* history seems to define us more than any other. The Second World War is the screen upon which we like to project all our national sentiments. Our monuments are the images on that screen.

What will become of these monuments in future years is anyone's guess. We build them out of granite and bronze because we hope that they will last for ever. But in reality it is only the monuments that have the capacity to change with the times that will survive, because history, and memory, have a habit of developing in the most unpredictable ways.

Bibliography

Most of the information in this book was gleaned from visits to the monuments themselves and the museums and information centres associated with them.

For the present day controversies surrounding these monuments, I consulted a wide variety of newspapers and websites too numerous to list here. For example, the 2018 protests about the Katyn memorial in Jersey City made headlines in various national American and Polish newspapers, was covered in more detail by the Jersey Journal and its website www.nj.com, and with great passion and humour on the local community website, http://jclist.com. Likewise, the saga of the 'Four Sleepers' monument in Warsaw was described by newspapers in both Poland and Russia, particularly in Warsaw's *Gazeta Wyborcza*. The controversies over Budapest's Monument to the Victims of German Occupation were covered extensively in the international press, but the development of its counter-monument, the 'Living Memorial', can be traced in real time on its Facebook page, https://facebook.com/groups/elevenemlekmu.

The bibliography below, therefore, lists only works with substantial material on the monuments in this book, or which readers might find useful for further general reading.

Journal articles and dissertations

Chin, Sharon; Franke, Fabian & Halpern, Sheri, 'A Self-Serving Admission of Guilt: An Examination of the Intentions and Effects of Germany's Memorial to the Murdered Jews of Europe', available online: https://www.humanityinaction. org/knowledgebase/225-a-self-serving-admission-of-guilt-an-examination-of-the-intentions-and-effects-of-germany-s-memorial-to-the-murdered-jews-of-europe

Clark, Benjamin, 'Memory in Ruins: Remembering War in the Ruins of Coventry Cathedral' M.A. dissertation (21 September 2015), Bartlett School of Architecture, University College London

Ellick, Adam B., 'A Home for the Vilified', *World Sculpture News* (Autumn 2001), pp.24-9

Glambek, Ingeborg, 'The Council Chambers in the UN Building in New York', *Scandinavian Journal of Design History*, vol. 15 (2005), pp.8–39

Kumagai, Naoko, 'The Background to the Japan–Republic of Korea Agreement: Compromises Concerning the Understanding of the Comfort Women Issue' in *Asia–Pacific Review*, vol.23, No.1 (2016), pp.65–99

Kim, Mikyoung, 'Memorializing Comfort Women: Memory and Human Rights in Korea–Japan Relations', in *Asian Politics and Policy*, Vol.6, No.1 (2014)

Okuda, Hiroko 'Remembering the atomic bombing of Hiroshima and Nagasaki: Collective memory of post-war Japan', *Acta Orientalia Vilnensia* Vol.12, No.1 (2011), pp.11–28

Petillo, Carol M., 'Douglas MacArthur and Manuel Quezon: A Note on an Imperial Bond', *Pacific Historical Review*, Vol. 48 No. 1, Feb., 1979

van Cant, Katrin, 'Historical Memory in Post-Communist Poland: Warsaw's Monuments after 1989', available on the University of Pittsburgh's Dept. of Slavic Languages website: https://www.pitt.edu/~slavic/sisc/SISC8/docs/vancant.pdf

Varga, Aniko, 'National Bodies: The "Comfort Women" Discourse and Its controversies in South Korea' in *Studies in Ethnicity and Nationalism* Vol.9 No.2 (2009)

Yoshinobu, Higurashi, 'Yasukuni and the Enshrinement of War Criminals', 11 August 2013; English translation 25 November 2013 available online: https://www.nippon.com/en/in-depth/a02404/

Yad Vashem quarterly, especially issues 31 (Fall 2003) and 37 (Spring 2005)

Useful Websites

https://www.4en5mei.nl

http://auschwitz.org/en

https://www.medprostor.si/en/projects/project-victims-of-all-wars-memorial

https://www.topographie.de

https://www.oradour.info

www.stiftung-denkmal.de

https://www.gedenkstaetten-in-hamburg.de

www.yadvashem.org

https://liberationroute.com

https://www.bibliotecasalaborsa.it

https://www.storiaememoriadibologna.it

http://parridigit.istitutoparri.eu

http://www.museodellaresistenzadibologna.it

http://www.straginazifasciste.it
http://www.comune.bologna.it
www.nj.com
https://facebook.com/groups/elevenemlekmu

General books on collective memory

Bevernage, Berber & Wouters, Nico (eds.), *Palgrave Handbook of State Sponsored History After 1945* (Palgrave Macmillan, 2018)

Halbwachs, Maurice, *On Collective Memory* (University of Chicago Press, 1992)

Mrozik, Agnieszka & Holubek, Stanislav (eds.), *Historical Memory of Central and East European Communism* (Routledge, 2018)

Nora, Pierre (ed.), *Realms of Memory: Rethinking the French Past* (Columbia University Press, 1996)

Winter, Jay, *War Beyond Words: Languages of Remembrance from the Great War to the Present* (Cambridge University Press, 2017)

Yang, Daqing & Mochizuki, Mike (eds), *Memory, Identity, and Commemorations of World War II: Anniversary Politics in Asia Pacific* (Lexington Books, 2018)

Books on aspects of the Second World War

Beevor, Antony, *The Second Word War* (Weidenfeld & Nicolson, 2012)

Buruma, Ian, *Wages of Guilt* (Farrar, Straus & Giroux, 1994)

Constantino, Renato & Constantino, Letizia R., *The Philippines: The Continuing Past* (Foundation for Nationalist Studies, 1978)

Dower, John W., *War Without Mercy: Race and Power in the Pacific War* (Pantheon, 1986)

—*Embracing Defeat: Japan in the Wake of World War II* (WW Norton, 2000)

Duggan, Christopher, *Fascist Voices: An Intimate History of Mussolini's Italy* (Bodley Head, 2012)

Farmer, Sarah, *Martyred Village* (University of California Press, 2000)

Friedländer, Saul, *The Years of Extermination: Nazi Germany and the Jews 1939–1945* (Weidenfeld & Nicolson, 2007)

Ham, Paul, *Hiroshima Nagasaki* (Doubleday, 2011)

Hastings, Max, *All Hell Let Loose* (HarperCollins, 2011)

Hibbert, Christopher, *Mussolini: The Rise and Fall of Il Duce* (Palgrave Macmillan, 2008)

Hondius, Dienke, *Return: Holocaust Survivors and Dutch Anti-Semitism* (Praeger, 2003)

Inman, Nick & Staines, Joe, *Travel the Liberation Route Europe* (Rough Guides, 2019)

Jager, Sheila Miyoshi, *Brothers at War: The Unending Conflict in Korea* (WW Norton, 2013)

Kennedy, Paul, *The Parliament of Man* (Allen Lane, 2006)

Kershaw, Ian, *Hitler 1936–1945: Nemesis* (Allen Lane, 2000)

Landstra, Menno & Spruijt, Desmond, *Het Nationaal Monument op de Dam* (Landstra & Spruijt, 1998)

Lowe, Keith, *Inferno: The Devastation of Hamburg, 1943* (Viking, 2006)

—*Savage Continent: Europe in the Aftermath of World War II* (Viking, 2012)

—*The Fear and the Freedom* (Viking, 2017)

MacArthur, Douglas, *A Soldier Speaks* (Praeger, 1965)

Manchester, William, *American Caesar: Douglas MacArthur 1880–1964* (Hutchinson, 1979)

Mazower, Mark, *The Balkans* (Weidenfeld & Nicolson, 2000)

McCallus, Joseph P., *The MacArthur Highway and Other Relics* of American Empire in the Philippines (Potomac Books, 2010)

Milza, Pierre, Gli Ultimi Giorni di Mussolini (Longanesi, 2011)

Morgan, Philip, The Fall of Mussolini (Oxford University Press, 2007)

Moseley, Ray, Mussolini: The Last 600 Days (Taylor Trade, 2004)

Pavlowitch, Stefan K., Hitler's New Disorder: The Second World War in Yugoslavia (Hurst & Co, 2008)

Reep, Edward, A Combat Artist in World War II (University Press of Kentucky, 1987)

Roberts, Andrew, The Storm of War (Allen Lane, 2009)

Taylor, Frederick, Coventry (Bloomsbury, 2015)

Tomasevich, Jozo, War and Revolution in Yugoslavia (Stanford University Press, 2001)

Vinogradov, V. K.; Pogonyi, J.F.; & Teptzov, N.V., Hitler's Death: Russia's Last Great Secret from the Files of the KGB (Chaucer Press, 2005)

Yoshiaki, Yoshimi, Comfort Women (Columbia University Press, 2002)

Xianwen, Zhang & Jianjun, Zhang (eds.), Human Memory: Solid Evidence of the Nanjing Massacre (Nanjing, 2017)

Acknowledgements

This book would not have been possible without the help and support of all the institutions mentioned in the text, whose dedicated and knowledgeable staff were uniformly helpful. A few people, however, went out of their way to help me and deserve my deepest gratitude: they include Enrico Cavalieri; Luca Pastore of Istituto Parri; Otelo Sangiorgi of Museo Risorgimento; Máthé Áron of the Committee of National Remembrance in Budapest; Rémi Praud of Liberation Route Europe; and architect Daniel Libeskind.

The hospitality I received on my various trips to China and Japan was truly incredible. I owe special thanks to my friend and translator, Hans Lu and my Chinese publisher, Dong Fengyun; and also to Zou Dehuai, Liu Xiaoping, Wang Hao and Tang Kai who showed me round Nanjing with seemingly endless patience. I am also extremely grateful to Xue Gang, deputy curator of the Private Museum of the Anti-Japanese War in Nanjing; and Zhang Jianjun, curator of the Nanjing Massacre Memorial Hall. Jarl and Tomoko Smidt-Olsen were extremely generous in putting me up during my travels; and my Japanese agents Atsushi Hori and Tsutomu Yawata also entertained me generously in Tokyo.

As always, I owe thanks to my brilliant agent of twenty years, Simon Trewin; my American agent Jay Mandel; and to my principal editors, Arabella Pike and Michael Flamini, who helped shape the book. I would also like to thank my copy-editor, Steve Gove, as well as Katy Archer, Jo Thompson and all at HarperCollins who contributed to making this book come to fruition.

But the greatest thanks must go to my wife, Liza, who is also my greatest friend and fiercest critic, and who had to put up with long absences while I travelled abroad in the name of research. Without her this book, and much else, would have fallen apart long ago.

Picture Acknowledgements

The majority of photographs in this book are from the author's personal collection. The remainder are reproduced from the following sources, with thanks:

Monument to Brotherhood in Arms, p.14 – Cezary Piwowarski/ Wikimedia Commons CC BY-SA 4.0

Marine Corps Memorial, p.24 – Idawriter/Wikimedia Commons CC BY-SA 3.0

Douglas MacArthur Landing Memorial, p.34 – Jelpads/ Wikimedia Commons CC BY-SA 4.0

'I have returned' – Gaetano Faillace/US Army Signal Corps (NARA ID 531424)

The original shrine, 1945, p.37 – Edo Ansaloni/Museo Memoriale della Libertà

National Monument in 1958, p.83 – Harry Pot/Anefo/ Nationaal Archief, Amsterdam

Peace Statue, South Korea, p.104 – Yun-Ho Lee/Wikimedia Commons CC0 1.0

Katyn Memorial, Jersey City, p.116 – Colin Knowles/ Wikimedia Commons CC BY-SA 2.0

Monument for the Victims of the German Occupation, p.128 – Abel Tumik/Shutterstock

Counter-monument, 20 July 2014, p.137 – Dina Balogh/ Eleven Emlékmű

Auschwitz–Birkenau, p.140 – Logaritmo/Wikimedia Commons CC BY-SA 3.0

Mussolini's tomb, p.186 – Sailko/Wikimedia Commons CC BY-SA 3.0

Oradour-sur-Glane, p.226 – Alf van Beem/Wikimedia Commons CC0 1.0

Cross of Nails, p.318 – Photograph permission of Coventry Cathedral

LRE hiking trail, p.320 – Liberation Route Europe

Hypothetical 'Vector' design, p.324 – Studio Libeskind

Every effort has been made to obtain permission to reproduce these photos. Any omissions or inaccuracies brought to the attention of the author or publisher will be corrected in subsequent editions.